The Deprivation of Liberty of Children and Young People

The Deprivation of Liberty of Children and Young People

Authors

Chloe Lee
Barrister, Spire Barristers

Pippa Pudney
Barrister, Spire Barristers

Contributor

Jacqueline Thomas KC
Head of Chambers, Spire Barristers

Bloomsbury Professional

LONDON • DUBLIN • EDINBURGH • NEW YORK • NEW DELHI • SYDNEY

BLOOMSBURY PROFESSIONAL
Bloomsbury Publishing Plc
50 Bedford Square, London, WC1B 3DP, UK
1385 Broadway, New York, NY 10018, USA
29 Earlsfort Terrace, Dublin 2, Ireland

British Library Cataloguing-in-Publication Data

A catalogue record for this book is available from the British Library.

ISBN: PB: 978 1 52653 005 9
ePDF: 978 1 52653 007 3
ePub: 978 1 52653 006 6

Typeset by Evolution Design and Digital (Kent)
Printed and bound by CPI Group (UK) Ltd, Croydon, CR0 4YY

To find out more about our authors and books visit www.bloomsburyprofessional.com. Here you will find extracts, author information, details of forthcoming events and the option to sign up for our newsletters

DEDICATION

For Chloe,

To my fiancé Jake Keating, my greatest supporter, for his love, patience and encouragement throughout this journey. Thank you for always believing in me, for encouraging me to pursue my dreams and for making me smile every single day.

To my dad Stephen Gannon who has always guided me in the right direction, given me endless support and encouraged me to always strive for more. Thank you for giving me my love for reading and writing, and for always reminding me that my words are powerful.

Finally, this work is dedicated to baby Keating, due November 2024. Thank you for already making me happier than I ever could have imagined.

For Pippa,

To Kyle and Lucie – for the unwavering support, cheerleading and blind confidence that I always 'can do it'

To my parents – for allowing me to grow up believing anything was possible

To Alex Collingwood – for teaching me how to write, and to trust in my own potential

FOREWORD

Six years ago, when I became President of the Family Division, I said that the area of the court's work that 'kept me awake at night' was that of deprivation of liberty ['DOLs'] cases. In DOLs cases judges are frequently asked to authorise the restraint of children and young people in placements which are often unregulated and frequently sub-optimal, but which are said to be the only placements available. The judge, as indeed are all of the professionals in the case, in such circumstances is between a rock and a hard place and, where restraint is necessary, there will be no alternative but to give the required authorisation. During the ensuing six years, my level of worry about DOLs cases has in no manner diminished, indeed, as the number of cases has risen from around 250 per year to 1,250 per year in that time, it has inevitably increased.

The concern that I have has a number of dimensions. First and foremost it arises from the often astonishingly disturbed behaviour of the young person at the centre of each case, and from the need to understand how best they may be cared for, whilst keeping them, and those around them, safe. These are very troubling cases. Secondly, it is plain that the number of those who need secure placements far outstrips the available resources in the registered and regulated children's homes that make up 'the secure estate'. It is the norm for the court to be told that, on any day, there are some 60 or so young people needing a secure placement, yet there are only one or two beds available in the system. Thirdly, it is not infrequently the case that the only option presented to the court is not wholly satisfactory, yet the need for the child to be held there means that the judge has no real option other than to authorise the proposed restrictive regime. The potential for a tragedy to occur in the future in such circumstances, and for it to be said 'well, the judge approved the plan', is all too plain to me. Fourthly, Parliament has made statutory provision for children whose welfare requires them to be held in secure circumstances (by secure accommodation orders under the Children Act 1989, s 25), yet, because of the need to do so, the High Court has used its inherent jurisdiction to authorise restriction of a child's liberty outside the statutory scheme, without formal Parliamentary approval.

Addressing, and reducing, these various concerns is, rightly, beyond the constitutional reach of the judges. They, and each of the social work and legal professionals involved in the individual cases, must simply do the best they can to meet the needs of the very troubled young person at the centre of proceedings. They need to do so with their eyes wide open to the fact that authorising a DOL represents a very high level of state intrusion into the life of a young person and that it is a basic requirement that they should act in a way which strictly accords with the law and European Convention on Human Rights.

It follows that every judge and professional involved in a DOLs case must be fully familiar with the law and practice that applies to this fast developing area of work. Chloe Lee and Pippa Pudney are therefore to be congratulated for producing this comprehensive and very accessible account of the law and practice relating to DOLs cases. Within these pages the reader, whether experienced or new to the field, is guided from authoritative overview down to granular practical detail through a clear and well organised narrative. The authors have done a thorough job in describing the modern law and practice, and a professional faced with a DOLs case need look no further for guidance. Whilst it is a matter of profound concern and regret that the circumstances of troubled young people make it necessary for courts to exercise a DOLs jurisdiction, as long as they have to do so the detailed support offered by this volume will be of genuine value and I very much welcome its publication.

The Rt Hon Sir Andrew McFarlane
President of the Family Division

20 September 2024

PREFACE

This book was borne out of a recognition by both authors, working increasingly within the field, that the system was not working. It was not working for the children and young people it was designed to support, and it was not working for practitioners who were often dealing with emergency situations without the requisite guidance and information to achieve the best outcomes for the children at the heart of these cases. The purpose of this book, therefore, is to be helpful in those situations. To allow practitioners, parents and lawyers alike easy access to information and guidance which will assist in circumstances where a child or young person is deprived of their liberty. The book strays into other, related, topics and may also be helpful for a wider scope of issues, but its focus is to assist in situations when children and young people are being confined and need the support of the social care system to stay safe.

Chapter 8 of this book is guest written by the brilliant Jacqueline Thomas KC, who generously gave her time to share her expertise in the field of transitions from children's services to adult services. Such is her experience that Jacqueline has published a book dedicated to this topic, entitled *A Practical Guide to Transitions from Child to Adult Social Care* which is a staple read for practitioners in the field. Not only has Jacqueline contributed to this book, but she has acted as a mentor for both authors since their practices began and throughout their early years within this profession. Without that guidance, paths may have been forged differently and this book may never have come into existence. The authors are extremely grateful for the unwavering support, enthusiasm and guidance that she has provided to both of them.

The foreword to this book is written by Sir Andrew McFarlane, President of the Family Division. Sir Andrew McFarlane's contribution to the development of the law and practice on the deprivation of liberty of children and young people has been astounding. His judgments are thoughtful, considered and always with the child at their heart. The authors are privileged to include his words within this book, and are grateful for the time he has taken to provide them.

Beyond those who have written words for this book, special thanks are also required to Lauren Gardner and Eleanor Suthern for their invaluable assistance in bringing together the pages of this book. As junior practitioners within the fields of child protection and the Court of Protection, Lauren and Eleanor have provided an exceptional contribution to this work and assistance to the authors, and they will both no doubt be part of shaping the landscape of these fields in the future.

The authors extend further thanks to all those from Spire Barristers who have supported both their practices and the process of writing this book. Without the brilliant clerking team and colleague support, this would not have been possible. Particular thanks are required for the clerking magic worked by Shannon Hart to accommodate our diaries for such a large project.

Finally, the authors are very grateful to all at Bloomsbury for taking a chance on two junior practitioners without any previous published work, and allowing us to create a resource which we hope will serve practitioners for years to come.

Chloe Lee
Pippa Pudney

September 2024

CONTENTS

AUTHORS

Chloe Lee

Chloe is a Family law and Court of Protection barrister specialising in cases involving the Deprivation of Liberty of children, young people and adults. She has a particular interest in representing vulnerable clients and ensuring that they are able to participate fully in proceedings.

Her expertise spans a range of complex issues including; serious medical treatment, physical and chemical restraint, coercion and control, capacity/consent, best interests' disputes, contact restrictions, and challenges to contact arrangements, as well as cases involving Mental Health Act and Mental Capacity Act crossovers. She regularly deals with transitional cases for young people in the care system who are moving under the jurisdiction of the Court of Protection. Chloe is frequently instructed to act on behalf of NHS bodies, local authorities, children, family members and protected parties.

Coming from a Northern working-class background herself, Chloe is keen to promote wider access and diversity to the legal profession for young people from disadvantaged backgrounds. She also has a strong commitment to pro-bono work.

Pippa Pudney

Pippa is a barrister specialising in child protection and Court of Protection work, in particular cases involving the deprivation of a person's liberty. Pippa has a developed practice representing local authorities, NHS bodies, parents, children and protected parties. Her expertise across both children's and adult's work lends itself to the tricky transitional cases involving young people as they progress towards adulthood and require support and intervention from statutory bodies.

She is regularly instructed in complex cases involving issues around a young person's consent to the arrangements for them, including their medical treatment or confinement. She has a particular interest in the framework of Article 5 of the ECHR, its purpose and domestic deployment.

Jacqueline Thomas KC (contributor, Chapter 8)

Jacqui is the joint head of Spire Barristers, a specialist family and public law set based in Leeds. She is the co-author of the book *Reforming Family Justice* and author of the Law Brief Practical Guide to Transitions from Children to Adult's social care. She has a Masters degree in Safeguarding Vulnerable Adults and is currently studying for a Masters in Medical law and ethics.

Jacqui sits as a Recorder and First Tier Mental Health Tribunal Judge. She took silk in 2020 and specialises in Family and Court of Protection work.

TABLE OF CASES

[all references are to paragraph numbers]

D

E

F

G

H

TABLE OF STATUTES

[all references are to paragraph numbers]

TABLE OF STATUTORY INSTRUMENTS

[*all references are to paragraph numbers*]

Chapter 1

INTRODUCTION

WHAT THIS BOOK IS AND WHO IT IS FOR

1.01 The deprivation of liberty of children and young people is an important topic, and a developing area of law. It concerns some of the most vulnerable children within our society and the arrangements that are made to raise them, and to keep them safe. The deprivation of liberty of children and young people centres around the physical liberty of under 18s and measures which may be imposed on them which curtail their liberty. This can include their supervision, their restraint, and monitoring or controlling their movements. All of those measures, individually and holistically, have a drastic impact on the lives of the children and young people concerned which contribute to the shape of their future.

1.02 The notion of a deprivation of liberty finds its roots in the European Convention on Human Rights (ECHR), and the protected right to liberty and security of person. The ECHR sought to establish fundamental rights which all people are entitled to and which member states, signing up to the Convention, must respect. Although the fundamental rights may be interfered with in accordance with the content of the ECHR, its aim is to protect certain rights for all citizens of the signatory countries. The right to liberty and security of person is a crucial part of the ECHR, and to interfere with that right significantly constitutes a deprivation of liberty. Since the ratification of the ECHR, countries have been required to implement domestic laws and safeguards to secure the liberty of their citizens, including their children and young people.

1.03 The aim of this book is not just to regurgitate the law relevant to a deprivation of liberty, but to help readers in their understanding of what it means, why it is important and what wider framework is in place to support children and young people who may be deprived of their liberty. It is well-established that the way we are raised helps to determine who we become as adults. So, we need to get it right. In getting it right, we need to understand what the law says about deprivations of liberty and use its guidance to navigate through these sometimes difficult waters. It is for that reason that we have written this book. We hope to contribute to the understanding of the deprivation of liberty of children and young people to make it easier to navigate for those involved, and to assist everyone to get it right for the child or young person they are concerned with.

1.04 Who are we talking to? This book is not just for lawyers. It is written for anyone who may be involved within a situation where a child or young person is, or is proposed to be, deprived of their liberty. This includes their parents, family, social worker, children's guardian or the young person themselves. It is not only important that the lawyers involved in court proceedings about a child know what the law says. The law is a helpful tool which governs the duties of state bodies, the support available for children and their families and the outcomes we must all seek to achieve for a child or young person. Knowing and understanding what the law says can help anyone involved with a child or young person who is deprived of their liberty. It shines a light on a situation which may at times feel very dark. The law gives us a framework in which to all work together to secure the right, and best, outcome for the child or young person.

1.05 In doing our best to make this book as helpful as it can be, we have included explanations throughout of concepts and phrases which may be unfamiliar to some. We have also dedicated a chapter to explaining who is who when it comes to situations in which a child or young person is deprived of their liberty. The book covers the deprivation of liberty of children and young people in England and Wales. It covers the statutory duties of state bodies that are within England and Wales, and court proceedings that take place in England and Wales. It will, at times, consider interrelated issues that extend to Scotland, but the law in Scotland is not covered within this book.

WHAT TO EXPECT

1.06 Each chapter focuses on a different element or issue relating to the deprivation of liberty of children and young people. Within the confines of this book, we will not explore deprivation of liberty issues related to adults. The chapters and paragraphs explaining the law are explanations of the law as it stands at the time this book goes to print. As case law continues to develop, there may be judgments which change or alter the legal position following the publication of this book. We therefore write with a word of warning to always check the law as it stands at the time it is being used because things may have developed since we finished writing. Future editions will come, with updates included, but that process takes time and there may be changes in the law in the intervening period. We also must stress that this book is not intended as legal advice but is a general, practical guide to this area of law.

1.07 The book will explore the concept of the deprivation of a person's liberty, including how it is interpreted in legal terms and how it looks practically. This includes walking through the journey of case law definitions a deprivation of liberty and how that definition has evolved over time, through judgments in the European Court to domestic decisions. The book will explain a deprivation of liberty through the lens of Article 5 of the ECHR, and what Article 5 requires us to consider when faced with a situation in which a child or young person is deprived of their liberty. This will extend to considering whether a specific deprivation of liberty may be lawful and if so, how it can be authorised. Discussions around authorisation will cover the scope of the inherent jurisdiction of the Family Division of the High Court, the Children Act 1989 (CA 1989), the Mental Health Act 1983 (MHA 1983) and the Mental Capacity Act 2005 (MCA 2005).

1.08 As part of exploring all things which may be relevant for a child or young person who may be deprived of their liberty, the book will also look at what duties a local authority has to a child who may require its support. This may be relevant to parents or family members who are not involved in circumstances which include a deprivation of liberty, but who require the wider support of a local authority in caring for a child or young person. The chapter's discussion will include what type of support can be offered to children and families, what support must be provided in certain circumstances, and what happens when a child is considered to be likely to suffer harm to such an extent that the Family Court is required to intervene.

1.09 A chapter is also dedicated to the tricky issue of what happens for children as they approach adulthood and require a transition between support services provided for children and those provided for adults. This period for young people which comes when they are 16 or 17 years' old is often difficult because there are different frameworks in place for supporting children and supporting adults, and regulating any deprivation of their liberty. This can create a vacuum of support for a young person who is reaching the end of the support provided to them by children's services, but does not yet have a support package devised by adult services. In order to properly assist everyone involved in getting it right for young people, the book will also explore what the issues are for 16 and 17 year olds, and how those issues can be tackled. The chapter dedicated to a young person's transition to adulthood is guest written by Jacqueline Thomas KC, a fantastic barrister, to whom we are eternally grateful for her contribution. The wealth of knowledge which she has shared within this chapter will be hugely beneficial to us all in getting it right for children and young people.

WHY THIS BOOK IS IMPORTANT

1.10 The law and practice which surrounds deprivation of liberty issues is not new. The ECHR which established the right to liberty is over 70 years' old. Much of the case law discussed within this book is a decade or two old. So, it is not because it is new or novel that this book is important. This book is important because children and young people are increasingly being deprived of their liberty and whilst the figures continue to rise, it is essential that everyone involved in this area understands what is happening for the child or young person, what the law says should happen, and what support is available.

1.11 The Nuffield Family Justice Observatory has gathered some of the statistics produced by the Ministry of Justice. From July to September 2023, 388 applications were made to the Family Division of the High Court for orders authorising the deprivation of liberty of a child or young person.[1] Over the same period, 151 applications were made for orders under the CA 1989 for a child or young person to reside within secure accommodation. During a 12-month pilot period of the National DoL Court, operating within the Royal Courts of Justice in London, 1,249 children were deprived of their liberty. Between January and December 2023, 1,368

1 Family Court Statistics Quarterly, Ministry of Justice (21 December 2023).

children and young people were the subject of applications made to the High Court to authorise their deprivation of liberty. The overall trend from 2017 shows a huge annual increase in the number of applications being made which relate to children and young people being deprived of their liberty. These statistics provide some insight into how widespread the issues that this book discusses are, making it even more important that those involved directly within them understand them.

1.12 This rise in case numbers was so great that the Nuffield Family Justice Observatory conducted an investigative report to provide some insight into the cases coming before the court and the issues they were raising. Their findings are summarised within the report entitled 'Children subject to deprivation of liberty orders: Key findings from 12 months of research at the national deprivation of liberty court'.[2] The report considers only the applications made within the remit of the High Court. There are many more applications and authorisations being dealt with under statutory regimes including the CA 1989 and the MCA 2005 which did not form part of the investigation or findings. The report found that the children about whom applications were made had multiple complex needs which included mental health challenges for which those children were not receiving adequate support. The findings included that the children who were made subject to these orders often had adverse early life experiences including having suffered abuse, neglect and presenting with complex trauma. The report highlights that although many of the applications before the court sought short-term orders, intending the child to be deprived of their liberty for a short time, they often endured for many months.

1.13 The figures demonstrate that there are substantially more applications to authorise a child or young person's deprivation of liberty under the High Court's inherent jurisdiction than there are applications for children to be placed in secure accommodation placements. From July 2022 to March 2023, 1,051 applications were made to the High Court compared with 155 applications to the Family Court for secure accommodation orders.[3] This reflects the situation on the ground that there are very few secure accommodation placements for the children and young people who require them. When a secure accommodation placement is not available, in many cases, the only other alternative is to apply for an order authorising a child's deprivation of liberty in another type of setting. Although both orders under the High Court's inherent jurisdiction and secure accommodation orders achieve the authorisation of a child or young person's deprivation of liberty, they operate within different frameworks and relate to different settings which can have a huge impact on the relevant child's experience.

1.14 One central reason why more deprivation of liberty applications are made to the High Court, as opposed to secure accommodation order applications in the Family Court, is a lack of approved secure accommodation placements which is a prerequisite to the Family Court order. The shortage in suitable secure accommodation

---

2 Children Subject to Deprivation of Liberty Orders: Key findings from 12 months of research at the national deprivation of liberty court, Nuffield Family Justice Observatory (September 2023).

3 Children Subject to Deprivation of Liberty Orders: Key findings from 12 months of research at the national deprivation of liberty court, Nuffield Family Justice Observatory (September 2023).

placements for children and young people is now well-documented in case law. One of the most referenced judgments setting out the scale of the issue is *Lancashire CC v G,* handed down by MacDonald J in October 2020.[4] Within his judgment, MacDonald J noted not only the lack of secure accommodation placements for children but also the limited number of clinical provisions available for children and young people suffering mental health difficulties and who require a specialist setting for assessment and treatment. The judgment refers to comments made by Sir James Munby in a reported decision three years earlier in which he describes 'a well known-scandal' being 'the disgraceful and utterly shaming lack of proper provision in this country of the clinical, residential and other support services so desperately needed'.[5]

1.15 MacDonald J summarised the issue before the court in saying:

> 'It is plain that, despite the issue being highlighted in multiple court decisions since 2017, and by the Children's Commissioner, the shortage of clinical provision for placement of children and adolescents requiring assessment and treatment for mental health issues within a restrictive clinical environment, the shortage of secure placements and the shortage of regulated placements remains. In this context, children like G with highly complex needs and behaviour continue to fall through the gaps that exist between secure accommodation, regulated accommodation and detention under the mental health legislation.'[6]

1.16 That crisis outlined in 2020 has not subsided. In 2023, the President of the Family Division, Sir Andrew McFarlane, handed down a judgment in *Re X (Secure Accommodation: Lack of Provision)* which again stresses the dire situation for children and young people who are falling through the gaps of what is available to them.[7] The court described the current situation as a 'substantial deficit that exists nationally in the provision of facilities for the secure accommodation of children'.[8] In summarising the concerns highlighted throughout its judgment, the court accepted that there is little that can actually be done by judges to change the position on the ground for children and young people who need specialist or secure placements. Sir Andrew McFarlane P urged action to be taken by the government and those responsible for the shortage of provisions, otherwise the court will continue to routinely find itself in a position of being asked to authorise arrangements for a child which do not meet their holistic needs, but which are the only available option.

1.17 For some children and young people, the setting that they require is a specialist mental health one. Whilst mental health support can and is provided in secure accommodation or residential settings, some children and young people require more specialist clinical care which can lead to their deprivation of liberty under the MHA 1983 within a hospital or inpatient setting. In January 2024, the House of Commons produced a research briefing on children and young people's

---

4 *Lancashire CC v G (Unavailability of Secure Accommodation)* [2020] EWHC 2828.

5 *Re X (A Child)(No.3)* [2017] EWHC 2036 (Fam), para 37.

6 *Lancashire CC v G (Unavailability of Secure Accommodation)* [2020] EWHC 2828, para 59.

7 *Re X (Secure Accommodation: Lack of Provision)* [2023] EWHC 129 (Fam).

8 *Re X (Secure Accommodation: Lack of Provision)* [2023] EWHC 129 (Fam), para 1.

mental health.[9] The statistics within the report evidence an overall increase in children and young people suffering mental disorders and probable mental disorders from 2017 to 2023. During the period of 2022 to 2023, from the providers who submitted data for the research, 997 children and young people were detained under the MHA 1983. The report raises concerns about the resource provision for children and young people who require mental health beds, and their placement in units out of area or within adult settings. The research cites a conclusion drawn by the Education Committee in 2023 which describes the capacity of children and young people's mental health services as 'grossly inadequate', a particularly startling description in the context of an increasing number of children and young people requiring these services.[10] It is important therefore for the scope of this book to include consideration of how the MHA 1983 operates for children and young people, and when this may be used to authorise a deprivation of liberty.

1.18 The availability and quality of mental health services is not only relevant for children and young people detained under the MHA 1983. The provision of suitable mental health services is important for many children and young people who require their liberty to be curtailed and who are confined under the other statutory schemes or the inherent jurisdiction. Many children and young people suffer mental health difficulties and disorders which cause or contribute to behaviours that challenge, resulting in care arrangements for them that deprive them of their liberty. Mental health services are therefore a crucial element of the overarching plans for children and young people who are deprived of their liberty. For many children and young people, access to the right specialist or therapeutic support can make a huge difference to their childhoods and can be an integral part of the path towards regaining their liberty in a safe way. It is so important that judges frequently reiterate the need for the children with whom they are concerned to be provided with specialist mental health support if there is to be any discernible progress for them.

1.19 At the core of this book's aim is a hope that it can contribute to building a better foundation of support for the most vulnerable and in-need children and young people within society. As part of achieving that aim, it is crucial that lessons are learned from past experience and a system is developed which is properly able to support the children who require it. Some of these lessons have been collated by the Nuffield Family Justice Observatory in its report 'Principles of care for children with complex needs and circumstances: principles of care framework'.[11] The report is aimed at providing guidance to statutory bodies and government for changes which are required 'to better meet the needs of children with complex needs and circumstances, including those subject to deprivation of liberty orders.' This includes better supporting children with complicated emotional and behavioural needs, those who have suffered childhood adversity and have complex trauma, and children with mental health and neurodevelopmental conditions. The report identifies that many

---

9 Children and young people's mental health: policy and services (England), House of Commons (26 January 2024).

10 Children and young people's mental health: policy and services (England), House of Commons (26 January 2024), page 8.

11 Principles of care for children with complex needs and circumstances: principles of care framework, Nuffield Family Justice Observatory (September 2023).

of the children assessed have disrupted relationships with family and professionals, their mental health support is minimal, they are supported by inexperienced staff and they have no say in their support planning. The report recommends that these children are provided agency and respect: that they are supported by experienced multidisciplinary teams who can offer a wide-range of tailored services and that they have a core and stable support team with whom they can build trusting relationships. Getting these fundamental services right will, the report concludes, be a significant step towards getting it right for these children and young people overall.

CONCLUSION

1.20 We hope this book is helpful. We hope it serves as a guide through a difficult and emotionally-turbulent area of law. We hope the contents of this book can be used by practitioners, family members and young people to make a complicated area of law and practice easier to tackle. In our own work within this field, we have grown to appreciate how inaccessible the law and regulations seem to those who are not regularly working within these cases. It has become clear that this inaccessibility creates barriers to making progress for children and young people, which we hope to break down. We have also come to appreciate the impact that the language around the deprivation of liberty of children and young people has on the families involved. Lawyers working within the field are hardened to the sterile and blunt words and phrases used within the legal arena to describe regimes and arrangements for children and young people, which can be daunting for their families. We have found that even the phrase 'deprivation of liberty' creates connotations for families of a prison-like routine which is scary for parents and young people, and often a misrepresentation of the situation on the ground. This book is designed to explain those words and phrases, drawing the ammunition out of them with understanding and insight. In doing this, we hope to contribute towards promoting the rights and welfare of the children and young people who these cases are about, bringing together all of those involved in their care and support to work collaboratively to get it right.

Chapter 2

WHO'S WHO

INTRODUCTION

2.01 Many words, phrases and titles used throughout this book will be familiar to those that work within the the courts or who have experience of the court process; however, to many others, they will be unfamiliar. This chapter provides definitions and explanations of the words, phrases and titles used throughout this book which may be new to some.

THE COURTS

2.02 **The Family Court** – The Family Court in England and Wales is the court which deals with issues related to children and families, including disputes about children spending time with their parents or which parent they live with, divorce applications or issues of child protection (separate to the process of prosecution for a criminal offence which is dealt with in the Criminal Court). Family Court proceedings relating to children are divided into private law proceedings, which involve applications made by parents and relating to internal family issues, and public law proceedings when there is some involvement by the state. Some limited cases, usually more complex cases, are heard in the Family Division of the High Court. These cases may involve international child abduction, particularly complex issues or consideration of using the inherent jurisdiction of the High Court. The Family Division of the High Court also hears appeals from certain decisions made by Circuit Judges and Recorders in the Family Court. The Family Court and the Family Division of the High Court are headed by the President of the Family Division.

2.03 **The Family Division** – The Family Division consists of 19 High Court Judges who deal with some of the most complex issues, including:

(a) Complicated divorce proceedings, including disputes over children, property or money;

(b) Adoption, wardship and other matters involving children with elements of complexity; and

(c) Serious medical treatment decisions.

2.04 **The European Court of Human Rights (ECtHR)** – The European Court of Human Rights, also known as the Strasbourg Court, is an international court that was set up in 1959. The ECtHR rules on individual or State applications which allege violations of the rights that are set out in the European Convention on Human Rights.

2.05 The European Convention on Human Rights (ECHR) – The European Convention on Human Rights is an international convention to protect human rights and political freedoms in countries within Europe. It is a document signed by 46 member states of the Council, including the United Kingdom, and which those member states have agreed to uphold. The ECHR protects a person's right to life; to freedom and security; to respect for a private life; to freedom of expression, thought, conscience and religion; to vote in and stand for election; to a fair trial; and for property and peaceful enjoyment of possessions.[1]

2.06 The inherent jurisdiction – The term inherent jurisdiction describes a power vested within the High Court to make orders which otherwise could not be made under existing statute. The inherent jurisdiction is often described as the 'great safety net'. It is used in proceedings involving vulnerable adults and children.

THE PROFESSIONALS INVOLVED AND THEIR ROLES

2.07 Accredited Legal Representative (ALR) – An ALR is a solicitor who has been authorised to represent P (the person who lacks capacity) in Court of Protection Proceedings.

2.08 Approved Mental Health Professional (AMHP) – An AMHP is a person involved in situations which engage the Mental Health Act 1983 (MHA 1983). They are professionals working within the mental health field who are approved to carry out duties under the MHA 1983. They are trained to implement elements of the MHA 1983 and they are responsible for organising, co-ordinating and contributing to MHA assessments. An AMHP may also be a social worker, nurse, occupational therapist or psychologist.

2.09 Barrister – A barrister is an independent lawyer whose role is to advocate for their client within court proceedings. A barrister's role includes providing legal advice, representing a client in court and addressing a judge on their client's behalf. All barristers in England and Wales are regulated by the Bar Standards Board.

2.10 CAFCASS – Cafcass stands for 'the Children and Family Court Advisory and Support Service'. The service is designed to represent the interests of children and young people in Family Court cases in England and Wales. As an organisation, it is independent of the local authority, court or any NHS service. Its role within proceedings is to represent the best interests of the children and young people involved.

2.11 CAMHS – CAMHS stands for 'Child and Adolescent Mental Health Services'. CAMHS is the NHS mental health service for children and young people. It has been established to help children and young people up to the age of 18 who are finding it hard to cope with their everyday life, and as such are struggling with

---

1 The Convention for the Protection of Human Rights and Fundamental Freedoms (Rome, 4 November 1950).

their mental health. The role of CAMHS is to undertake assessments and provide treatment and support for children and young people who require their services. CAMHS may offer cognitive behavioural therapy (CBT), dialectical behavioural therapy (DBT), family therapy, psychotherapy or a solution focussed practice.

2.12 Children's Guardian – Children's Guardians work within Cafcass. They are qualified social workers who are experienced in working with children and families. They are appointed by the court to represent the child or young person in family law proceedings. As part of their role, Children's Guardians will undertake direct work with the children at the heart of proceedings, where appropriate, and provide reports to the court about what is in the child's best interests.

2.13 Clerk – Every judge is assigned a clerk who is an officer of the court providing administrative support to the judge. Clerks are an essential part of the justice system, facilitating the smooth-running of court hearings and ensuring judges are provided with the documents they require to efficiently manage their cases.

2.14 Experts – This is a person who provides expert advice for use in family proceedings. They provide the court with their specialist professional knowledge and expertise, and sometimes technical knowledge. They have appropriate professional qualifications, experience and skills to provide an expert opinion to the court. Experts can come within a range of different fields, and may include: psychologists, psychiatrists, paediatricians, independent social workers, phone analysts, and hair and blood sample analysts.

2.15 High Court judges – High Court judges sit in the Family Division of the High Court. They deal with complex cases relating to children and families and can exercise the inherent jurisdiction of the High Court. High Court judges sitting in the Family Division also deal with the appeals from certain decisions of Circuit judges sitting in the Family Court. Some judges sitting in the Family Division of the High Court will be Deputy High Court Judges, allowing them to sit in this role on a part-time basis.

2.16 Independent Mental Capacity Advocate (IMCA) – The IMCA's role is to support and represent P in any decision making process and to ensure that the Mental Capacity Act 2005 is being followed in respect of decisions about their. The Mental Capacity Act 2005 (Independent Mental Capacity Advocates) (General) Regulations 2006 set out the IMCA's role and functions, which includes: gathering information, evaluating information, making representations and challenging decisions.

2.17 Independent Mental Health Advocate (IMHA) – An IMHA is a mental health advocate who is trained in the Mental Health Act 1983 (MHA 1983). Their role is to support people who fall within the scope of the MHA 1983's powers to understand their rights under the statute and support them to access information, explore options, raise queries and concerns and ensure their voice is heard. In England, you have a right to an IMHA if: you are detained under the MHA 1983 (save for in certain circumstances); you are 'liable to be detained'; you are subject to a community treatment order; you are subject to guardianship; you are a conditionally discharged restricted patient; or you are a voluntary/informal patient and certain treatments are being considered.

2.18 Litigation friend – A litigation friend is required when a person lacks capacity to participate in or make certain decisions within court proceedings. Litigation friends can be appointed in civil cases, family cases or cases within the Court of Protection. When a person is supported by a litigation friend, they are referred to as a 'protected party'. A wide range of people can be appointed to act as a litigation friend, including but not limited to a: parent or guardian; a family member; a friend; a solicitor; or a professional advocate. The primary duties of a litigation friend are to: make decisions in the best interests of the protected party; to do what is possible to keep the protected party informed about the proceedings and ascertain their wishes and feelings; and to obtain legal advice on behalf of the protected party and provide instructions to the solicitor.

2.19 Local Authorities – Local authorities are state bodies. Every local area has a local authority which has statutory duties to safeguard and promote the welfare of different children and adults in their area. Local authorities are divided into different departments which oversee different elements of their work and responsibilities. When dealing with children and young people, the relevant local authority department is children's services, also known as children's social care. Children's services deliver services to children, young people and families in their area.

2.20 Official Solicitor – The Official Solicitor is a civil servant appointed by the government. The Official Solicitor acts as litigation friend within court proceedings for individuals who lack capacity to conduct litigation and when there is no one else suitable and willing to act as a litigation friend. The Official Solicitor is known as 'the litigation friend of last resort'.

2.21 Ofsted – Ofsted is the 'Office for Standards in Education, Children's Services and Skills'. It is the organisation which inspects services providing education and skills for learners of all ages. It also inspects and regulates services that care for children and young people. Ofsted's role is to safeguard and promote the welfare of children and vulnerable young people.

2.22 P – P is a short-hand term used to refer to the person who is the subject of the court proceedings in the Court of Protection.

2.23 President of the Family Division – The President of the Family Division is the head of the Family Division of the High Court of Justice in England and Wales and the Head of Family Justice. The current President of the Family Division and Head of Family Justice is The Right Honourable Sir Andrew McFarlane. Sir Andrew McFarlane succeeded Sir James Munby who retired as President in July 2018.

2.24 Rule 1.2 Representative – A rule 1.2 representative is a person who represents an individual who lacks capacity to consent to restrictions on their liberty which amount to a deprivation of liberty. Their role as representative is to have oversight of P's best interests in circumstances where their liberty is curtailed. When appointed, a rule 1.2 representative will obtain the wishes and feelings of the person they are representing, check the care and treatment they are being provided with is the least restrictive of their rights and freedoms possible, and help the person to understand the arrangements for them and support them to exercise their rights in relation to their liberty. The role can be undertaken by a family member or friend, or in cases where there is no one familiar with P who is suitable to appoint, an independent advocate may be appointed. Rule 1.2 representatives are appointed by the court.

2.25 **Section 12 Doctor** – A section 12 doctor is a doctor approved by the Secretary of State under the MHA 1983, s 12(2). They are doctors with special experience in the diagnosis or treatment of mental disorders. Whenever a process governed by the MHA 1983 requires recommendations from two doctors, one of those doctors must be a section 12 doctor.

2.26 **Social Worker** – A social worker in the context of children and young people is an employee of the local authority or Cafcass. References to social workers most commonly refers to local authority social workers, as Cafcass employees are called Children's Guardians. Each child or young person in local authority care has an allocated social worker who plays a key role in safeguarding and promoting the welfare. As part of the social worker's role within child protection, they will get to know the child concerned (where appropriate), gather their wishes and feelings and work closely with children and families to secure the child's welfare.

2.27 **Solicitor** – A solicitor is a qualified legal professional who provides legal support, specialised legal advice and sometimes representation to clients within proceedings.

Chapter 3

WHAT IS A DEPRIVATION OF LIBERTY?

INTRODUCTION

3.01 The deprivation of a child or young person's liberty is the concept at the centre of this book. Although the focus herein will be on what this means in relation to children (who are under 16) and young people (aged 16 or 17), adults too can be deprived of their liberty and there is a significant overlap of the factors which are relevant to work out if a person, of any age, is deprived of their liberty. What it means to be deprived of liberty has been formulated over time, through lengthy discussion within case law, to arrive at the principles which are now determined to be crucial in order for a person to be considered deprived of their liberty.

3.02 This chapter will explore the background which preceded the domestic court's definition of a deprivation of liberty, the elements of a deprivation of liberty, and what circumstances in practice may satisfy the criteria for the deprivation of liberty of a child or young person. There will be a focus in this chapter on what is termed the 'objective element' of a deprivation of liberty, also referred to as the 'confinement' element.[1] The 'subjective element' of the criteria, an absence of valid consent, will be explored in the next chapter. Many of the cases referred to in this chapter concern adults although, save where specified, the principles which arise will apply equally to children and young people.

ARTICLE 5

3.03 The European Convention on Human Rights (ECHR) is a collection of principles, categorised into articles, which the member states signing up to the Convention agree to uphold.[2] The ECHR includes 16 protocols which guide the implementation of the ECHR. There are 46 member states signed up to the ECHR, including the United Kingdom, Ireland, France, Spain and Germany. The ECHR was drafted by the Council of Europe, established in 1949, to promote democracy, human rights and the rule of law. It is a requirement of joining the Council of Europe that member states sign up to the ECHR. The United Kingdom ratified the ECHR in 1951 and it was given direct effect in English and Welsh law by the Human Rights Act 1998. The ECHR protects a person's right to life; to freedom and security; to respect

---

1 *Re A-F* [2018] EWHC 138 (Fam), para 9.

2 The Convention for the Protection of Human Rights and Fundamental Freedoms (Rome, 4 November 1950).

for a private life; to freedom of expression, thought, conscience and religion; to vote in and stand for election; to a fair trial; and for property and peaceful enjoyment of possessions. The ECHR prohibits acts which contravene those rights, save for the following exceptions:

(a) 'qualified' rights which may be interfered with in order to protect the rights of another or the wider public interest;

(b) certain rights are subject to specific exceptions set out within the body of the ECHR. Article 5 (the right to liberty and security) falls into this category and there are provisions within the article itself which provide an exception to the right not to be deprived of liberty.[3]

3.04 The rights and freedoms contained within the ECHR apply to everyone living within the jurisdiction of a member state.[4] For the avoidance of doubt, this includes people with mental and physical disabilities.[5] Article 5, the right to liberty and security, is the key part of the ECHR which relates to the deprivation of a person's liberty.[6] It reads:

> '1. Everyone has the right to liberty and security of person. No one shall be deprived of his liberty save in the following cases and in accordance with a procedure prescribed by law:
>
> (a) the lawful detention of a person after conviction by a competent court;
>
> (b) the lawful arrest or detention of a person for non-compliance with the lawful order of a court or in order to secure the fulfilment of any obligation prescribed by law;
>
> (c) the lawful arrest or detention of a person effected for the purpose of bringing him before the competent legal authority on reasonable suspicion of having committed an offence or when it is reasonably considered necessary to prevent his committing an offence or fleeing after having done so;
>
> (d) the detention of a minor by lawful order for the purpose of educational supervision or his lawful detention for the purpose of bringing him before the competent legal authority;
>
> (e) the lawful detention of persons for the prevention of spreading of infectious diseases, or persons of unsound mind, alcoholics or drug addicts or vagrants;
>
> (f) the lawful arrest or detention of a person to prevent his effecting an unauthorised entry into the country or of a person against whom action is being taken with a view to deportation or extradition.
>
> ...

---

3 Article 5 of the Convention for the Protection of Human Rights and Fundamental Freedoms (Rome, 4 November 1950).

4 Article 1 of The Convention for the Protection of Human Rights and Fundamental Freedoms (Rome, 4 November 1950).

5 The Convention on the Rights of Persons with Disabilities, United Nations (2006), although implemented by the United Nations not the Council of Europe, this Convention provides for the equal treatment of people with disabilities.

6 Article 5 of the Convention for the Protection of Human Rights and Fundamental Freedoms (Rome, 4 November 1950).

4. Everyone who is deprived of his liberty by arrest or detention shall be entitled to take proceedings by which the lawfulness of his detention shall be decided speedily by a court and his release ordered if the detention is not lawful.

5. Everyone who has been the victim of arrest or detention in contravention of the provisions of this article shall have an enforceable right to compensation.'

3.05 The guidance accompanying the ECHR clarifies that reference to a person's liberty within the article is to their physical liberty, not related to freedom of movement save for where any restrictions are of a degree or intensity to warrant consideration of a deprivation of liberty.[7] 'Security of person' has been interpreted as incorporating a requirement that a person's liberty may not be deprived in an arbitrary fashion.[8] The accompanying guidance further explains that the overarching purpose of the article and its requirements is to 'prevent arbitrary or unjustified deprivations of liberty'.[9] What is meant by an 'arbitrary or unjustified' deprivation will depend upon the circumstances of each case. It may include a deprivation of liberty in the following circumstances: one which is not compliant with domestic law; where there is an element of bad faith or deception on the part of the authorities; when the restrictions implemented do not genuinely conform with their purpose; or where the restriction is not proportionate to the ground of Article 5(1) relied upon to justify it.[10]

3.06 Before delving into the permitted exceptions under Article 5 whereby a person may be deprived of their liberty, it is necessary to begin with how a deprivation of liberty is defined. The guidance which accompanies Article 5 is a helpful starting point in deciphering what is meant by a deprivation of liberty.[11] The guidance refers to the case *Guzzardi v Italy* and the principles set down therein by the European Court of Human Rights (ECtHR).[12] By way of background, the ECtHR in this case was considering the circumstances of an Italian man, Mr Guzzardi, who had been released from detention on remand and placed in a compulsory residence on a small island. Mr Guzzardi complained that he was being deprived of his liberty by virtue of the circumstances in which he was living, and this was the issue which the court had to determine. The court held that Mr Guzzardi was being deprived of his liberty, setting down that the starting point to determine a deprivation of liberty must be the person's 'concrete situation', which includes the 'type, duration, effects and manner of implementation of the measure in question'.[13] The court continued by explaining 'the difference between deprivation of and restriction upon liberty is nonetheless merely one of degree or intensity, and not one of nature or substance'.[14]

---

7 Guidance on Article 5 of the European Convention on Human Rights: Right to liberty and security, Council of Europe (August 2022), paras 1–2.

8 *East African Asians v United Kingdom* [1973] 3 EHRR 76.

9 Guidance on Article 5 of the European Convention on Human Rights: Right to liberty and security, Council of Europe (August 2022), para 23.

10 Guidance on Article 5 of the European Convention on Human Rights: Right to liberty and security, Council of Europe (August 2022), paras 39–42.

11 Guidance on Article 5 of the European Convention on Human Rights: Right to liberty and security, Council of Europe (August 2022), para 2.

12 *Guzzardi v Italy* 7367/76 [1980] ECHR 5.

13 *Guzzardi v Italy* 7367/76 [1980] ECHR 5, para 92.

14 *Guzzardi v Italy* 7367/76 [1980] ECHR 5, para 93.

Therefore, whilst the word 'restrictions' is often used to describe measures which cumulatively amount to a deprivation of liberty, a restriction on liberty itself is not the same as being deprived of liberty. A deprivation involves a more intense regime or invasive degree of measures in order to be distinguished from a restriction. The guidance to the ECHR incorporates the salient factors of this judgment and urges domestic courts, when considering potential deprivations of liberty, to have regard to the specific context and circumstances surrounding the restrictions imposed on each individual.[15]

3.07 The guidance goes on to set out the following principles to assist courts and practitioners to decipher if a deprivation of liberty is present and the corresponding cases from which they arise:

(a) Measures intended for the protection of or made in the interests of the person concerned may still amount to a deprivation of liberty, taken from *Khlaifia and Others v Italy* (GC) 16483/12 (2016);

(b) The purpose of measures taken in depriving a person of their liberty is not determinative of whether there has been a deprivation of liberty, from *Rozhkov v Russia (No 2),* 38898/04 (2017);

(c) A deprivation of liberty within the meaning of Article 5 contains an objective element of a person's confinement in a particular restricted space for a not negligible length of time, and a subjective element that the person has not validly consented to the confinement, principles arising from *Storck v Germany* (2005) 43 EHRR 6 and *Stanev v Bulgaria* 36760/06 [2012] ECHR 46 (both of which will be considered in more detail later);

(d) Relevant factors to consider include the possibility to leave the restricted area, the degree of supervision and control, the extent of isolation and the availability of social contacts, provided for within *Guzzardi v Italy* [1980] ECHR 5; *HM v Switzerland* [2002] ECHR 157; *HL v The UK* [2004] ECHR 471;

(e) The relatively short duration of any measures being in place will not affect the conclusion that a deprivation of liberty has arisen if the other facts of the case indicate a deprivation, from *Rantsev v Cyprus and Russia* (2010) 51 EHRR 1; *Iskandarov v Russia* 17185/05 (2010).[16]

3.08 The case of *Storck v Germany* was and continues to be an influential and important decision in outlining what constitutes a deprivation of liberty. It underpins much of the guidance set out above.[17] For this reason, it is helpful to look at this case in more detail. The ECtHR was concerned with a woman, the applicant, who was 18 years old at the time when the circumstances in question arose, and her placement in psychiatric institutions and hospital. The applicant argued before the court that she had been deprived of her liberty during her confinement to a clinic to which she

15 Guidance on Article 5 of the European Convention on Human Rights: Right to liberty and security, Council of Europe (August 2022), para 6.

16 Guidance on Article 5 of the European Convention on Human Rights: Right to liberty and security, Council of Europe (August 2022), paras 8–12.

17 *Storck v Germany* (2005) 43 EHRR 6.

objected.[18] The government rejected that argument and stated that the applicant had not been deprived of her liberty as she had consented to the stay.

3.09 In analysing the arguments and coming to a conclusion, the ECtHR distilled the complicated concept of a deprivation of liberty into a three-stage test, subsequently described as the '*Storck* limbs':

(a) the objective component of confinement in a particular restricted place for a not negligible length of time;

(b) the subjective component of a lack of valid consent; and,

(c) the attribution of responsibility to the state.[19]

3.10 On the evidence before it, the court determined that the applicant had been deprived of her liberty and the criteria set out were satisfied. The salient elements of the applicant's circumstances were as follows:

> 'The applicant had been placed in a locked ward of that clinic. She had been under continuous supervision and control of the clinic personnel and had not been free to leave the clinic during her entire stay there of some 20 months. When the applicant had attempted to flee it had been necessary to fetter her in order to secure her stay in the clinic. When she had once succeeded in escaping from there she had to be brought back by the police. She had also not been able to maintain regular social contacts with the outside world.
>
> …
>
> [T]he applicant had attained majority at the time of her admission to the clinic and had not been placed under guardianship. Therefore, she had been considered to have the capacity to consent or object to her admission and treatment in hospital.
>
> …
>
> [T]he applicant, on several occasions, had tried to flee from the clinic. She had to be fettered in order to prevent her from absconding and had to be brought back to the clinic by the police when she had managed to escape on one occasion. Under these circumstances, the Court is unable to discern any factual basis for the assumption that the applicant – presuming her capacity to consent – had agreed to her continued stay in the clinic.'[20]

3.11 The judgment in *Stanev v Bulgaria* reiterated and applied the test as set down within *Storck.*[21] The applicant in this case similarly argued that he had been deprived of his liberty pursuant to Article 5 but in circumstances where he was living in a care home. The care home was in an isolated area and provided little access to the community. The applicant argued that he could not choose to leave of his own initiative and he required permission to go out. It was submitted that his occupational activities and movements were subjected to thorough supervision by employees

18 *Storck v Germany* (2005) 43 EHRR 6, para 69.

19 *Storck v Germany* (2005) 43 EHRR 6, paras 73–89.

20 *Storck v Germany* (2005) 43 EHRR 6, paras 73–76.

21 *Stanev v Bulgaria* 36760/06 [2012] ECHR 36.

of the care home and a strict daily routine was implemented. The government, responding to the application, refuted the notion that the applicant was deprived of his liberty, stating that the placement was a protective measure taken within the applicant's interests. The court ultimately determined that the circumstances did amount to a deprivation of the applicant's liberty, placing weight on the fact that the applicant could not leave without permission (although the building itself was not locked); his time outside of the care home was controlled; and he was subject to constant supervision in one way or another.[22] In respect of the subjective element, a lack of valid consent, the court held that this had been satisfied as the applicant's consent was not sought prior to his placement in the care home and at no time after the move did the applicant express a wish to remain there.[23]

3.12 Both cases provide an important landscape on which the evolving definition of a deprivation of liberty has been formulated. They make clear that there needs to be simultaneous objective and subjective elements satisfied in order to establish a deprivation of liberty. The next section will focus on the first element, the objective component of confinement in a particular restricted place for a not negligible length of time.

THE OBJECTIVE ELEMENT

3.13 The landmark judgment in England and Wales concerning the objective element of a deprivation of liberty came in the case of *Cheshire West.*[24] The Supreme Court in this case was considering two appeals together, relating to three people. The issue before the court was 'the criteria for judging whether the living arrangements made for a mentally incapacitated person amount to a deprivation of liberty'.[25] The judgment makes clear that the court was only concerned with this objective element and not the second and third limbs of the *Storck* criteria.[26]

3.14 The court was, in this case, bound by the definition of a deprivation of liberty as used for the purposes of Article 5, by virtue of Mental Capacity Act 2005 (MCA 2005), s 64(5) which requires it.[27] Therefore, the Supreme Court's discussion on the law focused on the principles arising from the European jurisprudence. However, the court noted that European case law had not, at the time, dealt with a case which had the same features as the circumstances which arose here, namely:

---

22 *Stanev v Bulgaria* 36760/06 [2012] ECHR 36, paras 124–129.

23 *Stanev v Bulgaria* 36760/06 [2012] ECHR 36, paras 130–132.

24 *1) P (by his litigation friend the Official Solicitor) v Cheshire West and Chester Council & Anor (2) P and Q (by their litigation friend the Official Solicitor) v Surrey County Council* [2014] UKSC 19.

25 *(1) P (by his litigation friend the Official Solicitor) v Cheshire West and Chester Council & Anor (2) P and Q (by their litigation friend the Official Solicitor) v Surrey County Council* [2014] UKSC 19, para 1.

26 *(1) P (by his litigation friend the Official Solicitor) v Cheshire West and Chester Council & Anor (2) P and Q (by their litigation friend the Official Solicitor) v Surrey County Council* [2014] UKSC 19, para 37.

27 MCA 2005, s 64(5) which requires that for the purposes of that Act, references to deprivation of a person's liberty have the same meaning as in Article 5(1) of the ECHR.

being about a person who lacks legal and factual capacity to decide upon their placement but who has not indicated an objection to the placement; concerning a placement in a small group or domestic setting, close to 'normal' home life; and, with the initial authorisation of the placement by a court as being in the person's best interests.[28]

3.15 Within its analysis, the court considered the circumstances of the people at the centre of the case. This included the court asking whether the 'relative normality' of each person's living circumstances should be considered as part of the evaluation of their confinement, and how normality could be defined by comparison with a person's peers.[29] As part of this discussion, Lady Hale gave what has now become one of the most well-known phrases from domestic case law, saying 'The fact that my living arrangements are comfortable, and indeed make my life as enjoyable as it could possibly be, should make no difference. A gilded cage is still a cage.'[30]

3.16 What can be inferred from this phrase is that determining whether a person is confined for the purposes of the objective element of their deprivation of liberty should not be reduced to looking at whether their living arrangements are comfortable or with a good standard of care being provided. A confinement can be established whether a person is living in a cell without social interaction or living in a well-decorated care home with activities and stimulation. Lady Hale agreed with the approach taken by the National Autistic Society and Mind (who were interveners in the application) who considered the following to be not relevant in establishing a deprivation of liberty: the person's compliance or lack of objection; the relative normality of the placement; and the reason or purpose behind a particular placement. The court set out the following factors which could determine whether or not a mentally incapacitated person was being deprived of their liberty:

(a) whether or not the person was under continuous supervision and control; and

(b) whether the person was free to leave or not.[31]

3.17 In setting out those crucial elements, Lady Hale was conscious to note that the two may arise independent of one another. Lady Hale commented:

> 'A person might be under constant supervision and control but still be free to leave should he express the desire so to do. Conversely, it is possible to imagine situations

---

28 *(1) P (by his litigation friend the Official Solicitor) v Cheshire West and Chester Council & Anor (2) P and Q (by their litigation friend the Official Solicitor) v Surrey County Council* [2014] UKSC 19, para 32.

29 *(1) P (by his litigation friend the Official Solicitor) v Cheshire West and Chester Council & Anor (2) P and Q (by their litigation friend the Official Solicitor) v Surrey County Council* [2014] UKSC 19, paras 46–47.

30 *(1) P (by his litigation friend the Official Solicitor) v Cheshire West and Chester Council & Anor (2) P and Q (by their litigation friend the Official Solicitor) v Surrey County Council* [2014] UKSC 19, para 46.

31 *(1) P (by his litigation friend the Official Solicitor) v Cheshire West and Chester Council & Anor (2) P and Q (by their litigation friend the Official Solicitor) v Surrey County Council* [2014] UKSC 19, para 49.

in which a person is not free to leave but is not under such continuous supervision and control as to lead to the conclusion that he was deprived of his liberty.'[32]

3.18 It is therefore necessary to consider the circumstances of the person as a whole in order to establish whether the objective element of their confinement is established. Lord Neuberger commented that:

> 'whether a particular case involves deprivation or restriction must depend on the specific facts of the case, but that does not mean there can be no focussed guidance. It is also true that, however clear the guidance, there will be cases where it will be difficult to decide which side of the line the facts fall, but that is not a reason for the court not seeking to minimise the uncertainty.'[33]

He went on to agree with the comments of Lady Hale, clarifying that:

> 'the Strasbourg court decisions do indicate that the twin features of continuous supervision and control and lack of freedom to leave are the essential ingredients of deprivation of liberty (in addition to the area and period of confinement)'.[34]

Continuous Supervision and Control

3.19 The Supreme Court in *Cheshire West* did not define what is meant by 'continuous supervision and control'. However, the wording used reflects the integral principle outlined within *Storck* as taken from *HL v United Kingdom* that to establish a confinement, the intensity and degree of the circumstances must be assessed to distinguish a deprivation from a restriction on liberty.[35] The emphasis therefore is on considering the regime and situation as a whole, with a focus on identifying what supervision and control is in place and whether that is continuous.

3.20 The case of *HL v United Kingdom* brought about a defining moment in establishing the criteria for a deprivation of liberty in first including the phrase 'continuous supervision and control' in its analysis.[36] The facts of this case provide insight into what may constitute continuous supervision and control. The ECtHR was concerned with circumstances in which the relevant health professionals exercised 'strict control' over the detained person's assessment, treatment, contacts, movement and residence.[37] The court did not consider that the objective element necessitated that a person must be within a locked or lockable ward in order to be

---

32 *(1) P (by his litigation friend the Official Solicitor) v Cheshire West and Chester Council & Anor (2) P and Q (by their litigation friend the Official Solicitor) v Surrey County Council* [2014] UKSC 19, para 49.

33 *(1) P (by his litigation friend the Official Solicitor) v Cheshire West and Chester Council & Anor (2) P and Q (by their litigation friend the Official Solicitor) v Surrey County Council* [2014] UKSC 19, para 60.

34 *(1) P (by his litigation friend the Official Solicitor) v Cheshire West and Chester Council & Anor (2) P and Q (by their litigation friend the Official Solicitor) v Surrey County Council* [2014] UKSC 19, para 63.

35 *Storck v Germany* (2005) 43 EHRR 6; *HL v United Kingdom* (2004) 40 EHRR 761.

36 *HL v United Kingdom* (2004) 40 EHRR 761.

37 *HL v United Kingdom* (2004) 40 EHRR 761, para 91.

considered deprived of their liberty.[38] However, the intensity and degree of control that was in place was deemed sufficient to conclude that a deprivation of liberty had arisen. Whilst the court expressly recognised the measures which amounted to control of the applicant, the regime also strayed into preventing the applicant being free to leave as his movement was so closely controlled and monitored. This is a helpful example of a regime in which the measures focused on the supervision and control of a person, but which were so intense that they satisfied the holistic test for the objective deprivation of liberty.

3.21 What is clear from the jurisprudence is that each case must be considered on its own facts. The regime in place must be considered as a whole, rather than looking at individual measures in isolation. It is for this reason that the court has so far declined to set down a collection of facts which need to be in place to meet the criteria of continuous supervision and control. Sir Mark Hedley shone some light on the interpretation of the phrase 'continuous supervision and control' in *A Local Authority v AB* in surmising:

> '[I]t seems to me that the question of supervision and control must be viewed in the context of the prescribed condition of residence. Thus whilst she may be free to leave the property as she chooses, she is always subject to state control requiring her return should she be otherwise unwilling to do so… whilst the supervision of her coming and going is not intrusive, it is the fact that all her movements are known and noted.'[39]

3.22 It follows from this judgment and the wider jurisprudence concerning this limb of the test that a large number of measures may be considered to be an exercise of 'supervision and control', beyond the more obvious imposition of constant direct supervision by a carer, support worker or other professional. It may include supervision when a person is out in the community, their movements being monitored within or outside of a placement or when rules are implemented to govern their community access. Supervision and control may include dictating where a person is and is not allowed to go.[40] Sedative medication including that provided covertly may also amount to continuous supervision and control.[41] It can also include the presence of a carer during aspects of personal care and supervising a person's daily living activities. As technology advances, the court is also tasked with considering the use of technology as a means of effecting continuous supervision or control, and tracking devices are now seen increasingly within care plans that amount to a young person or adult's deprivation of liberty.

3.23 Case law has not gone so far as to suggest that 'continuous' imposes a requirement on the supervision and control that it must be in place for every minute of the day. In order to determine whether a regime is continuous, practitioners should consider the overall impact it has on a person's life even if there are short gaps in direct supervision, for example. Senior Judge Hilder considered the meaning of

---

38 *HL v United Kingdom* (2004) 40 EHRR 761, para 92.

39 *A Local Authority v AB* [2020] EWCOP 39, para 13.

40 *HL v United Kingdom* (2004) 40 EHRR 761, paras 91–92; *An NHS Trust v HT, NT, Manchester City Council, ST* [2022] EWHC 719 (Fam), para 15.

41 *AG v BMBC* [2016] EWCOP 37.

'continuous' within *London Borough of Havering v AEL* and found that the woman concerned was subject to continuous supervision and control because 'she has 24-hour support and she is thereby under continuous control in the sense that her freedom may be interfered with at any moment'.[42] This gives a broad interpretation to what 'continuous' may look like for a person, encompassing situations where someone may be alone for periods of the day but with the possibility of intervention lingering.

3.24 Cobb J provided some further guidance on the interpretation of continuous supervision and control in *Re RD (Deprivation of Restriction of Liberty)*.[43] The court held, in that case, that when considering if the supervision and control reaches the threshold of being 'complete or constant', it must be deemed to be 'something like 'total', 'unremitting', 'thorough', and/or 'unqualified' '.[44] This helpful guidance reiterates the general approach adopted by the court to this phrase being a common sense approach, analysing the regime as a whole and its effect practically on the child or young person concerned.

Free to leave

3.25 Freedom to leave was also not defined within the *Cheshire West* judgment. However, the court did make reference to the definition provided earlier by Munby J *JE v DE* as follows:

> 'And when I refer to leaving the X home and the Y home, I do not mean leaving for the purpose of some trip or outing approved by SCC or by those managing the institution: I mean leaving in the sense of removing himself permanently in order to live where and with whom he chooses…'[45]

3.26 This creates one clear circumstance in which a person will be considered 'not free to leave': if they are not permitted, by virtue of the regime, to choose to live elsewhere. However, this element of the criteria can be satisfied in other ways too, inferred by Munby J's reference to an 'approved' outing and the passage he quoted from the dissenting judgment in *HM v Switzerland*.[46] A person may be considered not free to leave if they are unable to leave without permission or without arrangements being approved by the body exercising supervision and control, even if that is not for the purposes of relocating elsewhere. Munby J agreed with the submissions put before him that the person concerned was not free to leave as the authority implementing restrictions decided the 'essential matters' of where the person concerned lived and whether he could leave.[47]

---

42 *London Borough of Havering v AEL* [2021] EWCOP 9, para 47.
43 *Re RD (Deprivation of Restriction of Liberty)* [2018] EWFC 47.
44 *Re RD (Deprivation of Restriction of Liberty)* [2018] EWFC 47, para 31.
45 *JE v DE* [2007] 2 FLR 1150, para 115.
46 *JE v DE* [2007] 2 FLR 1150, para 116; *HM v Switzerland* (2002) 38 EHRR 314.
47 *JE v DE* [2007] 2 FLR 1150, para 117.

3.27 The notion that a person will be considered 'not free to leave' by measures other than preventing their relocation was reinforced in the short comment made by His Honour Judge Burrows in *Lancashire & South Cumbria NHS Foundation Trust, Lancashire County Council v AH*.[48] The judge summarised that 'She would be deprived of her liberty there because she was not free to leave and could only leave the placement for visits to her own flat with the permission of staff and was required to return in accordance with her care plan.'[49] This is an example of a circumstance which frequently arises for adults residing in care homes who do not have unfettered community access to ensure their safety, and would be sufficient to determine that a person is not free to leave for the purpose of this element of the deprivation of liberty analysis.

3.28 Although the interpretation of the concepts of 'continuous supervision and control' and 'free to leave' have been dealt with separately in this chapter, in practice, they must be considered together. As Lady Hale noted, it is possible for one of the two criteria to be satisfied alone and that will not necessarily amount to a deprivation of liberty. It is therefore essential that the entirety of the regime in place for a person is considered, looking at its intensity and degree, and the cumulative impact of the arrangements, in order to determine if an objective deprivation of liberty is present.

Not negligible length of time

3.29 Whilst the focus of this section has been on the 'acid test' as set down in *Cheshire West,* to satisfy the objective component of a deprivation of liberty, the arrangements must also extend for a period of time which is not negligible.[50] This is another concept which has not been neatly defined within case law, but a common sense approach is sufficient to address this element. Whether a period of time is negligible or not will be assessed on the facts of the individual case. It is related to the intensity of the measures implemented, with an understanding that 'negligible' is ordinarily defined to mean small, unimportant, or insignificant. It is clear from the different reported judgments on this issue that determining a 'negligible length of time' must be done on a case by case basis. Within *ZH v Commissioner of the Police for the Metropolis,* the court found that a confinement for a period of 40 minutes was sufficient to fit within the definition of a deprivation of liberty because of its intensity.[51] Conversely, within *R (Sessay) v South London and the Maudsley NHS Foundation Trust,* the court commented that a person would ordinarily not be considered to be deprived of their liberty by virtue of their detention in a Mental Health Act 1983 (MHA 1983), s 136 suite for a period of eight hours.[52] It is evident, therefore, that in order to determine whether a period of time is negligible or not,

48 *Lancashire & South Cumbria NHS Foundation Trust, Lancashire County Council v AH* [2023] EWCOP 1.

49 *Lancashire & South Cumbria NHS Foundation Trust, Lancashire County Council v AH* [2023] EWCOP 1, para 7.

50 ' *Storck criteria'* as summarised within *Stanev v Bulgaria* 36760/06[2012] ECHR 36, paras 117 and 120; *Storck v Germany* (2005) 43 EHRR 6, para 74.

51 *ZH v Commissioner of the Police for the Metropolis* [2012] EWHC 604 (Admin).

52 *R (Sessay) v South London and the Maudsley NHS Foundation Trust* [2011] EWHC 2617 (QB).

it is necessary to assess the circumstances arising and their degree and intensity as implemented over the relevant time period.

THE SUBJECTIVE ELEMENT

3.30 Consent is the subjective element of the deprivation of liberty criteria. It requires that the arrangements in place must be absent valid consent. The topic of consent insofar as it relates to deprivations of liberty for children and young people is complicated. There are circumstances in which a child may provide valid consent or their parents may. Because the law in this area is so complex, it has been dedicated its own chapter which must be considered alongside the principles herein when determining if a deprivation of liberty is present. For an explanation and discussion around the issue of consent, turn to chapter 4.

ATTRIBUTION OF RESPONSIBILITY TO THE STATE

3.31 The third and final limb of the *Storck* criteria is to establish the state's responsibility for the arrangements, often referred to as the 'imputability to the state' element. Whilst Article 5 sets out a prohibition on deprivations of liberty save in the circumstances provided for therein, it also includes positive obligations on a state. These are to refrain from active infringement in a person's right to liberty and security of person, and to take appropriate steps to provide protection against an unlawful interference with those rights.[53] These positive obligations give rise to a responsibility of a member state in circumstances where a person is being deprived of their liberty. A state's responsibility may be engaged if it 'acquiesces in a person's loss of liberty by private individuals or fails to put an end to the situation'.[54] These principles are the 'attribution of responsibility to the state' requirement at limb (c) of the *Storck* criteria.

3.32 Lady Hale summarised what limb (c) amounts to in *Re D* by saying:

> 'As already mentioned, limb (c) of Storck is no longer disputed and rightly so. Not only was the State actively involved in making and funding the arrangements, it had assumed statutory responsibilities – albeit not parental responsibility – towards D by accommodating him under section 20 of the Children Act 1989, thereby making him a "looked after child". Even without all this, it is clear that the first sentence of article 5 imposes a positive obligation on the State to protect a person from interferences with liberty carried out by private persons, at least if it knew or ought to have known of this.'[55]

3.33 This quote refers to the judgment of *Storck* and the thought given by the ECtHR in that case to state involvement and the role the state should play in identifying

---

53 Guidance on Article 5 of the European Convention on Human Rights: Right to liberty and security, Council of Europe (August 2022), para 20.

54 Guidance on Article 5 of the European Convention on Human Rights: Right to liberty and security, Council of Europe (August 2022), para 22.

55 *Re D (A Child)* [2019] UKSC 42, para 43.

a deprivation of liberty and preventing an arbitrary or unlawful one.[56] In its judgment, the ECtHR considered the positive obligation imposed by Article 5 and three ways in which the circumstances before the court could engage those provisions of Article 5. First, it was held that a deprivation of liberty may be imputable to the state if there is direct involvement by a public body in the detention of a person. Secondly, in the circumstances of *Storck*, the state may have violated Article 5 in the failure by the domestic court to interpret the provisions of civil law in the spirit of Article 5. Thirdly, the court considered the state may have violated its positive obligations under Article 5 in failing to protect the applicant against interferences with her liberty carried out by private persons.[57] In looking at the third possibility in more detail, the court recorded that it has been 'consistently held that the responsibility of a State is engaged if a violation of one of the rights and freedoms defined in the Convention is the result of non-observance by that State of its obligation under Article 1 to secure those rights and freedoms in its domestic law to everyone within its jurisdiction.'[58] The judgment goes on to confirm that 'the Court considers that Article 5(1), first sentence, of the Convention must equally be considered as laying down a positive obligation on the State to protect the liberty of its citizens.'[59]

3.34 *Stanev v Bulgaria* added more flesh to the bones of this proposition by outlining:

> 'In addition, the Court has had occasion to observe that the first sentence of Article 5(1) must be construed as laying down a positive obligation on the State to protect the liberty of those within its jurisdiction. Otherwise, there would be a sizable gap in the protection from arbitrary detention, which would be inconsistent with the importance of personal liberty in a democratic society. The State is therefore obliged to take measures providing effective protection of vulnerable persons including reasonable steps to prevent a deprivation of liberty of which the authorities have or ought to have knowledge.'[60]

3.35 The case law makes clear that when the objective and subjective components of a deprivation of liberty are satisfied, the positive obligations of Article 5 give rise to an attribution of responsibility to the state which is required to take measures to protect its citizens against any unlawful or arbitrary deprivation of liberty. State responsibility may also be satisfied, as is often the case for children and young people, when the state is directly involved in the arrangements which give rise to a deprivation of liberty, or the state ought to know about those arrangements. Sir James Munby summarised the responsibility for children who are the subject of care orders in *Re A-F* when he stated '[i]t is so obvious that where a child is subject to a care order (whether interim or final) there is involvement and "responsibility" by the State satisfying Storck component (c) – both the State in the form of the court and the State in the form of the local authority named in the care order'.[61] Similarly, Lady Hale's comments in *Re D* make clear that the far-reaching duties of the Children

---

56 *Storck v Germany* (2005) 43 EHRR 6, para 89.
57 *Storck v Germany* (2005) 43 EHRR 6, para 89.
58 *Storck v Germany* (2005) 43 EHRR 6, para 101.
59 *Storck v Germany* (2005) 43 EHRR 6, para 102.
60 *Stanev v Bulgaria* 36760/06 [2012] ECHR 36, para 120.
61 *Re A-F* [2018] EWHC 138 (Fam), para 10.

Act 1989 (CA 1989) extend to include preventing interferences with the liberty of children and young people.[62]

APPLYING THE PRINCIPLES TO CHILDREN

3.36 Having defined a deprivation of liberty, the discussion must then turn to how the criteria is applied to children and young people. Much of the case law discussed above considered the circumstances of adults and examples of what may amount to their deprivation of liberty. For children and young people, the outline criteria for a deprivation of liberty is the same but there are different factors which must be taken into account and weighed into the balance owing to the different age and status of under 18s. The different approach to deprivations of liberty for children and young people stems from the fact that by virtue of being parented, restrictions will be in place for a child or young person that would not be in place for an adult. These restrictions of parenting must be factored into the analysis of whether a child or young person is objectively confined, preventing unnecessary interventions with ordinary parenting. This section will consider the objective element of a deprivation of liberty insofar as it relates to children and young people. The subjective element of consent as it applies to children and young people is explored in chapter 4.

3.37 One of the most significant decisions in which the principles of a deprivation of liberty were applied to a child came from the ECtHR in 1988 within *Nielsen v Denmark*.[63] Whilst harking back slightly to European case law, it is not possible to consider the application of the test for a deprivation of liberty to children without looking at *Nielsen*. This case concerned a 12-year old boy who was placed in a children's psychiatric unit by his mother, exercising her sole parental responsibility. Whilst the court's decision in this case, determining that the child was not deprived of his liberty, turned on the mother's exercise of consent, the ECtHR also provided some guidance on the objective element of a deprivation of liberty relating to a child. In determining whether or not the circumstances of the child fit into the objective element of the criteria, the court undertook a comparative exercise. It looked at the current circumstances for the child compared with the circumstances that may be implemented for another child in an 'ordinary hospital' and the protective purpose of any restrictions imposed for children generally in hospitals.[64] The court determined that measures including locked wards and the accompaniment of staff would be expected for any child in hospital and so did not amount to an objective confinement of the child. This decision preceded the formulation of the 'acid test' in *Cheshire West* and has been the subject of criticism in subsequent jurisprudence. However, it signifies the emergence of a comparative approach when determining if a child is deprived of their liberty under the objective element of the criteria.

---

62 *Re D (A Child)* [2019] UKSC 42, para 43.

63 *Nielsen v Denmark* (1988) 11 EHRR 175.

64 *Nielsen v Denmark* (1988) 11 EHRR 175, para 70.

3.38 *Cheshire West* also considered how the defining principles of a deprivation of liberty apply to children, and the role of a comparative approach within this. Lord Kerr, in his judgment, stated:

> '77. The question of whether one is restricted (as a matter of actuality) is determined by comparing the extent of your actual freedom with someone of your age and station whose freedom is not limited. Thus a teenager of the same age and familial background... is the relevant comparator for them. If one compares their state with a person of similar age and full capacity it is clear that their liberty is in fact circumscribed. They may not be conscious, much less resentful, of the constraint but, objectively, limitations on their freedom are in place.
>
> 78. All children are (or should be) subject to some level of restraint. This adjusts with their maturation and change in circumstances. If MIG and MEG had the same freedom from constraint as would any child or young person of similar age, their liberty would not be restricted, whatever their level of disability. As a matter of objective fact, however, constraints beyond those which apply to young people of full ability are – and have to be – applied to them. There is therefore a restriction of liberty in their cases.'[65]

3.39 Lord Kerr's comments established some key principles which guide the assessment of whether a deprivation of liberty is present for a child or young person. The first is that when adopting the comparative approach to determine if the objective element is met, the child or young person's circumstances should be compared to those of another child of 'full capacity' and 'whatever their level of disability'. This requires comparison with children or young people who do not have diagnoses or disabilities impacting their physical, mental and psychological presentation and needs. The second principle is of comparing a child or young person with another of the 'same age and familial background'. This element seeks to reinforce the need to look at a child or young person's circumstances as a whole, including their family situation, and compare that with a child or young person in a similar situation. Finally, Lord Kerr recognised that all children will be subject to some level of restrictions imposed upon them by their parent or the person caring for them. The type of restrictions which are applied generally and ordinarily to children as part of parenting them will not be considered a confinement for the purposes of the objective element of a deprivation of their liberty.

3.40 Following on from the notion of comparison envisaged by Lord Kerr came the case of *Re A-F* in 2018 before the President of the Family Division at the time, Sir James Munby.[66] In this case, the court was considering the circumstances of seven children, all of whom were subject to care orders and restrictions on their movement or liberty.[67] The court's focus was the objective element of the deprivation of liberty criteria, termed 'confinement' for the purposes of the judgment. The court gave a thoughtful judgment and outlined some preliminary matters which must be

65 *(1) P (by his litigation friend the Official Solicitor) v Cheshire West and Chester Council & Anor (2) P and Q (by their litigation friend the Official Solicitor) v Surrey County Council* [2014] UKSC 19, paras 77–78.

66 *Re A-F (Children)* [2018] EWHC 138 (Fam).

67 *Re A-F (Children)* [2018] EWHC 138 (Fam), para 3.

taken into account when determining if a child or young person was 'confined'. It is helpful to set this out in full:

> 'i) First, the realities of the modern world, driven in significant part because the school leaving age is now sixteen and by consequential changes in the employment patterns of young people, mean that the typical child who is not yet sixteen years old is not economically active and lives – in reality has no choice but to live – at home. So, the typical child of fifteen is, in the sense in which the expression is used in the case-law, not free to leave the place where they live. If the fifteen-year old child runs away, wanting to live on their own, they will probably not get social housing and, if not taken into care, are likely to be returned home to live either with the parents or with other relatives.
>
> ii) Secondly, and another reality of the modern world, children nowadays tend to live more regulated and controlled lives than children of the same age would have been used to a generation or two back. The ubiquity of the motor vehicle in modern Britain, accompanied by changes in social attitudes as to what is or what is not 'responsible parenting', mean that the street is no longer as safe (or seen as being as safe) an environment as it once was. It is no longer as safe (or seen as being as safe) as it once was for children to play in the street, to be allowed to roam or even to go to and from school under their own steam.
>
> iii) Thirdly, and as I have already explained (…), many aspects of the normal exercise of parental responsibility that interfere with a child's freedom of movement do not involve a deprivation of liberty engaging Article 5.'[68]

3.41 In explaining these preliminary points, Sir James Munby clarified how the elements of the 'acid test' should be applied to children. The judgment confirms that, in reality, the notion that a child aged 15 or under is 'not free to leave' for the purpose of relocating elsewhere is unlikely to be the central issue nor determinative of the objective element of the deprivation of liberty criteria.[69] The court recognised that most children aged 15 and under would not be provided with the freedom of choosing to live elsewhere. This will, however, be a more prevalent consideration for young people who have reached 16 and who are, by virtue of their age, generally afforded more autonomy and may be expected to be making independent decisions about where they live.

3.42 The court went on to explore the circumstances in which the measures in place for a child may constitute their confinement, although being cautious to note that every case is determined on its individual facts.[70] Sir James Munby referred to the decision of Her Honour Judge Rowe KC in *Re B* concerning an 11-year-old boy with autism spectrum condition.[71] In that case, the child was deemed to be confined and the objective element of the criteria met in circumstances where he was supervised from a distance by staff, with them being always aware of where he was and what he was doing; he was not left alone with another child in the placement; he was always accompanied into the community; he was occasionally subject to

---

68 *Re A-F (Children)* [2018] EWHC 138 (Fam), para 31.

69 *Re A-F (Children)* [2018] EWHC 138 (Fam), para 32.

70 *Re A-F (Children)* [2018] EWHC 138 (Fam), para 38.

71 *Re B* [2017] EWFC B93.

the removal of or limited access to a computer and Xbox; and staff used measures including physical restraint upon the child.[72]

3.43 Sir James Munby then set out a 'rule of thumb' which has since been cited in many cases concerning the deprivation of liberty of children and gives guidance on what may amount to a child's confinement by reference to their age. The court suggested as follows:

> 'i) A child aged 10, even if under pretty constant supervision, is unlikely to be "confined" for the purpose of Storck component (a).
>
> ii) A child aged 11, if under constant supervision, may, in contrast be so "confined", though the court should be astute to avoid coming too readily to such a conclusion.
>
> iii) Once a child who is under constant supervision has reached the age of 12, the court will more readily come to that conclusion.
>
> That said, all must depend upon the circumstances of the particular case and upon the identification by the judge in the particular case of the attributes of the relevant comparator as described by Lord Kerr.'[73]

3.44 The relevant comparator, described by Lord Kerr, was summarised earlier in the judgment of Sir James Munby who confirmed that when a comparative approach is being used, the comparison should be with the 'restrictions which would apply to a child of the same "age", "station", "familial background" and "relative maturity" who is "free from disability"'.[74] These are the salient factors of a child's situation which should be looked at when undertaking a comparison to establish whether the measures in place go beyond what may be considered 'normal' or 'ordinary' parenting. If the measures or regime do go beyond what is considered ordinary parenting, having undertaken the comparative exercise, consideration must then turn to whether the arrangements are absent of valid consent which is explained in detail in chapter 4. If the subjective element is also satisfied, alongside an attribution of responsibility to the state, then a deprivation of liberty arises. The process for seeking authorisation of any deprivation of liberty is considered at chapter 5.

3.45 More light has been shed on the use of the comparative approach by Lieven J in a recently handed down judgment concerning SM, a 12-year old girl.[75] SM was diagnosed with 'profound and enduring disabilities… She is non-mobile and non-verbal and she is fed via a gastrojejunal button'. The court was tasked with determining whether the arrangements in place for SM, who was living in foster care pursuant to a care order, amounted to her deprivation of liberty. Lieven J began by distinguishing that a number of measures which formed the basis of the local authority's application were not restrictions intended to deprive SM of her liberty, but they were essential components of her care provision. This included carers moving SM, feeding her and administering medication, undertaking personal care

72 For further discussion on the removal/monitoring of electronic devices, see **3.52**.

73 *Re A-F (Children)* [2018] EWHC 138 (Fam), para 43.

74 *Re A-F (Children)* [2018] EWHC 138 (Fam), para 33.

75 *Peterborough City Council v Mother & Ors* [2024] EWHC 493 (Fam).

tasks and SM having bars on the side of her bed to prevent falling.[76] The court found that these measures were not, in SM's circumstances, intended to curtail her physical liberty. The judge then went on to consider whether SM's arrangements met the criteria to be considered a deprivation of liberty, recognising that by virtue of her significant disabilities, SM could not be free to leave her placement as she was physically unable to do so and this was not imposed upon her by any action of the state. Lieven J considered the suitability of the comparative approach for cases such as SM's, where the child concerned had significant disabilities which profoundly impacted their physical liberty. The court determined it nonsensical to undertake a comparative analysis of a child such as SM with another 12-year old who is free from disability in order to determine whether the disabled child was deprived of their liberty. Lieven J commented that 'The able bodied 12-year old is plainly not an appropriate comparator because there is a material difference between them and SM as regards the matter in question, here the constant control and supervision.'[77] In finding that SM was not deprived of her liberty, the court noted that SM's physical liberty was significantly impacted by her disabilities but it was not being curtailed by actions of the state which did not serve to impose on her more restrictions than those which flowed from her disabilities.

3.46 This case may provide a steer for practitioners when assessing whether a regime or proposed regime amounts to a child's deprivation of liberty in circumstances where the child concerned is significantly disabled. First, practitioners should be careful to distinguish between what measures are implemented in order to deprive the child of their liberty, as opposed to measures which make up their essential care provision. Secondly, practitioners should be cautious in using the comparative model for children with significant disabilities. Lieven J advocated for a realistic and logic-based approach to be taken in evaluating whether a regime amounts to continuous supervision and control of a significantly disabled child. That may not always include comparing the child's circumstances to those of a non-disabled child of the same age, particularly where the disability itself is so significant as to prevent the child exercising their right to physical liberty. Consideration must be given to whether the child's physical liberty is being curtailed by measures which are imposed upon them for that purpose, or by virtue of their disability.

3.47 Whilst each case must be determined on its own facts, and it is not possible within the confines of this chapter to consider all of the reported cases on the issue, it is illuminating to look closer at some of the reported decisions which deal specifically with the objective element of a child or young person's deprivation of liberty.

3.48 *Re RD (Deprivation or Restriction of Liberty)* was handed down shortly after Sir James Munby's decision in *Re A-F*.[78] The judge was concerned with a 14-year old girl (R) and the measures in place for her at a rural residential placement. R was not free to leave the placement and the court accepted that this was typical of any 14-year old child whose parents would not permit the same. Consideration then

---

76 *Peterborough City Council v Mother & Ors* [2024] EWHC 493 (Fam), para 8.

77 *Peterborough City Council v Mother & Ors* [2024] EWHC 493 (Fam), para 43.

78 *Re RD (Deprivation or Restriction of Liberty)* [2018] EWFC 47.

turned to whether R's arrangements amounted to continuous supervision and control. The court recognised that R presented as younger than her chronological age and so the restrictions which may be imposed upon her by a reasonable parent would likely be greater than those imposed on a more mature 14-year old.[79] The court considered the regime in place to be boundaried but supportive. The boundaries included monitoring of R when on the placement grounds, deemed to be akin to ordinary quasi-parenting, noting that the placement stood on a busy road which would lead any parent to implement safety measures for their child. Ultimately, the court did not consider the regime to possess the degree or intensity required to fit within the definition of complete control or supervision.

3.49 Another case which followed the decision of Sir James Munby was that of *Re HC*.[80] This case concerned a 13-year old boy living in a residential unit. The court was tasked with determining whether the regime in place amounted to his confinement, being of such a degree or intensity to constitute continuous supervision and control. The measures in place for the child included external doors being locked; limited access to the kitchen within the placement; constant staff supervision; restricted access to money; monitored social media and internet access; and the use of physical restraint when necessary. The child was reportedly happy living at the placement although expressed a preference to be in foster care.[81] Whilst the court recognised that by virtue of the child's age, ordinary parenting would include various restrictions on his liberty, it concluded that the degree and intensity of the regime in place at the residential unit was sufficient to satisfy limb (a) of the *Storck* criteria.

3.50 The incremental approach suggested by Sir James Munby infers that as children get older, less restrictions and boundaries would be expected in the course of ordinary parenting. This is helpful guidance when assessing whether measures in place for young people constitute their confinement and go above and beyond what a parent may lawfully implement in the course of their parenting. The case of *Blackpool BC v HT* provides a more extreme example of restrictive measures that were deemed to fall within limb (a) of the *Storck* criteria for a 17-year-old, going above and beyond ordinary parenting.[82] In this case, the young person was 'prevented from leaving the placement by the use of physical restraint and 3:1 staff supervision by staff 24 hours per day, including supervision by waking watch and 3:1 supervision outside the accommodation building'.[83] This, in the court's judgment, fell clearly within the remit of continuous supervision and control and being not free to leave. The level of adult supervision and its intensity went far beyond what a parent may reasonably impose.

3.51 A similar set of measures was implemented for a 16-year old girl, G, within *Lancashire CC v G*.[84] Although that regime did not expressly include physical restraint, it did permit 'reasonable and proportionate measures' to restrain G when

79 *Re RD (Deprivation or Restriction of Liberty)* [2018] EWFC 47, para 39.
80 *Re HC (A Child: Deprivation of Liberty)* [2018] EWHC 2961 (Fam).
81 *Re HC (A Child: Deprivation of Liberty)* [2018] EWHC 2961 (Fam), para 13.
82 *Blackpool BC v HT* [2022] EWHC 1480 (Fam).
83 *Blackpool BC v HT* [2022] EWHC 1480 (Fam), para 46.
84 *Lancashire CC v G* [2020] EWHC 2828 (Fam), para 63.

she was distressed. The court found that this regime in its entirety fell within the definition of continuous supervision and control and being not free to leave.

3.52 As part of the evolving interpretation of the objective element of a deprivation of liberty, the court has also had cause to determine what does not fall to be considered as a restriction on a child or young person's liberty. This came most clearly within *Manchester City Council v CP.*[85] In his judgment, MacDonald J clarified what measures should be considered when analysing any restriction on a child or young person's liberty for the purposes of Article 5. The court was concerned with a 16-year old girl for whom a care order had been made. The local authority's application to the court included seeking the authorisation of restrictions on the young person's ability to use a mobile phone, tablet, or laptop and on their social media access. The court clarified that for the purposes of a deprivation of liberty under Article 5, the court was concerned with measures which impacted upon a person's physical liberty. The court held that whilst using a phone or social media may equate to liberty in the young person's mind, it did not impact upon her liberty for the purposes of Article 5.[86] The measures in place were communication restrictions designed to ensure physical and emotional safety and potentially engaging Article 8, rather than falling within Article 5. It follows that when assessing the circumstances of a child or young person, caution should be taken to focus upon the measures which relate to their physical liberty, rather than all of the boundaries and safeguards that may form part of the arrangements for the child or young person.

COMPLIANCE WITH ARTICLE 5

3.53 Having considered what is meant by a 'deprivation of liberty', the discussion must then turn to what Article 5 says about a lawful deprivation of liberty. There are two requirements for a deprivation of liberty to be lawful. First, it must be in accordance with a procedure prescribed by law and, secondly, it must fit within the list of circumstances within the article.

3.54 The first requirement of Article 5 for a lawful deprivation of liberty is for any deprivation to be in accordance with a procedure prescribed by law.[87] This refers to domestic law but includes other legal standards such as international or European law which may apply. It requires each member state's domestic law to be in accordance with the principles of the ECHR including the principles of proportionality and protection against arbitrariness.[88] In England and Wales, the procedure prescribed by law in respect of cases concerning a deprivation of liberty include the CA 1989, s 25 (and the Social Services and Well-being (Wales) Act 2014 (SSWWA 2014), s 119), the MHA 1983 and the MCA 2005. Where those statutory

---

85 *Manchester City Council v CP (Refusal of Restrictions on Mobile Phone)* [2023] EWHC 133 (Fam).

86 *Manchester City Council v CP (Refusal of Restrictions on Mobile Phone)* [2023] EWHC 133 (Fam), para 45.

87 Guidance on Article 5 of the European Convention on Human Rights: Right to liberty and security, Council of Europe (August 2022), para 29.

88 Guidance on Article 5 of the European Convention on Human Rights: Right to liberty and security, Council of Europe (August 2022), para 32.

routes are not available, the legal basis often turned to is the CA 1989, s 100, and the High Court's inherent jurisdiction. The various elements of these procedures and when they may be used are considered in detail in chapter 5.

3.55 The second requirement imposed by Article 5 is that any deprivation of liberty must fit within one of a list of exceptions, including the detention of a minor for the purpose of educational supervision.[89] What is meant by 'educational supervision' has been discussed within domestic case law and is summarised within *Re T*.[90] The judgment explains:

> 'In this regard, the relevant guidance from the European Court of Human Rights ("ECtHR") must be noted. It establishes that, in the context of the detention of minors, the concept of "educational supervision" is particularly broad, see *Koniarska v United Kingdom* 30 EHRR CD 139. It is not to be equated rigidly with notions of classroom teaching. The court observed, at p.143: "In particular, in the present context of a young person in local authority care, educational supervision must embrace many aspects of the exercise, by the local authority, of parental rights for the benefit and protection of the persons concerned."'

3.56 In *Re K*, the court made similar observations about the wide scope of 'educational supervision'. It stated:

> 'This goes far beyond school. It is not just about the restriction on liberty involved in requiring a reluctant child to remain at school for the school day. It arises in the context of the responsibilities of parents which extend well beyond ensuring the child's attendance at school. So it involved education in the broad sense, similar, I would respectfully suggest, to the general development of the child's physical, intellectual, emotional, social and behavioural abilities, all of which have to be encouraged by responsible parents, as part of his upbringing and education, and for this purpose, an appropriate level of supervision of the child to enhance his development, where necessary, by restricting his liberty is permitted.'[91]

3.57 The court has recently reaffirmed the importance of the provision of education, in the broad sense, in order to comply with the ECHR in cases which purport to fall under Article 5(1)(d). Within *EBY (A Child) (Deprivation of Liberty Order: Jurisdiction) (17-year-old)*, Deputy High Court Judge Bowen KC considered whether the circumstances for the child concerned fell within the definition of being 'for the purpose of educational supervision'.[92] In this case, the court was satisfied that the provision of counselling for the child and steps being taken to enable her to access schoolwork were sufficient to fit into the criteria of 'educational supervision'.[93] The court is likely to be satisfied that this criteria is met if there is a sufficient form

---

89 Article 5(1)(d) of the Convention for the Protection of Human Rights and Fundamental Freedoms (Rome, 4 November 1950).

90 *Re T (A Child)* [2021] UKSC 35, paras 83–87.

91 *Re K (A Child) (Secure Accommodation Order: Right to Liberty)* [2001] Fam 377, para 107.

92 *Re EBY (A Child) (Deprivation of Liberty Order: Jurisdiction) (17-year-old)* [2023] EWHC 2494 (Fam).

93 *Re EBY (A Child) (Deprivation of Liberty Order: Jurisdiction) (17-year-old)* [2023] EWHC 2494 (Fam), para 59.

of educational input for the young person, which does not necessarily need to be curriculum-based education delivered within a school setting. Education related to the young person's overall development including core life skills such as cooking, budgeting or maintaining a home may also be sufficient to fit within the criteria of Article 5(1)(d), provided that there is a discernible programme of education input for the child or young person.

3.58 The other set of circumstances which may give rise to a lawful deprivation of liberty and may be of relevance to the children and young people with whom this book is concerned is found at Article 5(1)(e). This is the lawful detention of a person of unsound mind.[94] The article is purposefully broad in referring to a 'person' rather than 'adult' so as to include children and young people. In order for a person to be lawfully deprived of their liberty under this category, the following conditions must be satisfied:

(a) the individual is shown reliably to be of unsound mind;

(b) the mental disorder must be of a kind or degree warranting compulsory confinement; and

(c) the mental disorder must be persisting.[95]

3.59 The ECtHR considered the criteria of Article 5(1)(e) within *HL v the United Kingdom*.[96] It was recognised within the court's decision that national authorities have 'a certain margin of appreciation on the question of the merits of clinical diagnosis since it is in the first place for them to evaluate the evidence in a particular case' when determining if a person meets the criteria of being of unsound mind.[97] The ECHR itself does not require a clinical diagnosis, and the term 'unsound mind' is intended to be somewhat fluid and able to evolve with medical and social attitudes.[98] The term should be given an autonomous meaning, without strict boundaries being placed on its interpretation.[99]

3.60 His Honour Judge Burrows has provided some clarification on the domestic interpretation of the term 'unsound mind' in the context of Court of Protection proceedings. His conclusion in the case of *Stockport MBC v KB* distilled the principles that: unsoundness of mind refers to a mental disorder; it is for the court to be satisfied that the person concerned is of unsound mind; and, the unsoundness of mind is to be 'proved by those seeking to assert it on sound medical evidence'.[100]

---

94 Article 5(1)(e) of the Convention for the Protection of Human Rights and Fundamental Freedoms (Rome, 4 November 1950).

95 *Winterwerp v Netherlands* (1979) 2 EHRR 387; *Johnson v UK* (1997) 27 EHRR 296; see also Guidance on Article 5 of the European Convention on Human Rights: Right to liberty and security, Council of Europe (August 2022), paras 116–134.

96 *HL v United Kingdom* (2004) 40 EHRR 761.

97 *HL v United Kingdom* (2004) 40 EHRR 761, para 98.

98 Guidance on Article 5 of the European Convention on Human Rights: Right to liberty and security, Council of Europe (August 2022), para 116 .

99 *Petschulies v Germany* 6281/13 [2016] ECHR.

100 *Stockport Metropolitan Borough Council v KC* [2023] EWCOP 58, para 4.

3.61 The guidance accompanying the ECHR confirms that a mental disorder warranting compulsory confinement may include where a person needs therapy, medication or other clinical treatment, and also where the person needs control and supervision to prevent them causing harm to themselves or others.[101] The opinion of a medical expert should be sought before depriving the relevant person of their liberty under this provision.[102] When considering whether the mental disorder in question is persisting, changes in the mental condition of the person must be taken into account and signs of recovery may prompt the authority concerned to review the confinement and relevant criteria.[103] The ECtHR has recently considered the criteria under Article 5(1)(e) within *Rooman v Belgium* and what that criteria seeks to achieve.[104] The court summarised that the provisions of Article 5(1)(e) provide both a social function of protection alongside a therapeutic function related to the person who is of unsound mind and their receipt of appropriate treatment. This judgment brings back into focus the requirement not to arbitrarily deprive people, including children, of their liberty by emphasising the importance of providing appropriate treatment or other services for those whose liberty is curtailed.

CONCLUSION

3.62 In distilling the definition of a deprivation of liberty, this chapter has focused on the right to liberty and security of person itself (as set out within Article 5 of the ECHR), what may constitute an interference with that right and how it may lawfully be interfered with. As noted throughout, this chapter has not considered element (b) of the *Storck* criteria which is essential to establish a deprivation of liberty. That element, an absence of valid consent, is a complicated one in respect of children and young people, requiring its own chapter at chapter 4. The influx in cases concerning the deprivation of liberty of children and young people continues in the High Court and the Court of Protection, therefore, it is likely that the definitions and concepts herein will be subject to further refinement by the court over time. This will be essential in ensuring that the approach taken to deprivation of liberty cases remains in line with societal norms and practices, and is reflective of the society in which the children and young people concerned are being raised. It is important for all those involved in cases concerning a deprivation of liberty to be up to date with the case law developments as they arise, particularly those which materially alter the approach taken by the court to defining a deprivation of liberty.

---

101 Guidance on Article 5 of the European Convention on Human Rights: Right to liberty and security, Council of Europe (August 2022), para 120; *Ilnseher v Germany* [GC] 10211/12 and 27505/14 [2018] ECHR; *Hutchison Reid v UK* 50272/99 [2003] ECHR 94.

102 *Ruiz Rivera v Switzerland* 8300/06 [2014] ECHR 156.

103 Guidance on Article 5 of the European Convention on Human Rights: Right to liberty and security, Council of Europe (August 2022), paras 123–125.

104 *Rooman v Belgium* [2019] ECHR 105.

Chapter 4

CONSENT

INTRODUCTION

4.01 Consent is permission provided by a person for something to happen. This can include an agreement to do something, be involved in something or for something to be done to the person. The notion of consent is an important element within the promotion of autonomy and independence enshrined within the European Convention on Human Rights (ECHR).[1] Its significance as a concept within human rights is solidified by its inclusion within the *Storck* limbs of a deprivation of liberty (explored further in chapter 3) which requires 'valid consent' to be absent for a deprivation of liberty to arise. If valid consent is provided to a regime of confinement, a deprivation of liberty will not be present as limb (b) of the *Storck* components is not satisfied.[2] This chapter explores the concept of valid consent insofar as it relates to the deprivation of liberty of children and young people, including who can provide valid consent to a child or young person's confinement and when.

4.02 Valid consent, generally, refers to consent provided by a person who:

(a) Has sufficient information to make the decision, including the purpose and nature of the arrangements being put in place and any alternatives to them;

(b) Gives their consent voluntarily, without unfair or undue pressure;

(c) Has the ability to make the decision.

4.03 Within *Cheshire West*, Lord Kerr provided guidance on what valid consent means by distinguishing it from what it is not. He stated: 'The subjective element in deprivation of liberty is the absence of valid consent to the confinement in question… This must be distinguished from passive acquiescence to the deprivation, particularly where that stems from an inability to appreciate the fact that one's liberty is being curtailed'.[3] Keehan J in *A Local Authority v D* and Mostyn J in *A Local Authority v SW* both discussed valid consent as needing to be 'authentic and enduring'.[4] Although the use of the term 'enduring' was subsequently questioned in an appeal

---

1 The Convention for the Protection of Human Rights and Fundamental Freedoms (Rome, 4 November 1950).

2 *Storck v Germany* (2005) 43 EHRR 6.

3 *(1) P (by his litigation friend the Official Solicitor) v Cheshire West and Chester Council & Anor (2) P and Q (by their litigation friend the Official Solicitor) v Surrey County Council* [2014] UKSC 19, para 81.

4 *A Local authority v D* [2016] EWHC 3473 (Fam); *A Local Authority v SW, MT, NT* [2018] EWHC 576 (Fam), para 10.

to Keehan J's decision, the persistence of consent over time, not just being a fleeting agreement, remains a relevant consideration when establishing valid consent.

4.04 The question of who can consent to the confinement of a child or young person which would, without that consent, be a deprivation of their liberty has been an issue that the court has grappled with for some time. A person, including a child or young person, can consent to a restriction or set of restrictions on their physical liberty. If their consent is deemed valid by reference to the criteria at **4.02**, this will negate a deprivation of liberty arising. In respect of children, valid consent to a restriction on their physical liberty may also be provided by their parents or a person with parental responsibility, in some circumstances. Valid consent, whomever provided by, prevents a deprivation of liberty arising.

4.05 Each element of valid consent will be considered within this chapter, alongside exploring the options for who may provide valid consent. This chapter will begin by exploring the consent that may be provided by the child or young person themselves, and then consider the circumstances in which a parent or person with parental responsibility may be able to provide consent to restrictive arrangements for their child. The scope of parental responsibility will be considered at length when looking at a parent's consent.

4.06 This chapter is divided by the provider of consent, but also by the age of the child. The law approaches the issue of consent differently for children, who are under 16 years of age, and young people who are 16 and 17 years of age. The distinction between children and young people reflects the growing maturity and understanding of children as they age, and is substantiated in a number of statutory provisions. This includes the Family Law Reform Act 1969, s 8 which provides that:

> '(1) The consent of a minor who has attained the age of sixteen years to any surgical, medical or dental treatment which, in the absence of consent, would constitute a trespass to his person, shall be as effective as it would be if he were of full age; and where a minor has by virtue of this section given effective consent to any treatment it shall not be necessary to obtain any consent for it from his parent or guardian.'

4.07 Similarly, the Mental Health Act 1983 (MHA 1983) recognises that children and young people should be approached differently with regard to their informal admission to hospital. Section 131 reads:

> '(1) Nothing in this Act shall be construed as preventing a patient who requires treatment for mental disorder from being admitted to any hospital… in pursuance of arrangements made in that behalf and without any application, order or direction rendering him liable to be detained under this Act, or from remaining in any hospital… in pursuance of such arrangements after he has ceased to be so liable to be detained.
>
> (2) Subsections (3) and (4) below apply in the case of a patient aged 16 or 17 years who has capacity to consent to the making of such arrangements as are mentioned in subsection (1) above.
>
> (3) If the patient consents to the making of the arrangements, they may be made, carried out and determined on the basis of that consent even though there are one or more persons who have parental responsibility for him.

(4) If the patient does not consent to the making of the arrangements, they may not be made, carried out or determined on the basis of the consent of a person who has parental responsibility for him.'

4.08 Perhaps most significantly, the Mental Capacity Act 2005 (MCA 2005) created a clear divide between children and young people. The Act brought into place a presumption of capacity (the ability to make informed decisions for oneself) for all adults and, importantly, anyone aged 16 or over. The statute recognised that from the age of 16, young people generally should be regarded as having sufficient understanding and decision-making abilities to consider information for themselves and make an informed choice. This presumption, and the MCA 2005 generally, does not apply to children who are under 16.

4.09 These statutory provisions provide examples of the law separating out children and young people with regard to their ability to make decisions for themselves. This is relevant both in respect of a child providing consent in their own right and the consent of a parent acting under their parental responsibility. There is now a clear dividing line at the age of 16 at which point a child becomes a young person and is assumed to have capacity to make decisions for themselves, a presumption which does not apply to under 16s. This development in the law has created natural categories in which consent must be considered, related to who the consent relates to. They are: the consent provided by the child; the consent provided by the young person; the consent of a parent in relation to a child; and, the consent of a parent in relation to a young person.

VALID CONSENT:

The person has sufficient information to make the decision including the purpose and nature of the arrangements being put in place and any alternatives to them;

The person gives their consent voluntarily without unfair or undue pressure;

The person has the ability to make the decision (see the explanations of *Gillick* competence and mental capacity).

CHILD AND YOUNG PERSON'S CONSENT

Consent and children under 16 years of age

4.10 The first circumstance in which consent may be provided to negate a deprivation of liberty is where the child themselves provides valid consent to the arrangements. When children are under 16, the first consideration must be whether they are able to provide valid consent, as defined above. One crucial element of valid consent is the person's ability to make the decision. One of the most significant decisions made by the court in respect of a child's decision-making abilities came in the House of Lords decision in *Gillick v West Norfolk and Wisbech Area Health*

Authority.[5] This case was initially brought by a mother seeking a determination that her daughter, who was under 16, could not be provided with contraceptive advice and medication by a doctor as she was too young to consent to the medication, and it should be a matter determined by her parents. The court was therefore tasked with considering at what point a child becomes able to make decisions for themselves, without consultation with their parents. At the time the judgment was handed down, the MCA 2005 was not in force and so the presumption of capacity for those aged 16 and over had not yet been provided for in statute. In any event, this court was tasked with considering a child under the age of 16 and her decision-making abilities.

4.11 In reaching its decision, the court considered at length the case law, statute and guidance dealing with the ability of children to provide consent and the rights of the parents to provide consent for their children. The court held that children under the age of 16 are able to make decisions about and provide consent to their own medical treatment, if they have reached a 'sufficient understanding and intelligence' to be capable of making up their own mind on the matter requiring a decision.[6] This principle is not tied to the age of the child and there cannot be a 'judicially fixed age limit' on when a child can or cannot have sufficient understanding and intelligence to be considered competent to make decisions for themselves. Each situation must be considered individually, having regard to the child's specific abilities and competencies. The concept which arose from this judgment, of a child being of sufficient understanding and intelligence to make their own decisions, became known as '*Gillick* competence'.

4.12 In order for a child to have '*Gillick* competence' or '*Gillick* capacity' they must be able to:

(a) Understand the nature and implications of the decision and the process of implementing that decision;

(b) Understand the implications of not pursuing the decision;

(c) Retain the information long enough for the decision-making process to take place;

(d) Be of sufficient intelligence and maturity to weigh up the information and arrive at a decision;

(e) Be able to communicate that decision.[7]

4.13 The concept of *Gillick* competence reflects a child's increasing development through to maturity. If a child is assessed as being *Gillick* competent, then their consent to a decision alone is sufficient and consent from a parent or person with parental responsibility is not required. Valid consent provided by a *Gillick* competent

---

5 *Gillick v West Norfolk and Wisbech Area Health Authority* [1985] UKHL 7.

6 *Gillick v West Norfolk and Wisbech Area Health Authority* [1985] UKHL 7.

7 *Gillick v West Norfolk and Wisbech Area Health Authority* [1985] UKHL 7; [1986] 1 FLR 224; *Gillick* competence is sometimes referred to as '*Gillick* capacity', see *X (A Child)* [2014] EWHC 1871, para 12.

child also cannot be overruled by a parent.[8] A *Gillick* competent child can consent to a range of different interventions including; their confinement and restriction, instruction of their own lawyer, and medical treatment and interventions.[9]

4.14 The ability of a child to make a decision for themselves has since been considered in case law, with guiding principles set down as to how a child's competence should be assessed. Within *Re S*, Cobb J considered the principles of the MCA 2005 and how they are relevant to decision-making by children and young people.[10] He stated that whilst the MCA 2005 does not apply to under 16s, some principles could usefully be applied to determinations on whether a child has *Gillick* competence, and any determination of a child's competence must be decision-specific and child-specific, and made on the current evidence available.[11] The court made clear that assessments should be appropriate to the child's age and circumstances, to enhance their decision-making potential and that the more significant the issue, the greater onus there should be on ensuring that the child understands and is able to weigh up the relevant information.[12]

4.15 As the House of Lords made clear, there is no lower age limit for *Gillick* competence to be obtained. Whether a child is able to consent to a decision about them depends upon the professional judgement of the assessor and not on the age of the child. The Mental Health Act Code of Practice 2015 provides guidance in respect of assessing *Gillick* competence and sets out questions that assessing practitioners should consider:

(a) Does the child understand the information that is relevant to the decision that needs to be made?

(b) Can the child hold the information in their mind for long enough so that they can use it to make the decision?

(c) Is the child able to weigh up that information and use it to arrive at a decision?

(d) Is the child able to communicate their decision (by talking, using sign language or any other means)?[13]

4.16 The next important consideration when looking at a child's *Gillick* competence is who should conduct the assessment. The President of the Family Division at the time, Munby J, considered the suitability of social workers to provide evidence on *Gilick* competence in *Re A-F.*[14] The court determined that evidence of *Gillick* competence should normally come from either a child and adolescent psychologist or, depending upon the nature of the child's difficulties, a child and adolescent psychiatrist. The court recognised that evidence from a social worker

---

8 *Re W (A Minor) (Medical Treatment: Court's Jurisdiction)* [1993] Fam 64.

9 *Re D (A Child)* [2019] UKSC 42; *S v SBH* [2019] EWHC 634 (Fam); *An NHS Foundation Trust v A & Others* [2014] EWHC 920 (Fam).

10 *Re S (Child as parent: Adoption: Consent)* [2017] EWHC 2729 (Fam).

11 *Re S (Child as parent: Adoption: Consent)* [2017] EWHC 2729 (Fam), paras 16-17 and 19.

12 *Re S (Child as parent: Adoption: Consent)* [2017] EWHC 2729 (Fam), para 62.

13 The Mental Health Act Code of Practice 2015, Department of Health (2015), paras 19.36 – 19.37.

14 *Re A-F (Children) (Care Proceedings: Deprivation of Liberty)* [2018] EWHC 138.

could not be excluded from consideration, if a social worker felt qualified to express an opinion, but that it would be undesirable for the only evidence to come from an employee of the local authority responsible for the child's confinement.[15]

4.17 In coming to this determination, the court recognised that this somewhat departs from *A Local Authority v D, E and C*, in which Keehan J gave weight to a social worker's evidence on *Gillick* competence.[16] In that case, submissions had been made that to disregard social work evidence on the basis that a social worker might be tempted to 'pass' a child as *Gillick* competent in order to rely on their consent to a regime of confinement would be, in effect, to say that social workers cannot be trusted.[17] Keehan J did not make that bold assertion but found on the totality of evidence before the court that this child, aged 15, was *Gillick* competent. The child was described as understanding fully what was involved in his placement including the restrictions on his liberty, why they were necessary and how they benefited him.[18]

4.18 Once an assessment of *Gillick* competence has been conducted, its conclusions must then be considered as part of the evaluation of whether valid consent can be provided. Children who are assessed as not being *Gillick* competent will not have sufficient understanding or intelligence in order to provide consent to arrangements that would otherwise amount to a deprivation of their liberty. No valid consent can be obtained from children who are not *Gillick* competent. In these circumstances, the possibility of obtaining consent from a child's parents must be considered and this is explored later in the chapter.

4.19 If a child is assessed as being *Gillick* competent, the other elements of valid consent need to be considered. These are that the child has sufficient information to make the decision and that their consent is given without unfair or undue pressure.

4.20 Assessors and practitioners should ensure that a child has been provided with sufficient information in order to make a decision about whether or not to consent to restrictions on their liberty. The information provided must be sufficient to allow the child to appreciate the measures that will be implemented and the impact they will have on them and their life. In respect of adults, the court has guided practitioners that the relevant information provided should include the context in which the restrictions are being imposed, including the setting and wider circumstances.[19] What information is considered relevant for a child to make an informed decision will vary on a case by case basis. It will likely include detail about the placement, the type of restrictions, how they will be imposed and by whom, alongside the risks were the restrictions not imposed.

4.21 In order to be valid, the consent must be provided without undue or unfair pressure. Practitioners should be satisfied that the child has not been persuaded to

---

15 *Re A-F (Children) (Care Proceedings: Deprivation of Liberty)* [2018] EWHC 138, para 53.

16 *A Local Authority v D, E and C* [2016] EWHC 3473 (Fam).

17 *A Local Authority v D, E and C* [2016] EWHC 3473 (Fam), para 44.

18 *A Local Authority v D, E and C* [2016] EWHC 3473 (Fam), para 54.

19 *A PCT v LDV* [2013] EWHC 272 (Fam).

provide their consent, that the child understands their right not to provide consent, and there has been no coercion or manipulation to obtain the consent of the child.

4.22 In summary, a child aged under 16 may provide valid consent to their living and care arrangements which impose restrictions on their physical liberty to such an extent that without consent, they would be considered to be deprived of their liberty. The child must be assessed as being *Gillick* competent and provide their consent having been given sufficient information to understand the proposed regime and its consequences, and that consent being freely given without undue or unfair pressure. This would constitute valid consent for the purposes of the *Storck* limb (b). Where a child is not *Gillick* competent, or is competent but does not provide consent, the next step for practitioners to consider is whether their parent may be able to provide valid consent to the arrangements. This is explored further in the section below.

4.23 To put these principles into context, it is helpful to consider the case of *T (A Child)*. This decision was handed down by the Supreme Court in 2021, considering two distinct questions:

(a) Firstly, whether it is a permissible exercise of the High Court's inherent jurisdiction to make an order authorising a local authority to deprive a child of his or her liberty in unregistered secure accommodation when a registered secure children's home would be appropriate but is not available; and,

(b) Secondly, if the High Court can have recourse to its inherent jurisdiction to make an order of the type in question, what is the relevance of the child's consent to the proposed living arrangements?

4.24 T, the child, aged 15, was in the care of the local authority by virtue of a care order. Due to T's complex needs and behaviours, there was no dispute that she required secure accommodation: however, no placement was available in a setting registered to provide secure accommodation for children. The accommodation shortage forced the local authority to seek an order from the High Court under its inherent jurisdiction to authorise T's deprivation of liberty in an unregistered placement. T's position from the outset of proceedings was that she had the capacity to consent to the care regime proposed in each of the identified placements for her, that she wanted to be in those placements, and that she consented to any restrictions placed on her liberty. T's case was that there was no need for court involvement because her consent was all that was required to legitimise the arrangements which restricted her physical liberty.

4.25 At first instance, Mostyn J took the view that a court order was required because in his assessment, T's consent did not have the 'authentic and enduring' quality which, he held, was necessary to establish consent for the purposes of Article 5.[20] In considering Keehan J's decision in *A Local Authority v D*, the court summarised that authentic and enduring consent is not necessarily established by

20 *A Local Authority v SW, MT, NT* [2018] EWHC 576 (Fam).

the child saying 'I do'.[21] The child must say it and mean it. The authentic consent must be deemed to endure in the short to medium term, not being 'merely evanescent consent'.[22] Whilst the judgment does not set out the specific comments made by T providing her consent, Mostyn J was satisfied that the consent was not authentic and enduring and as such, a deprivation of liberty authorisation was granted.

4.26 T then unsuccessfully appealed to the Court of Appeal against the authorisation of both placements, challenging the judge's approach to the question of consent, and the Court of Appeal found no basis to conclude that on the facts of T's case that Mostyn J was wrong to exercise his discretion by making an order. Sir Andrew McFarlane, President of the Family Division, stated at paragraph 86:

> 'T's appeal, as it had become by the close of argument, is now no more than a challenge to the judge's discretion and could only succeed if this court were to be satisfied that the judge was wrong to grant authorisation to the local authority notwithstanding the apparent consent of the young person. There is no basis for holding that Mostyn J was 'wrong' to authorise restriction of liberty in this case. Indeed, as the judge himself observed, the breakdown of the placement so soon after the January order had been made vindicated his determination on that occasion; it also justified the making of a further order in respect of the new placement.'[23]

4.27 The Supreme Court dismissed the appeal and held that the use of the inherent jurisdiction to authorise the deprivation in cases such as this was permitted. In respect of consent, Lady Black commented that the ground of appeal which related to consent could not have led to success in the appeal on the facts, and that the ground raises points of more general importance:

> '161. The President was rightly anxious to stress (para 79 of the Court of Appeal judgment) the importance, for the protection of a child, of the court's involvement in authorising a deprivation of liberty, whether under section 25/section 119 or under the inherent jurisdiction. This is not the occasion for a comprehensive exploration of the complications attending consent to deprivation of liberty. For the moment, it is enough to observe that, even leaving to one side difficult issues about the pressures that circumstances may place on a child to consent to a proposed arrangement, an apparently balanced and free decision made by a child may be quickly revised and/or reversed. The facts of this case clearly demonstrate how insecure may be the child's apparent consent. Having said that, there may also be cases in which the child is expressing a carefully considered and firm view.
>
> 162. When the court considers the local authority's application, any consent on the part of the child will form part of the circumstances that it evaluates in deciding upon its order. I would not presume to forecast, still less dictate, what its implications would be for any particular case. That must depend upon the facts. The child needs to be, and is, protected by the institution of the proceedings and the consequent involvement of the court. His or her personal autonomy will be respected by being fully involved in those proceedings, and able to express views about the

21 *A Local Authority v D* [2016] EWHC 3473 (Fam); *A Local Authority v SW, MT, NT* [2018] EWHC 576 (Fam), para 10.

22 *A Local Authority v SW, MT, NT* [2018] EWHC 576 (Fam), para 10.

23 *Re T (A Child)* [2018] EWCA Civ 2136.

> care that is being proposed, as ensured by the procedures stipulated by statute (for section 25) and by case law (for the inherent jurisdiction). It is worth noting that, in a case where the local authority is authorised to deprive the child of his or her liberty but, when it comes to putting the restrictive arrangements into practice, the child is in fact consenting to them in circumstances where that consent is valid and sufficient, there would be no deprivation of liberty. In that situation, the local authority would simply be providing the child with accommodation.'[24]

4.28 The Supreme Court also made clear that the court is not bound by a required absence of valid consent in order to intervene and exercise its inherent jurisdiction.[25] The court may, therefore, make an order authorising a child's deprivation of liberty irrespective of whether the child themselves has provided consent to the arrangements. Whilst an absence of consent is a requirement under the *Storck* limbs for a deprivation of liberty to arise, the presence of consent provided by a child does not prevent the court making a permissive order to authorise the deprivation of a child's liberty.

Young people aged 16 and 17

4.29 The law distinguishes between children under 16 and young people aged 16 to 17 years in many areas and this extends to their ability to make decisions for themselves. As set out above, the law recognises that generally, as a child gets older, their understanding grows and their ability to make informed decisions progresses. *Gillick* competence ceases to be relevant once a child reaches 16, and the starting point when considering a 16 or 17 -year old's ability to make decisions for themselves (including to provide valid consent) is 'capacity', derived from the MCA 2005. Capacity is defined within the MCA 2005 in the negative, with the MCA 2005 setting out what it means to lack capacity.[26] A person does not have capacity if, at the material time, they are unable to make a decision in relation to a matter because of an impairment of or disturbance in the functioning of their mind or brain. To be unable to make a decision, a person must be: unable to understand the information relevant to the decision; unable to retain that information; unable to use or weigh that information as part of the process of making a decision; or, unable to communicate their decision.[27] Everyone aged 16 or over is assumed to have capacity to make a decision for themselves unless it is established that they lack capacity to do so.[28]

4.30 It is not always clear whether or not a young person has capacity and therefore whether or not they can provide valid consent to their living arrangements which would otherwise amount to a deprivation of their liberty. If a young person's capacity is uncertain and there is any doubt as to their ability to understand, retain, use or weigh the relevant information, a capacity assessment must be carried out.

---

24 *Re T (A Child)* [2021] UKSC 35, paras 161-162.
25 *Re T (A Child)* [2021] UKSC 35, para 100.
26 MCA 2005, s 2.
27 MCA 2005, s 3.
28 MCA 2005, s 1(2).

Capacity assessments are often carried out by social workers, psychologists or mental health practitioners and determine whether or not a person is deemed to have the requisite capacity in order to make a decision for themselves in the relevant area.

4.31 In the Supreme Court case of *A Local Authority v JB,* Lord Stephens clarified the test for assessing a person's capacity.[29] He made clear that this is a two-stage test and the assessor should begin with the functional aspect, being whether the person can undertake the tasks set out above, before considering any impairment of or disturbance in the functioning of their mind or brain, and whether there is a causative link between the impairment or disturbance and the person's ability to undertake the identified tasks.[30] Capacity is a decision-specific concept and each issue which requires a decision should be considered separately. A person may have capacity to make decisions about where they live, for example, but lack capacity to make decisions about their medical treatment. In cases relating to a deprivation of liberty, the relevant information includes the arrangements for residence, care and support including the nature of restrictions that would amount to a deprivation of liberty and their consequences.[31]

TWO-STAGE TEST:

Stage 1 – Is the young person unable to make a particular decision? (the functional test)

Stage 2 – Is the inability to make a decision caused by an impairment of or disturbance in the functioning of the person's mind or brain? This requires identification of an impairment or disturbance, and then consideration of whether that impairment or disturbance is causing the young person to be unable to make a particular decision. (the diagnostic test)

4.32 Care must be taken when assessing a young person's capacity as their cognitive functioning is still developing and they have not fully matured. This may mean that a young person may lack capacity when initially assessed, but may develop capacity over time. A person's capacity to make decisions may also fluctuate. A young person may have capacity to consent to their living arrangements at one point in time but may lack that capacity later. The MCA 2005 Code of Practice offers some guidance and describes fluctuating capacity as 'a problem or condition that gets worse occasionally and affects their ability to make their own decisions.' The examples given of diagnoses which may cause capacity to fluctuate are manic depression or psychotic illness which may have a temporary effect on a person's decision-making abilities, causing them to lose the functions needed to make a capacitous decision, but regain those abilities when they are more stable.[32] Fluctuating capacity is a complicated area and requires careful assessment of the young person involved. The Court of Protection has provided guidance which should

29 *A Local Authority v JB* [2021] UKSC 52.

30 *A Local Authority v JB* [2021] UKSC 52, para 78.

31 *A Primary Care Trust v LDV & Ors* [2013] EWHC 272 (Fam).

32 The MCA 2005 Code of Practice, Department for Constitutional Affairs (2007), para 4.26.

be considered when the circumstances and presentation of the young person suggest their capacity may fluctuate.[33]

4.33 If a young person is assessed as having capacity in the relevant area, the other elements of valid consent must then be considered. The provision of sufficient information to the young person and ensuring the consent is freely given apply equally to 16 and 17-year olds as they do to under 16s. If those elements are satisfied and valid consent is provided by a young person, this would render there to be no deprivation of liberty as limb (b) of the *Storck* components is not satisfied – there is not an absence of valid consent.

4.34 If a young person is assessed as having the capacity to consent to their living arrangements which include restricting their physical liberty, but does not provide their consent, the only means by which they can be lawfully deprived of their liberty is with the authorisation of the court acting under its inherent jurisdiction.[34] Whilst in some circumstances, the MCA 2005 can be used as a statutory instrument to authorise the deprivation of liberty of young people, it is not an available route to consider when the relevant person retains mental capacity to make the decision in question. The potential of seeking valid consent from a parent is not an available option for young people, and this is explored further later in this chapter.

4.35 When a young person is assessed as lacking capacity to make decisions about their residence, care and support arrangements which may amount to a deprivation of their liberty, they are unable to provide valid consent. In the absence of that consent, any confinement that meets the criteria set down in *Storck* amounts to a deprivation of liberty. In those circumstances, the confinement would need to be authorised by the court. The process of seeking authorisation from the court is considered further at chapter 5.

4.36 If a young person lacks capacity to consent to their confinement, they should still be kept as fully informed as possible in the decisions being made. The MCA 2005 Code of Practice states that 'people must be given all appropriate help and support to enable them to make their own decisions or to maximise their participation in any decision-making process'.[35] This applies to decisions about the care and treatment of young people and includes ensuring they are supported to engage fully in the process of assessing their capacity and making decisions.[36]

Overriding consent

4.37 Obtaining the valid consent of a child or young person to their arrangements should be sought where possible and appropriate. However, if a child or young person

---

33 *A Local Authority v H* [2023] EWCOP 4; *A Local Authority v PG & Ors* [2023] EWCOP 9.

34 *EBY (A Child) (Deprivation of Liberty Order: Jurisdiction) (17-year-old)* [2023] EWHC 2494 (Fam), paras 46-48.

35 The Mental Capacity Act 2005 Code of Practice, Department for Constitutional Affairs (2007), para 1.2.

36 The Mental Health Act Code of Practice 2015, Department of Health (2015), para 19.5.

is able to consent but refuses to provide consent, there are other routes available to lawfully deprive them of their liberty when that is necessary, proportionate and in their best interests. The High Court's powers are limitless unless they are constrained by case law or statute.[37] Where a *Gillick* competent child or capacitous young person refuses to give consent to restrictions on their physical liberty, the court may use its powers under the inherent jurisdiction to override their wishes and authorise the restrictive measures.[38] This power exists in furtherance of the court's overarching duty to make decisions in a child or young person's best interests where the child or young person is unable to do so, because they have not yet reached adulthood.[39]

4.38 In circumstances where a child or young person's refusal to provide consent is to be overridden, the court needs to be satisfied that it is in their best interests to do so.[40] Acting in opposition to a child's competent or capacitous wishes is usually confined to extreme situations, such as where a child or young person has refused a life-saving treatment.[41] However, this may extend to the court making an order when it is necessary to deprive a child of their liberty.[42] The notion of overriding a young person's wishes was considered recently by the Court of Appeal within *E&F (Minors: Blood Transfusion)*.[43] In this case, the court exercised its power to overrule the decisions of two capacitous young people (aged 16 and 17) in respect of their medical treatment. Within the judgment, the court emphasised that welfare is the overriding principle which the court must consider in making a decision like this, and that there is no presumption in favour of the mature adolescent's decision being upheld. Sir Andrew McFarlane, the President of the Family Division remarked:

> '63. Re W does not establish a presumption in favour of the mature adolescent's decision, but instead affirms welfare as the overriding principle. It speaks for the young person's decision to be upheld where possible but also speaks of those rare circumstances where the gravity of the consequences and the imperative to preserve life may require the court to intervene.'

4.39 It is clear from this judgment that the court will be willing to intervene and go against the wishes of a child or young person in circumstances where to do so is necessary and proportionate to secure their safety and, in extreme cases, save their life. Both the court and Mental Health Act Code of Practice 2015 provide clear guidance that each case should be considered individually on its specific facts.[44] All decisions 'require a close examination of the concrete situation on the ground'.[45] Therefore, whilst it is within the court's power to override a child or young person's wishes, to do so is recognised as being an extreme step which requires careful analysis.

---

37 Family Procedure Rules 2010, PD12D, para 1.1.

38 *A Local Authority v D and others* [2016] EWHC 3473 (Fam); *Re T (A child)* [2021] UKSC 35.

39 *Re J (A Minor) (Medical Treatment)* [1993] Fam 64.

40 *Re P (Medical Treatment: Best Interests)* [2003] EWHC 2327 (Fam); *NHS Foundation Trust Hospital v P* [2014] EWHC 1650 (Fam).

41 *Re W (A Minor) (Medical Treatment: Court's Jurisdiction)* [1993] Fam 64.

42 *Re J* [2020] EWHC 2395 (Fam).

43 *E&F (Minors: Blood Transfusion)* [2021] EWCA Civ 1888 (Fam).

44 The Mental Health Act Code of Practice 2015, Department of Health (2015).

45 *Re D* [2015] EWHC 922 (Fam), para 68.

PARENTAL CONSENT

4.40 In some circumstances, in the absence of valid consent from the child, parental consent may be an appropriate form of consent to the arrangements in place for a child which amount to their confinement. This section will focus on the circumstances in which parental consent may be obtained and deemed 'valid'.

4.41 Parental consent may be a form of valid consent; the subjective element at limb (b) of the *Storck* components of a deprivation of liberty.[46] In practice, this means that the arrangements in place for a child which amount to their confinement (in line with limb (a) of the *Storck* components) are not an unlawful interference with their Article 5 ECHR rights because the consent of their parent renders the arrangements not a deprivation of liberty within the meaning of Article 5.[47]

4.42 Before delving into the circumstances in which parental consent is available and appropriate, it is helpful to first look at the wider context. The notion of parental consent is derived from the traditional role of a parent as someone who makes decisions on behalf of or for their child who is too young to understand all of the relevant information in order to make an informed decision themselves. This concept has been translated into the law with the creation of parental responsibility. Parental responsibility is afforded: automatically to mothers, and fathers who are married to the mother or in a civil partnership with them; to second female partners who were married to or in a civil partnership with the mother at the time of conception (unless the partner did not consent to the conception); to fathers by naming on the birth certificate or by declaration; and to those in receipt of a child arrangements order or special guardianship order. Parental responsibility is also conferred to adoptive parents by way of an adoption order, which simultaneously removes the parental responsibility of birth parents. A similar process is in place for children born through surrogacy and a parental order confers parental responsibility to the intended parents and extinguishes the parental responsibility of the surrogate. Parental responsibility may also be conferred by way of a court appointed guardianship (which is not the same as a children's guardian for the purposes of court proceedings) or by a court order granting parental responsibility. References in this chapter to parents include all those who have parental responsibility for the child. Local authorities may also obtain parental responsibility for a child, explored further in chapter 6. A local authority with parental responsibility may act as 'corporate parent' but does not fall within the definition of a parent for the purposes of this chapter and discussions on consent.

4.43 The rights of parents have been discussed at length within case law and are summarised within *Gillick v West Norfolk and Wisbech Area Health Authority* as being a parent's powers which are required to perform their duties to their children.[48]

---

46 *Storck v Germany* (2005) 43 EHRR 6; *(1) P (by his litigation friend the Official Solicitor) v Cheshire West and Chester Council & Anor (2) P and Q (by their litigation friend the Official Solicitor) v Surrey County Council* [2014] UKSC 19.

47 *Stanev v Bulgaria* 36760/06 [2012] ECHR 36.

48 *Gillick v West Norfolk and Wisbech Area Health Authority* [1986] AC 112.

The judgment goes on to define this duty as to be 'responsible for the physical and moral upbringing of the child', but it is not an absolute right and has limits and qualifications to ensure the autonomy of the child is promoted alongside the child's wider welfare interests.

4.44 Parental responsibility is defined within the Children Act 1989 (CA 1989) at s 3(1) as being 'all the rights, duties, powers, responsibilities and authority which by law a parent of a child has in relation to the child and his property'. In practical terms, this includes decisions about a child's education, health and medical treatment, travel, religion and culture alongside smaller everyday decisions such as receiving dental treatment or which school the child attends. The House of Commons Research Briefing on parental responsibility further explains that parental responsibility requires a person to be responsible for the care and wellbeing of a child, including naming the child, determining their religion and education, consenting to medical treatment, protecting and maintaining the child and lawfully correcting the child.[49]

4.45 In setting out the scope of parental responsibility, it is important to recognise that this may include, in some circumstances, the use of reasonable force as may be appropriate to protect the best interests of the child.[50] The lawful correction of children includes reasonable punishment, with the reasonableness of any punishment being determined by considering the individual circumstances on a case by case basis. Knowles J described this right within *Re Z* by saying 'Parents can, pursuant to the exercise of their parental responsibility, permit or authorise the use of reasonable force on a child particularly if the child will suffer immediate and significant harm by them not acting.'[51] The use of force against a child by a parent, or by another but permitted by a parent, shall be a reasonable exercise of parental responsibility when it is to secure the immediate safety of the child and prevent them suffering significant harm. This envisages an emergency scenario whereby without some force being implemented, the child would suffer serious harm, injury or death.

4.46 The UN Convention on the Rights of the Child (UNCRC) sets out a framework within which parental responsibility must be exercised.[52] This includes at Article 2 that the best interests of the child shall be the primary consideration in all actions concerning that child. Article 5 requires the responsibilities, rights and duties of parents to be exercised in a manner 'consistent with the evolving capacities of the child'. The UNCRC recognises that whilst parents should and will act protectively towards their children, children should also be encouraged to exercise their rights independently as they grow up. Article 37 deals specifically with the deprivation of a child's liberty, clarifying that no child shall be deprived of their liberty unlawfully or arbitrarily. Any detention of a child, the UNCRC sets out, should be a last resort and for the shortest time appropriate.[53]

---

49 Parental responsibility in England and Wales, Commons Library Research Briefing 8760 (2023).

50 *A Metropolitan Borough Council v DB* [1997] 1 FLR 767.

51 *Re Z* [2020] EWHC 3038 (Fam), para 27.

52 The Convention on the Rights of the Child, United Nations (1989).

53 Article 37 of the The Convention on the Rights of the Child, United Nations (1989).

4.47 The Mental Health Act Code of Practice 2015 adds to the guidance on parental responsibility, seeking to make clear what needs to be considered when important decisions are being made for a child.[54] The Code of Practice states at paragraph 19.48:

> 'In determining the limits of parental responsibility, decision-makers must carefully consider and balance: (i) the child's right to liberty under article 5, which should be informed by article 37 of the UNCRC, (ii) the parent's right to respect for the right to family life under article 8, which includes the concept of parental responsibility for the care and custody of minor children, and (iii) the child's right to autonomy which is also protected under article 8'.

4.48 Owing to its wide definition, it has been necessary for the court to consider the scope of parental responsibility and what decisions fall within it. Parental responsibility encompasses a bundle of rights or powers, defined in the 1970s as including a 'personal power physically to control the infant until the years of discretion'.[55] The court went further 18 years later in setting some clear boundaries to parental responsibility, or parental authority as it was then called. Within *Nielsen v Denmark*, the European Court of Human Rights (ECtHR) recognised that parental responsibility includes a broad range of rights relating to the care and custody of a child.[56] The court stated that 'the care and upbringing of children normally and necessarily require that the parents or an only parent decide where the child must reside and also impose, or authorise others to impose, various restrictions on the child's liberty.' The court continued '… the rights of the holder of parental authority cannot be unlimited and that it is incumbent on the state to provide safeguards against abuse'.[57]

4.49 What is meant by the 'not unlimited scope of parental responsibility' has since been considered extensively by the court. In general terms, decisions which may fall outside of the scope of parental responsibility are ones which impede or curtail a child's core human rights, and have a significant impact upon the child. Parents may make decisions about where their child lives, how they are raised and what boundaries are in place to prevent them from coming to harm.[58] Parents can also consent to the medical treatment of their child in appropriate circumstances.[59] However, a parent does not have unfettered control over their child, and their parental responsibility may not extend to making decisions which significantly impact upon the child's rights under the ECHR and which would not be reasonable decisions for a parent to make. The case law explored within this chapter attempts to strike a balance between a parent's right to a private and family life, including to make decisions concerning their child, and the child's right to autonomy. One way in which the autonomy of children is promoted, and the rights of the parent curtailed, is

---

54 The Mental Health Act Code of Practice 2015, Department of Health (2015).

55 *Hewer v Bryant* [1970] 1 QB 357.

56 *Nielsen v Denmark* (1988) 11 EHRR 175.

57 *Nielsen v Denmark* (1988) 11 EHRR 175, paras 61 and 72.

58 *R v Gibbins and Proctor* [1918] 13 Cr App R 134; Children and Young Persons Act 1933 as amended by CA 1989, Sch 13.

59 *Gillick v West Norfolk and Wisbech Area Health Authority* [1986] AC 112.

a parent being unable to override the valid consent provided by a *Gillick* competent child to medical treatment.[60]

4.50 When considering the scope of parental responsibility and its appropriate exercise, the individual circumstances of each child must be looked at. Within *Trust A v X and A Local Authority*, Keehan J distinguished between what will be an appropriate exercise of parental responsibility for a 5-year old child and what may be appropriate for a 15-year-old.[61] The court considered that the age and development of a child impact upon what decisions are appropriate for a parent to make, recognising the increasing autonomy of a child as they move towards adulthood. It is expected that as children get older, there are more decisions which they are able to make for themselves and it is therefore inappropriate for their parents to make those decisions on their child's behalf. Keehan J also considered the diagnoses, or lack of diagnoses, of any child to be a relevant factor when determining what is an appropriate exercise of parental responsibility. Deciding to keep a 15-year-old who is free from disability under constant supervision and control will be undoubtedly inappropriate, Keehan J determined, whilst constant supervision of a 15-year-old with autism and erratic behaviours is more likely to be a justified exercise of parental responsibility.[62]

4.51 Lieven J touched upon this issue in *Lincolnshire County Council v TGA* by saying:

> 'More fundamentally, when dealing with children, whose ability to understand the issues will vary greatly depending not simply on their age, but on their psychological and emotional maturity, their family support and life experiences, in my view it is more appropriate to consider the characteristics of the individual child than to try compare them with a hypothetical child of the same age.'[63]

4.52 For this reason, Lieven J preferred the approach as set out within *Gillick,* to consider the characteristics of the particular child when determining the scope of appropriate parental responsibility in respect of that child. This will include taking into account the child's age, level of understanding and any diagnosis or condition which impacts their mental or physical functioning. It is important to consider the circumstances of the child holistically when determining what decisions are appropriate for a parent to make, and whether those decisions are in that child's welfare interests. It cannot be a 'one size fits all' approach or a sliding scale determined only on the age of a child. The scope of a parent's rights in relation to their child is determined by looking at a range of factors which determine what is appropriate in the individual circumstances of each child.

4.53 Having defined the concept and scope of parental responsibility, the discussion then turns to when that parental responsibility can be invoked to provide consent to arrangements which would otherwise amount to the deprivation of a child or young person's liberty. The law has divided this discussion into two categories,

60 *Re W (A Minor) (Medical Treatment: Court's Jurisdiction)* [1992] 3 WLR 758.

61 *Trust A v X and A Local Authority* [2015] EWHC 922 (Fam).

62 *Trust A v X and A Local Authority* [2015] EWHC 922 (Fam), paras 56 – 57.

63 *Lincolnshire County Council v TGA* [2022] EWHC 2323 (Fam), para 57.

children who are under 16 and young people who are 16 and 17. This distinction has been made in order to properly represent the autonomy of children as they get older, and to afford them the right to make decisions about their own lives.

Under 16s

4.54 Relying on a parents' consent to measures which amount to the confinement of a child is possible. The consent of a parent is relevant when a child lacks *Gillick* competence and so cannot consent themselves. If that consent is provided and is appropriate, no deprivation of liberty is present. However, obtaining consent and then relying upon it isn't straightforward. Due to the severe intervention in a child's life which is inherent within a child's confinement, limits are required on the circumstances in which consent can appropriately be provided by parents to negate the deprivation of the child's liberty. This section will consider the circumstances in which parental consent can be relied upon to authorise a child's confinement, and those in which it cannot.

4.55 An initial key principle to note is that parental consent to a child's confinement is not available in circumstances where a local authority shares parental responsibility for a child.[64] A local authority may share parental responsibility because it has been granted an interim care order or a care order. Owing to the circumstances which must be present before an interim care order or care order is granted (explained in chapter 6), the court has confirmed it would not be appropriate to rely on a parent exercising their parental responsibility in the best interests of their child when the circumstances are such that a local authority has been required to share that parental responsibility

4.56 A second consideration which arises when a local authority shares parental responsibility or is involved in accommodating a child is whether the local authority itself may provide consent to the arrangements, acting as 'corporate parent' or the body responsible for the arrangements. The role of 'corporate parent' allows a local authority to make some decisions for a child as a parent would, usually in relation to where the child lives and by whom they are cared for. However, the general, established, rule has been that this does not extend to permitting a local authority to provide consent to arrangements for a child which would otherwise amount to their deprivation of their liberty. Within *A Local Authority v D*, the court explained:

> 'In taking a child into care and instituting care proceedings, the local authority is acting as an organ of the state. To permit a local authority in such circumstances to consent to the deprivation of liberty of a child would (1) breach Article 5 of the Convention, which provides "no one should be deprived of his liberty save in the following cases and in accordance with a procedure prescribed by law", (2) would not afford the "proper safeguards which will secure the legal justifications for the constraints under which they

64 *Re AB (A Child) (Deprivation of Liberty: Consent)* [2015] EWHC 3125 (Fam); *Re D (A Child)* [2017] EWCA Civ 1695.

are made out", and (3) would not meet the need for a periodic independent check on whether the arrangements made for them are in their best interests.'[65]

4.57 For the reasons set out within *A Local Authority v D,* and subsequently reiterated in *Re AB,* it has been considered not possible for consent to be provided by a local authority to negate a deprivation of liberty.[66] Recently, the well-trodden ground of local authority consent in these circumstances has been shaken by a judgment provided by Lieven J in *Re J: Local Authority consent to Deprivation of Liberty*.[67] In this case, the court was concerned with J, a 14-year-old boy who was a looked after child under the CA 1989, s 20. The local authority sought a care order and for authorisation of the deprivation of J's liberty. In the face of an agreed position, the court had no hesitation in first granting a care order for J, providing the local authority with shared parental responsibility for him. Lieven J then considered whether she was required to make an order authorising the deprivation of J's liberty. The court accepted on the facts of the case that J was objectively confined, and that the arrangements for his confinement were imputable to the state. Limbs (a) and (c) of the *Storck* criteria were therefore met.[68] The question which arose related to limb (b) and consent.

4.58 Lieven J distilled the issue before her as 'whether a LA [local authority], which holds parental responsibility for a child under the age of 16, under a Care Order, can consent to a deprivation of liberty of that child.'[69] The court found that it could. Lieven J considered the scope of powers which fall within a local authority's parental responsibility, and considered that to consent to a deprivation of liberty was not a decision of '*such magnitude*' as to fall outside of a local authority's powers.[70] This decision by Lieven J is a very recent one, and it is not yet clear whether the decision will be appealed in light of its conflict with earlier case law. What can be said with certainty is that the scope of a local authority's powers in this regard, to consent to what would otherwise be a deprivation of liberty, is an issue which requires consideration by the appellate court promptly. There are now conflicting decisions from the High Court in relation to this and the route ahead for local authorities is unclear.

4.59 Moving then to consider the use of parental consent for children who are not the subject of interim care orders or care orders. Lieven J provided a helpful and explanatory judgment within *Lincolnshire County Council v TGA* in 2022 dealing with the issue of parental consent to the confinement of a child under 16.[71] In this case, the court was concerned with K. K was diagnosed with epilepsy, autism, attention deficit disorder and global developmental delay. K was accommodated by the local authority because his parents had provided consent for his placement in

65 *A Local Authority v D* [2015] EWHC 3125 (Fam), para 29.

66 *A Local Authority v D* [2015] EWHC 3125 (Fam); *Re AB (A Child) (Deprivation of Liberty)* [2015] EWHC 3125 Fam.

67 *Re J: Local Authority consent to Deprivation of Liberty* [2024] EWHC 1690 (Fam).

68 *Re J: Local Authority consent to Deprivation of Liberty* [2024] EWHC 1690 (Fam), para 14.

69 *Re J: Local Authority consent to Deprivation of Liberty* [2024] EWHC 1690 (Fam), para 22.

70 *Re J: Local Authority consent to Deprivation of Liberty* [2024] EWHC 1690 (Fam), para 35.

71 *Lincolnshire County Council v TGA* [2022] EWHC 2323 (Fam).

local authority care (sometimes referred to as 'section 20 consent').[72] K's parents passed away and testamentary guardians were appointed, acting in a role similar to that of parents. The arrangements for K's care amounted to his confinement. The key question before the court was whether a deprivation of liberty was present. This was because K's guardians had provided consent to the arrangements, which could mean that the second limb of the *Storck* criteria had not been satisfied. The court was asked whether that consent could be relied upon and, if it could, no deprivation of liberty would be present.

4.60 The court determined that a parent can consent to the confinement of a child, which would otherwise amount to their deprivation of liberty, in circumstances where the child lacks *Gillick* competence and there is no dispute as to the arrangements being in the child's best interests. Any potential dispute referred to here relates to a disagreement between the professionals involved in the care of the child (such as doctors and social workers) and the parents, or a dispute between the parents themselves.[73] The judge referred herself to *Nielsen* and the ECtHR's decision that in the circumstances before it, the scope of parental responsibility did extend to consenting to that child's confinement. The circumstances of *Nielsen* concerned a 12-year-old boy who was placed in a children's psychiatric unit by his mother, exercising sole parental responsibility. That court found that it was within the mother's parental rights to authorise her child's confinement in a psychiatric unit, drawing a comparison to a child's admission to hospital for medical treatment.[74] The court considered that the circumstances for the young boy in *Nielsen* were no more than the circumstances that may be imposed upon a child by their parent in the course of ordinary parenting. They were not of a nature and degree that would render them inappropriate for a parent to impose or consent to.

4.61 Lieven J's decision brings into focus one significant issue which arises in respect of relying on parental consent to a child's confinement. That is whether or not the decision to be made falls within the 'zone' of appropriate parental responsibility. The general interpretation and scope of parental responsibility has been explored earlier in this chapter, and must now be applied to the circumstances which surround a child's confinement.

4.62 This is an issue which the court has carefully considered over time. It boils down to whether or not the nature of the confinement, or restrictive regime, proposed or implemented is a confinement or regime which a parent should, pursuant to their parental rights, be making a decision about. Logically, in keeping with the principles of the ECHR and the UNCRC, the more severe the intervention, the less likely it is to be a matter which a parent should be making a decision about for their child. Similarly, as a child gets older and develops their autonomy, the limits on a parent's decision-making powers increase and gradually render more decisions inappropriate for a parent to make.

---

72 CA 1989, s 20.

73 *Lancashire CC v PX* [2022] EWHC 2379 (Fam).

74 *Nielsen v Denmark* (1988) 11 EHRR 175, para 61.

4.63 A helpful starting point in considering the appropriateness of relying on parental consent is the guidance provided within the Mental Health Act Code of Practice 2015.[75] The Code of Practice requires that consideration is given to the child's right to liberty and autonomy when determining the scope of decisions which their parents may be able to make for or about them. The wording of the Code suggests that where a decision or arrangement for a child interferes significantly with their right to liberty and autonomy, it is likely to fall outside of the scope of parental responsibility. Applying this to the confinement of a child, the nature, degree and intensity of the restrictions proposed or implemented must be considered. A regime of restrictions which interfere markedly with a child's liberty and autonomy, beyond what would be implemented in the course of ordinary parenting, is therefore more likely to be considered an inappropriate regime for a parent to be making a decision about and ultimately consenting to. The Code does not outline a particular set of circumstances which would fall outside the scope of parental responsibility, recognising that the boundaries of parental responsibility cannot be rigid and must be applied to each individual circumstance. However, the Code gives a helpful foundation on which to analyse whether or not the consent of a parent to a restrictive regime will be a matter that falls appropriately within their parental responsibility.[76]

4.64 The next place in which guidance about the appropriate scope of parental responsibility can be found is case law. There are a number of cases within which the court has found that consenting to restrictive arrangements for a child fell within the scope of parental responsibility. Within *Trust A v X*, Keehan J considered that it was an appropriate exercise of parental responsibility for the child's, D's, parents to consent to his residence in hospital which included a regime of locked doors, frequent observations by staff and 1:1 support in the community.[77] In that case, D was diagnosed with ADHD, asperger's syndrome and tourette's syndrome and was assessed as being not *Gillick* competent and so unable to provide valid consent himself.[78]

4.65 His Honour Judge Hayes KC found similarly within *RN (Deprivation of Liberty and Parental Consent)*.[79] The child in that case, RN, was subject to similar arrangements with a higher degree of intensity involving up to 2:1 supervision in the community and constant supervision at his placement at home. RN was diagnosed with attention deficit hyperactivity disorder and a significant learning disability.[80] She had very limited vocabulary and was deemed incapable of providing consent herself. The court found again that it fell within the scope of parental responsibility for the parents to provide consent to the arrangements for RN which amounted to her confinement.

4.66 However, the court has also made clear that there are arrangements which are, by virtue of their degree and intensity, outside of the scope of parental

75 The Mental Health Act Code of Practice 2015, Department of Health (2015), chapter 19.

76 The Mental Health Act Code of Practice 2015, Department of Health (2015), chapter 19.

77 *Trust A v X* [2015] EWHC 922 (Fam).

78 *Trust A v X* [2015] EWHC 922 (Fam), para 19.

79 *RN (Deprivation of Liberty and Parental Consent)* [2022] EWHC 2576 (Fam).

80 *RN (Deprivation of Liberty and Parental Consent)* [2022] EWHC 2576 (Fam), para 46.

responsibility to consent to. Knowles J considered this issue as part of the decision in *Re Z (A Child; Deprivation of Liberty: Transition Plan)*.[81] In its judgment, the court noted that the living arrangements for the child were restrictive but fell within the scope of parental responsibility to consent to (although the judgment does not provide detail of what those arrangements were). The question which arose in this case was whether the transition plan to transport the child to a proposed new placement went beyond measures which the parents could consent to. The arrangements included the use of force and physical and chemical restraint in order to move the child. The judge commented that there are 'limits to what a parent can reasonably authorise' and that 'what was contemplated here strained the boundaries of what was permitted by a parent with respect to the exercise of their parental responsibility.'[82]

4.67 It is clear from this judgment that there are measures which the court considers go beyond what can be consented to as part of the exercise of parental responsibility. In *Re Z*, the measures which were distinguished from those which the parents were already appropriately consenting to were those involving force, holds and sedative medication. This was a planned move with a gradual scale of restrictions to be implemented if required and not a situation of immediate necessity in which force may be required to prevent the child suffering significant harm.[83] For that reason, the court considered this was not a circumstance in which it would be reasonable to expect the parents to consent to the arrangements as part of the decisions made under their parental responsibility. The court determined that the level of force proposed in the transition plan required the authorisation of the court in order to be lawfully imposed.

4.68 The trend of recent case law follows the decision in *Re Z* and suggests that whilst parental responsibility may be exercised to consent to some arrangements which amount to the confinement of a child, there is a limit to this. The court has been willing to step back and allow parental consent to negate a deprivation of liberty in circumstances where a child is supervised, monitored and locked within a placement. However, the court has considered consent to be inappropriate and its authorisation to be necessary where the arrangements for a child include physical restraint in the form of holds, and chemical restraint by sedation. It follows that the more restrictive a regime for a child, taking into account the child's age and circumstances, the more likely it will be that this falls outside the scope of parental responsibility to consent to.

4.69 Within *Re AB (A Child) (Deprivation of Liberty)*, Keehan J considered the issue of parental consent from a different angle.[84] This was, whether or not the circumstances for the child as a whole, and the parents' past exercise of parental responsibility, would render relying on parental consent to a confinement inappropriate. The judge considered two extremes. Firstly, the judge surmised that

---

81 *Re Z (A Child; Deprivation of Liberty: Transition Plan)* [2020] EWHC 3038 (Fam).

82 *Re Z (A Child; Deprivation of Liberty: Transition Plan)* [2020] EWHC 3038 (Fam), paras 39 and 41.

83 *A Metropolitan Borough Council v DB* [1997] 1 FLR 767.

84 *Re AB (A Child) (Deprivation of Liberty)* [2015] EWHC 3125.

there will be cases where a child is accommodated by a local authority with the agreement of his parents to ensure that the child's needs are met, and the parents and local authority are working cooperatively together. In those circumstances, the fact that the child is not residing with their parents does not call into question their ability to appropriately exercise their parental responsibility, and arrangements have been agreed upon as being in the child's welfare interests. It may then be appropriate to rely on parental consent to the confinement of a child. The other extreme will arise when a child is removed from their parents' care by agreement pending the issuing of care proceedings and there are concerns that the child has suffered harm in the care of their parents. In those circumstances, the judge considered it not within the spirit of *Cheshire West* to determine it appropriate to rely upon parental consent because the past behaviour of the parents has not demonstrated that they are exercising their parental responsibility in line with the child's best interests. It is important therefore to consider whether it will be appropriate to seek a parent's consent to their child's confinement in light of the past exercise of parental responsibility, and whether past decisions for the child call into question the parent's ability to make decisions in their child's welfare interests.

4.70 Keehan J's approach feeds into the second element to consider when looking at the appropriate exercise of parental responsibility which is the concept of best interests. A decision being made in a child's best interests is a requirement for it to be an appropriate exercise of parental responsibility in any context. In relation to a child's confinement, it is crucial that the confinement be considered to be in the best interests of the child in order for parental consent to be relied upon. The concept of best interests is one regularly referred to in the Court of Protection when considering decisions for young people and adults. The MCA 2005, s 4 and the Codes of Practice which apply to best interests decision-making in the Court of Protection provide guidance as to what factors should be considered to determine if an act or decision is in a person's best interests, which also applies to a decision to deprive them of their liberty.[85] Best interests decisions should be made not only on the basis of the relevant person's age, appearance or condition. All relevant circumstances must be taken into account when assessing if a decision is in the relevant person's best interests, including that person's wishes, feelings, beliefs and values. Consideration must also be given to what harm the person may suffer if they are not deprived of their liberty, the seriousness of that harm and its likelihood. Thought must also be given to what the alternatives to a deprivation of liberty are and whether or not they could adequately achieve the same aims.

4.71 Within *Lincolnshire County Council v TGA*, Lieven J described the concept of best interests as being 'for the benefit of the child'.[86] All appropriate exercises of parental responsibility must amount to doing what is best for the child to prosper and succeed. As Keehan J alluded to in *Re AB*, for a parent's decision to be considered appropriate and within the scope of their parental responsibility, there should be no

---

85 Deprivation of Liberty Safeguards: Code of Practice to supplement the main Mental Capacity Act 2005 Code of Practice, Ministry of Justice (2008), para 4.61; Mental Capacity Act 2005 Code of Practice, Department for Constitutional Affairs (2007), para 5.13.

86 *Lincolnshire County Council v TGA* [2022] EWHC 2323 (Fam).

question as to whether that parent is exercising their parental responsibility to further their child's best interests.

4.72 The third requirement which has emerged through case law for appropriately relying on a parent's consent to their child's confinement is that the decision to place the child in a regime of confinement must not be disputed. This element is more straightforward. It must be agreed by the people involved in the care, treatment and support of the child that their confinement is the best thing for them. This will include considering both the immediate safety of the child and their development and progress as they grow up. Where there is a dispute in respect of whether or not the proposed confinement is in the child's best interests, or the arrangements which form part of the confinement are not agreed, it is inappropriate to rely upon parental consent to negate a deprivation of the child's liberty.

4.73 The final factor to consider when looking at the appropriateness of relying on parental consent is the child's wishes. Although featured at the end of this section, the wishes of the child are hugely important. They are a fundamental element of decision-making and ascertaining what is in each child's welfare interests. The court has for a long time been concerned with the exercise of parental responsibility against the wishes of the child, particularly when the decisions of a parent intervene in the child's human rights. Lord Denning MR encapsulated this concern in *Hewer v Bryant* when he said:

> '…the legal right of a parent to the custody of a child ends at the 18th birthday: and even up till then, it is a dwindling right which the courts will hesitate to enforce against the wishes of the child, and the more so the older he is. It starts with a right of control and ends with little more than advice.'[87]

4.74 There is, therefore, a recognition within case law that the older a child gets, the more pivotal their wishes will be in determining whether it is appropriate for their parents to make decisions and provide consent to arrangements for them. The ECHR is carefully drafted to require that people, including children, are involved in decisions that are being made about them. The UNCRC which followed also requires 'due weight' to be given to the views of children and young people.[88] There is an implicit expectation within these provisions that the wishes of a child are factored into all decisions being made about them, whether by their parents or by the court. The wishes of the child also feature as a required consideration when determining what is in their best interests. These principles collectively require practitioners to be cautious when seeking to rely on a parent's consent to their child's confinement if that confinement is against the wishes of the child. Parents can, of course, make decisions appropriately which go against their child's wishes. However, caution should be taken when seeking to rely on parental consent to the confinement of a child who is opposed to that confinement, particularly when considering an older child whose parents' rights are more limited in scope.

---

87 *Hewer v Bryant* [1970] 1 QB 357.

88 Article 12 of the Convention on the Rights of the Child, United Nations (November 1989).

4.75 It is an uncomfortable proposition that parental responsibility should extend to a parent consenting to their child's confinement in circumstances where that child is *Gillick* competent, is approaching 16 and is vehemently opposed to the arrangements. Applying the earlier discussion on the scope of parental responsibility, it would appear a contradiction to suggest that a parent's powers extend to making such significant decisions in opposition to their child's views at the time when their parental responsibility is dwindling in scope and the child is assessed as having sufficient understanding and intelligence on the subject matter.[89] At the time of writing, this is not an issue which has been finally determined by the court and there is no clear guidance on what age a child must reach before their competent views in opposition to their confinement would render a reliance upon parental consent inappropriate. However, the overarching principles which guide the court dealing with issues surrounding the deprivation of a child's liberty include that the voice of the child is an important element of any decision being made, and so this must be a relevant factor to take into account when determining if relying upon parental consent to avoid a deprivation of liberty arising is appropriate.

16 and 17-year olds

4.76 When children turn 16 and are considered young people, the law approaches them differently. The muddy waters of the law in relation to parental consent to the confinement of a young person have recently been distilled into a comprehensive judgment provided by the Supreme Court in 2019 within *Re D (A Child)*.[90] The court was tackling the issue of whether parental consent could be obtained to the confinement of a 16 or 17 year old, rendering it not a deprivation of that young person's liberty, if the *Storck* component of 'a lack of consent' was not satisfied. Lady Hale summarised the issue before the court in her opening paragraphs as:

> 'the interplay between the liberty of the subject and the responsibilities of parents, between the rights and values protected by article 5 and the rights and values protected by article 8, and between the relationship of parent and child at common law and the Convention rights. The principle issue can be simply stated: is it within the scope of parental responsibility to consent to living arrangements for a 16 or 17-year-old child which would otherwise amount to a deprivation of liberty within the meaning of article 5?'.[91]

4.77 In its lengthy and detailed judgment, the Supreme Court considered a number of related issues including the importance of a child's capacity, to what extent the principles could or should apply to children under 16, and the interplay with accommodating a child in secure accommodation pursuant to the CA 1989, s 25. The court ultimately declined to determine the applicability of its judgment to children under 16, simply suggesting that it may logically be applicable but it

---

89 *Lincolnshire County Council v TGA* [2022] EWHC 2323 (Fam); *RN (Deprivation of Liberty and Parental Consent)* [2022] EWHC 2576 (Fam); *Lancashire County Council v PX & Ors* [2022] EWHC 2379 (Fam).

90 *Re D (A Child)* [2019] UKSC 42.

91 *Re D (A Child)* [2019] UKSC 42, paras 1 – 4.

was not an issue before the court on this occasion. For the purposes of this section, the focus will be on the court's determination on the use of parental consent to arrangements which may amount to the deprivation of a young person's liberty.

4.78 The Supreme Court was concerned with a child, D, who, at the material times, was 16 and 17 years old (although by the time of the judgment being handed down by the Supreme Court, D was 20 years' old). D was diagnosed with attention deficit hyperactivity disorder, asperger's syndrome, and tourette's syndrome. D also had a mild learning disability. D had presented with challenging behaviour for much of his childhood and had spent periods of time in hospital settings for the purposes of assessment and treatment. D was discharged from hospital following his 16th birthday and placed in accommodation arranged by the local authority, pursuant to consent provided by his parents under the CA 1989, s 20. From this time, D was considered a looked after child for the purposes of the CA 1989. D moved to another placement arranged by the local authority. Within that placement, the doors were locked, the garden was secure, D had to ask for a door to be unlocked to access the garden, D was not allowed to leave the placement save for planned activities and 1:1 support was present during waking hours with staff present constantly at the placement overnight. The parties agreed throughout that the arrangements for D amounted to his confinement and if parental consent could not or would not be provided, D would be deprived of his liberty.

4.79 The appeal before the Supreme Court was lodged by the Official Solicitor, acting on D's behalf. The Official Solicitor argued that no person, parent or otherwise, could consent to arrangements which amount to the deprivation of liberty of a person who has reached the age of 16 and lacks capacity to make that decision themselves. D lacked capacity to consent to the arrangements for his residence and care, and this was not in dispute. As a secondary argument, the Official Solicitor proposed that even if the relevant consent is within the scope of parental responsibility to provide, the parent providing consent should apply the principles of the MCA 2005 in determining whether the arrangements are in the subject child's best interests. The local authority in this case argued that D's parents could provide consent to his confinement because he was not *Gillick* competent to consent himself.

4.80 The court undertook an extensive analysis of the principles arising in relation to the scope of parental responsibility and how the child's level of understanding and intelligence (*Gillick* competence) feeds into the consideration of what is an appropriate exercise of parental responsibility. The court also considered the importance of a child reaching the age of 16 and the extent to which this curtails the appropriate exercise of parental responsibility in line with other common law and statutory principles. Lady Hale then looked to the ECHR and the protection which that affords to everyone against being deprived of their liberty without lawful procedure. This has the effect of preventing a local authority consenting to arrangements which amount to the deprivation of liberty of a child for whom a local authority has parental responsibility. The court was tasked with considering why, in the case of 16 and 17-year olds, that should be any different for parents or those with parental responsibility providing consent.

4.81 The Supreme Court came to the ultimate conclusion that it was not within the scope of D's parents' parental responsibility to consent to a placement which deprived D of his liberty. Parental consent could not be relied upon to the confinement of a 16 or 17-year old to render limb (b) of the *Storck* criteria not met, and the young person would therefore be deprived of their liberty. The court recognised that this was the conclusion notwithstanding that D's placement was in his best interests and his parents had throughout acted with his best interests at the forefront. The judgment focused particularly on the safeguards which are afforded to anyone living in circumstances which amount to their deprivation of liberty by Article 5 of the ECHR. The court emphasised that those safeguards are implemented for good reason and are necessary to ensure that people, including young people, are not arbitrarily or disproportionately deprived of their liberty. To allow parental consent to be used to prevent a deprivation of liberty arising would strip a young person of those safeguards and likely place them in a more vulnerable position.

4.82 The Supreme Court was not tasked with considering the use of parental consent in circumstances where a child under 16 is confined, and therefore no binding judgment in respect of children was provided. However, the court did comment upon the likely applicability of the principles in respect of young people to children under 16. Whilst it was recognised that common law has drawn a distinction between children under 16 and those who have reached the age of 16, the Supreme Court noted a lack of clarity about how this distinction impacts upon the applicability of the principles of the Human Rights Act 1998 which were applied to young people in the judicial analysis and are intended to safeguard them.

4.83 Following this landmark judgment, it has become an established principle that notwithstanding a child's incapacity, or absence of *Gillick* competence, a parent to a child who is 16 or older cannot provide consent to arrangements in place for them which would otherwise amount to their deprivation of liberty. Where limbs (a) and (c) of the *Storck* criteria are satisfied, limb (b) will be satisfied if the young person does not or cannot provide valid consent, irrespective of their parents' views, and a deprivation of liberty will be present which requires authorisation by the court.

CONCLUSION

4.84 This chapter has explored the second limb of the *Storck* criteria which must be satisfied to establish a deprivation of liberty: an absence of valid consent. It has considered consent which may be provided by children and young people, and consent that may be given by parents acting within the scope of their parental responsibility. Valid consent as it relates to the deprivation of liberty of children and young people is complex and requires careful consideration. Relying on consent, either provided by the child or young person or by their parent, prevents a deprivation of liberty arising. When valid consent is present, the regime of confinement for the child or young person is not subject to the stringent safeguards and oversight which comes with court proceedings. For this reason, care must be taken when seeking to rely on valid consent to a regime of confinement, and thought must always be given to which route best meets the child or young person's welfare needs.

Chapter 5

AUTHORISATION OF THE COURT

INTRODUCTION

5.01 Once a deprivation of liberty is established, it may only be lawful if it fits within one of the criteria contained within Article 5 of the European Convention on Human Rights (ECHR) and is 'in accordance with a procedure prescribed by law'.[1] The guidance accompanying the article explains the rationale behind these requirements. The primary purpose which underpins Article 5 in its entirety is to 'prevent arbitrary or unjustified deprivations of liberty'.[2] Such deprivations must be prevented in order to secure the right to liberty and security of all citizens of the member states. Any deprivation of liberty which occurs and is not lawful is described as being a 'complete negation of the fundamentally important guarantees contained in Article 5... and discloses a most grave violation of that provision'.[3] The guidance goes on to set out three 'strands of reasoning' which appear as themes throughout the case law relating to Article 5 and its purpose. They are:

(a) The exhaustive nature of the exceptions and their strict interpretation which contrast with the broad range of justifications provided for under other sections of the ECHR;

(b) The repeated emphasis on the lawfulness of the detention, both procedurally and substantively, requiring adherence to the rule of law; and,

(c) The importance of the promptness of the requisite judicial controls as contained within Article 5(3) and (4).[4]

5.02 The specified circumstances within Article 5(1) are one element of the two-strand criteria for a deprivation of liberty to be lawful, and they are explored within chapter 3. The other element is for any deprivation to be in accordance with a procedure prescribed by law. Together, these elements create the requirement of lawfulness. In order to meet the second element, being in accordance with a procedure prescribed by law, any deprivation of liberty must be governed by a procedure set down within domestic law. This requires member states to pass laws which govern a

---

1 Article 5 of the Convention for the Protection of Human Rights and Fundamental Freedoms (Rome, 4 November 1950).

2 Guidance on Article 5 of the European Convention on Human Rights: Right to liberty and security, Council of Europe (August 2022), para 23.

3 Guidance on Article 5 of the European Convention on Human Rights: Right to liberty and security, Council of Europe (August 2022), para 24.

4 Guidance on Article 5 of the European Convention on Human Rights: Right to liberty and security, Council of Europe (August 2022), para 26.

person's deprivation of liberty and set out the circumstances in which a deprivation of liberty may be lawfully implemented. However, because deprivations of liberty engage such a fundamental and significant human right, that domestic law itself must conform with the principles of the ECHR too. The general principles of the ECHR can be summarised as: the principle of the rule of law and legal certainty; the principle of proportionality; and the principle of protection against arbitrariness.[5]

5.03 European jurisprudence has fleshed out these general principles to assist member states to enact compliant domestic laws. Domestic laws must clearly define the conditions required to be met when a deprivation of liberty arises or is foreseen, and the consequences of any deprivation of liberty so far as is reasonable to foresee.[6] Domestic law must be sufficiently accessible, precise and foreseeable in its application. This includes clear provisions for a permissible deprivation of liberty, for extending that deprivation of liberty and for setting time-limits on it. It also includes bringing into existence an effective remedy by which a person may contest the lawfulness or duration of their deprivation of liberty.[7]

5.04 The domestic statutes in England and Wales which govern the deprivation of liberty of children and young people include: the Children Act 1989 (CA 1989), s 25; the Social Services and Well-being (Wales) Act 2014 (SSWWA 2014), s 119; the Mental Health Act 1983 (MHA 1983), ss 2 and 3; and the Mental Capacity Act 2005 (MCA 2005), ss 4 and 16. There are other provisions within the MHA 1983 which may also allow for a deprivation of liberty to be lawful, and the police may also detain children and young people using their powers of protection and to secure necessary investigations. The inherent jurisdiction of the High Court is also a procedure prescribed by law, although not set down in statute, which may be used to bring about a lawful deprivation of liberty. This chapter will not explore all of the procedures as prescribed by law in England and Wales governing the deprivation of liberty of children and young people, but those which are most frequently used for the children and young people with whom this book is concerned. References in this chapter to a child include young people unless specified.

WHEN TO SEEK AUTHORISATION

5.05 Before delving into the methods of authorisation, it is important to first be clear about the point at which it becomes necessary to seek authorisation of the arrangements for a child. Authorisation, if granted, prevents a child being unlawfully deprived of their liberty and their Article 5 rights being infringed. Once the arrangements in place satisfy all three limbs of the *Storck* criteria, they amount to a deprivation of liberty and therefore must be authorised in some way in order to comply with Article 5 of the ECHR. Authorisation may be sought under statutory

---

5 Guidance on Article 5 of the European Convention on Human Rights: Right to liberty and security, Council of Europe (August 2022) para 32.

6 *Khlaifia and Others v Italy* 16483/12 [2016] ECHR ; *Del Río Prada v Spain* 42750/09 [2013] ECHR; *Creangă v Romania* 29226/03 [2012]; *Medvedyev and Others v France* 3394/03 [2010].

7 *JN v United Kingdom* 37289/12 [2016] ECHR.

provisions or by the use of the High Court's inherent jurisdiction, all of which will be considered in detail in this chapter.

5.06 In order to identify the point at which a deprivation of liberty will arise, all those involved in the care and support of a child must be careful to consider in detail the *Storck* limbs and continuously assess whether they are satisfied. This should focus on evaluating whether the child is or will be objectively confined (explained in chapter 3) or whether valid consent to the arrangements is or will be absent (explained in chapter 4). It is only once all three limbs are satisfied that a deprivation of liberty arises and authorisation is required. However, the framework of the court process allows for applications to be made for orders authorising deprivations of liberty before they arise, such that there is no gap between the deprivation of liberty coming about and its authorisation. This prevents a child being unlawfully deprived of their liberty, pending an application being processed to bring about that authorisatoin.

5.07 Theis J highlighted the importance of seeking timely authorisation of the deprivation of a child's liberty within *Trafford Borough Council v B, C, Manchester University NHS Foundation Trust, X*.[8] The court stated:

> '53. As outlined above, the purpose of this judgment is to emphasise the critical importance, in situations like this, where no party has sought to suggest X's situation did not amount to a deprivation of liberty, for the application under the inherent jurisdiction for declarations authorising the deprivation of liberty of children and young people to be issued without delay.
>
> 54. Where the child or young person is placed in a hospital in circumstances such as in this case there should be effective and robust procedures in place between the Trust and the local authority agreed in advance for situations such as that X was in as to who should be taking primary responsibility for issuing the application to this court. Once the application is issued the court should be requested by the applicant to join the child as a party, without delay, and setting out, with brief reasons in support, how urgently the application needs to be considered by the court.
>
> 55. Any delay in making the application is detrimental to the welfare of the child or young person, as there may be a lack of clarity about the legal structure under which they are being deprived of their liberty. Also, they do not have the safeguard of an effective voice in the process, as they do within proceedings if they are joined as a party and separately represented through a Children's Guardian within the proceedings under the inherent jurisdiction.'

5.08 When a child or young person is deprived of their liberty and this is not authorised in accordance with a procedure prescribed by law, this may give rise to a claim against the relevant state body for a breach of the child's human rights under the Human Rights Act 1998. The process of making an application for a breach of a child's human rights is not explored within this book. However, when any such application is made and is successful, the court may make a declaration that the child's Article 5 right has been breached and it may make an award of damages.

---

8 *Trafford Borough Council v B, C, Manchester University NHS Foundation Trust, X* [2022] EWHC 1406 (Fam), paras 53-55.

AUTHORISATION UNDER STATUTE

5.09 As required by Article 5 of the ECHR, England and Wales have implemented various statutory schemes which may be used in different situations to lawfully authorise a deprivation of liberty, setting up the requisite 'procedures prescribed by law'. This section will consider these statutory schemes, when they apply and what they entail. When these statutory schemes are not available, or the criteria is not met, practitioners may turn to the High Court's inherent jurisdiction for authorisation as a last resort. The use of the inherent jurisdiction will be considered in the next section of this chapter.

Children Act 1989 and Social Services and Well-being (Wales) Act 2014

5.10 The CA 1989, s 25 and the SSWWA 2014, s 119 permit the deprivation of liberty of children and young people in secure accommodation, subject to the criteria within the statute and applicable guidance. Secure accommodation is described as accommodation provided for the purpose of restricting liberty.[9] It is permissible as a form of accommodation for children when it appears that:

(a) The child has a history of absconding from any other description of accommodation and if they abscond, they are likely to suffer significant harm; or

(b) The child if kept in any other description of accommodation is likely to injure themselves or another person.

5.11 What constitutes secure accommodation has been the subject of discussion within case law. Within *Re B (Secure Accommodation Order)*, the Court of Appeal clarified that secure accommodation can be identified as accommodation which is 'designed for the restriction of liberty, or the primary purpose of the placement is to restrict liberty.'[10] This will not encompass accommodation which may impose a degree of restriction but which is designed for another primary purpose, for example, treatment. Lady Black shone further light on this issue in her observations made within the judgment in *Re D (A Child)*:

> '113. The exercise in which we have engaged has, however, been sufficient to persuade us that section 25 is not intended to be widely interpreted, so as to catch all children whose care needs are being met in accommodation where there is a degree of restriction on their liberty, even amounting to a deprivation of liberty. There is much force in the argument that it is upon the accommodation itself that the spotlight should be turned, when determining whether particular accommodation is secure accommodation, rather than upon the attributes of the care of the child in question. This fits with the language used in section 25(1), when read as a whole. It is also consistent with the objective of ensuring that the section is not so widely drawn as to prejudice the local authority's ability to offer children the care that

9 CA 1989, s 25; SSWWA 2014, s 119.

10 *Re B (Secure Accommodation Order)* [2019] EWCA Civ 2025.

they need, and it ought to make it more straightforward to apply than would be the case if the issue were dependent upon the features of a child's individual care regime, so that the child might be found to be in secure accommodation in all manner of settings.

114. A restrained construction of the section is also justified by the fact that, far from being concerned with the routine sort of problems that might require a child's freedom to be curtailed, the section has a "last resort" quality about it. It is concerned with accommodation which has the features necessary to safeguard a child with a history of absconding who is likely to abscond from any other description of accommodation or to prevent injury where the child in question would be likely to injure himself or others if kept in any other description of accommodation.

115. Of course, training the spotlight on the accommodation itself does not provide a complete answer to the question as to what falls within the definition of secure accommodation. Some secure accommodation will be readily recognisable from the fact that it is approved as such by the Secretary of State, but that is by no means a universal hallmark, as that approval is not needed for all types of secure accommodation. Moreover, given that it is contemplated that secure accommodation might be provided in places such as hospitals, it seems likely that there will not infrequently be more than one purpose of the child being in the accommodation, and there is much to commend Wall J's approach to such a situation, that is to count within the definition of secure accommodation "designed for or having as its primary purpose" the restriction of liberty. Equally, the section will have to be interpreted in such a way as to allow for situations where only a part of the premises is made over to restricting liberty.'[11]

5.12 It follows from the regulatory provisions and case law that to identify secure accommodation, the focus must be on the placement itself rather than on the care plan in place for the child. The provisions permitting secure accommodation to be used are limited to only certain children and young people. The CA 1989, s 25 and the SSWWA 2014, s 119 provide that the use of secure accommodation is limited to children who are looked after by a local authority. This may be by way of a care order or under the provisions of the CA 1989, s 20(1), (3) (which govern the provision of accommodation by a local authority to children in need). This is extended somewhat by the provisions of the applicable regulations which add in children who are accommodated by health authorities, NHS trusts, education authorities or children who live in residential care homes, nursing homes or mental nursing homes.[12] For children who are subject to a care order, it is not a prerequisite of making a secure accommodation order that the child must consent to being accommodated by the local authority.[13]

5.13 Children cannot be placed in secure accommodation if they are under 13 years of age without the prior approval of the Secretary of State or Welsh Ministers.[14]

---

11 *Re D (A Child)* [2019] UKSC 42.

12 Children (Secure Accommodation) Regulations 1991, reg 7; Children (Secure Accommodation) (Wales) Regulations 2015, reg 16; *Re D (A Child)* [2019] UKSC 42, para 94.

13 *Re W* [2016] EWCA Civ 804.

14 Children (Secure Accommodation) Regulations 1991, reg 4; Children (Secure Accommodation) (Wales) Regulations 2015, reg 13.

Secure accommodation cannot be used for children and young people who are detained under the MHA 1983 or who are subject to an order under the Children and Young Persons Act 1933, s 53 having committed serious criminal offences.[15]

5.14 An application must be made to the court to approve the use of secure accommodation for a child, save for when the accommodation is used for an aggregate 72-hour period or less within any 28-day period.[16] When an order is made authorising the use of secure accommodation, it must specify the maximum period in which the child can be kept there.[17] The maximum initial period a court can authorise secure accommodation can be no longer than three months.[18] This may then be extended by six months at any one time.[19]

5.15 When an application is before the court for a secure accommodation order, the court must be satisfied that the criteria within the CA 1989, s 25(1) and the SSWWA 2014, s 119(1) are made out, and determine the appropriate duration of any order. In coming to a conclusion on these two issues, the court must ask itself the following, as set out in *Re B*:

(a) Is the child being looked after by the local authority or falls within one of the other categories specified in regulation 7?

(b) Is the accommodation where the local authority proposes to place the child 'secure accommodation' designed for or having as its primary purpose the restriction of liberty?

(c) Is the court satisfied that the test as set down in the CA 1989, s 25(1) and the SSWWA 2014, s 119(1) is met?

(d) If the local authority is proposing to place the child in a secure children's home in England, has the accommodation been approved by the Secretary of State for use as secure accommodation?

(e) Does the proposed order safeguard and promote the child's welfare?

(f) Is the order proportionate? Do the benefits of the proposed placement outweigh the infringement of rights?[20]

5.16 When this criteria is met, the court is required by the CA 1989, s 25(4) to make an order authorising the use of secure accommodation and specifying the maximum period for which it may be used.[21] In making such an order, the court must consider the principle that secure accommodation should always be a last

---

15 Children (Secure Accommodation) Regulations 1991, reg 5.

16 Children (Secure Accommodation) Regulations 1991, reg 10; Children (Secure Accommodation) (Wales) Regulations 2015, reg 2.

17 CA 1989, s 25(4); SSWWA 2014, s 119(4).

18 Children (Secure Accommodation) Regulations 1991, reg 11; Children (Secure Accommodation) (Wales) Regulations 2015, reg 6.

19 Children (Secure Accommodation) Regulations 1991, reg 12; Children (Secure Accommodation) (Wales) Regulations 2015, reg 6.

20 *Re B (Secure Accommodation Order)* [2019] EWCA Civ 2025, para 98.

21 *Re B (Secure Accommodation Order)* [2019] EWCA Civ 2025, para 99.

resort and that alternative arrangements should be evaluated before determining that secure accommodation is necessary. Although the wording of the CA 1989, s 25(4) mandates that an order permitting secure accommodation shall be made if the criteria within the CA 1989 is satisfied, the court must also be satisfied that the order is necessary and proportionate as it engages the child's Article 5 ECHR rights.[22]

5.17 Prior to placing a child in secure accommodation, the local authority has a duty to consult the child's parents, if possible, and devise a placement plan.[23] This plan should set out the purpose of the placement, its expected duration and the procedure for bringing an end to the placement.[24] Once a child is placed in secure accommodation, the applicable regulations impose a duty on local authorities to ensure that the suitability of the placement remains under review. Reviews must be conducted for placements in England within one month of the placement beginning and then at least every three months whilst the child remains in secure accommodation.[25] In Wales, this differs slightly in that the initial review must take place within 15 working days of the placement commencing.[26]

5.18 A child should not be kept in secure accommodation for longer than is both necessary and proportionate. The requirements contained within the regulations for regular review of these placements highlight the need to continuously consider whether any less restrictive form of accommodation could meet the child's needs and secure their welfare or well-being. Regular reviews will also ensure that the limited placements in secure accommodation are not occupied by children who do not require that type of placement, creating spaces for children who do need to be placed in secure accommodation. The statistics published by the government for 31 March 2023 confirm that in England and Wales, at that time, there were only 230 approved places in secure children's homes.[27] The largest proportion of children living in secure accommodation were children aged between 15 and 16, and the most common period of time spent in secure accommodation was between one and three months. Recent published judgments from the High Court have made clear that there are still not enough placements available for children who require secure accommodation across the country. This has necessitated alternatives being created for children who meet the criteria to be placed in secure accommodation but for whom there are no vacancies.

5.19 For any accommodation which appears to meet the definition explained by Lady Black in *Re D (A Child)* but, as she recognises in the quote above, which

---

22 *Re W* [2016] EWCA Civ 804.

23 Children (Secure Accommodation) Regulations 1991, reg 14; Children (Secure Accommodation) (Wales) Regulations 2015, reg 5; Care Planning, Placement and Care Review (England) Regulations 2010, reg 9; Care Planning, Placement and Case Review (Wales) Regulations 2015, reg 10.

24 Children's Homes (England) Regulations 2015; Care Planning, Placement and Case Review (England) Regulations 2010.

25 Children (Secure Accommodation) Regulations 1991, reg 15.

26 Children (Secure Accommodation) (Wales) Regulations 2015, reg 10.

27 Children accommodated in secure children's homes, HM Government (18 May 2023) (https://explore-education-statistics.service.gov.uk/find-statistics/children-accommodated-in-secure-childrens-homes/2023).

is not approved as required by the Secretary of State, these statutory provisions of the CA 1989 are not available and this may be an occasion where the High Court's inherent jurisdiction is turned to for authorisation of the arrangements.

Mental Health Act 1983

5.20 The MHA 1983 provides another route by which a child or young person may be lawfully deprived of their liberty. Authorisation of a deprivation of liberty under the MHA 1983 is commonly referred to as 'being sectioned'. It is permissible under a number of sections of the MHA 1983, however, the most common provisions used for children are the MHA 1983, ss 2 and 3. The MHA 1983 is a piece of legislation designed to govern the assessment and treatment of people with a mental disorder. There is no lower age limit for the application of the MHA 1983 and its provisions therefore apply to children and young people in the same way as they do to adults. The MHA 1983, ss 2 and 3 permit the detention of people, including children, in hospital if they fall within the criteria set out in the Act. Whether or not the relevant child falls within the criteria to be 'sectioned' is determined by an assessment undertaken by a team of health professionals, who then provide a recommendation on whether or not to detain the child in hospital. If the assessment concludes that a child requires detention in hospital, an application will be made for that to be authorised by the Approved Mental Health Professional (AMHP). It is important to note that the process of authorising a person to be deprived of their liberty under the MHA 1983, ss 2 and 3, does not involve the court and is undertaken by health professionals.

5.21 The MHA 1983, s 2 governs short-term detentions in hospital for the purposes of assessment of the person concerned. The MHA 1983 provides that a patient (an adult or a child) may be admitted to hospital and detained there for no more than 28 days for the purposes of assessing them.[28] In order for a child or young person to be detained under this provision, they must be:

(a) Suffering from a mental disorder of a nature or degree which warrants the detention of the patient in a hospital for assessment (or for assessment followed by medical treatment) for at least a limited period; and

(b) The child or young person ought to be so detained in the interests of their own health or safety or with a view to the protection of other persons.

5.22 The MHA 1983, s 3 permits longer periods of detention for the purposes of providing treatment. For detention under this section, the child or young person must be:

(a) Suffering from a mental disorder of a nature or degree which makes it appropriate for them to receive medical treatment in a hospital; and

---

28 MHA 1983, s 2.

(b) It is necessary for the health or safety of the patient or for the protection of other persons that they should receive such treatment and it cannot be provided unless they are detained under this section; and

(c) Appropriate medical treatment is available for them.

5.23 The first criteria which must therefore be satisfied in order to be detained under the MHA 1983 is that the child or young person must be suffering from a mental disorder. The MHA 1983, s 1 sheds some light on what falls within the definition of a mental disorder. It is defined at s 1(2) to mean any disorder or disability of the mind. The section goes on to confirm that a person with a learning disability will not be considered, by reason of that disability, to be suffering a mental disorder unless that disability is associated with abnormally aggressive or seriously irresponsible conduct on their part, for the purposes of detention under s 3.[29] This qualification does not apply to detentions under s 2 for which a learning disability alone may be a sufficient mental disorder. It also confirms that dependence on alcohol or drugs is not considered to be a disorder or disability of the mind.[30] However, a dependence on alcohol or drugs may accompany a mental disorder and the presence of that dependence does not prevent a person being considered to have a mental disorder. The Code of Practice issued for the MHA 1983 specifically refers to organic mental disorders associated with prolonged abuse of drugs or alcohol, acute intoxication or withdrawal state with delirium as potential mental disorders for the purposes of the MHA 1983.[31]

5.24 The Code of Practice discusses the definition of a mental disorder at chapter 2.[32] It provides a non-exhaustive list of clinically recognised conditions which may fall within the definition of a mental disorder for the purposes of the MHA 1983. These include: bipolar disorder; schizophrenia; anxiety; obsessive compulsive disorders; post-traumatic stress disorder; dementia; personality and behavioural changes caused by brain injury or damage; personality disorders; mental and behavioural disorders caused by psychoactive substance use; eating disorders; non-organic sexual disorders; autism spectrum disorders; and behavioural and emotional disorders of children and young people. When assessing whether a child is suffering a mental disorder, it is important that assessors factor in that the child will still be in the process of developing physically, emotionally and cognitively as they approach adulthood and this may too affect their presentation.[33]

5.25 The second element to consider as part of the criteria for detention under the MHA 1983 is the nature and degree of the mental disorder. This forms part of the criteria for both ss 2 and 3 detentions. The degree of the mental disorder refers to the severity of the condition at the time the person is assessed for detention. The nature of the mental disorder requires a longer-term view of the condition including

---

29 MHA 1983, s 1(2A).

30 MHA 1983, s 1(3).

31 Code of Practice: Mental Health Act 1983, Department of Health and Social Care (2015), paras 2.9 – 2.12.

32 Code of Practice: Mental Health Act 1983, Department of Health and Social Care (2015), chapter 2.

33 Code of Practice: Mental Health Act 1983, Department of Health and Social Care (2015), para 19.5.

considering the likelihood of relapse. The Code of Practice has distilled case law guidance on the interpretation of the two terms into the following summary:

> 'The criteria require consideration of both the nature and degree of a patient's mental disorder. Nature refers to the particular mental disorder from which the patient is suffering, its chronicity, its prognosis, and the patient's previous response to receiving treatment for the disorder. Degree refers to the current manifestation of the patient's disorder.'[34]

5.26 Thirdly, the MHA 1983 dictates that the mental disorder must warrant detention of the patient in a hospital (under s 2) or that the mental disorder is of a nature or degree which makes treatment in hospital appropriate (under s 3). This element of the criteria necessitates an evaluation of the options available for the child to determine whether admission to hospital is required. Practitioners should consider if there are other effective forms of care or treatment which do not require detention in hospital, and if there are, the least restrictive alternative must be selected. The Code of Practice requires that, as part of this evaluation, consideration should be given to the patient's wishes and view of their own needs; the patient's age and physical health; any past wishes or feelings expressed by the patient and the patient's cultural background. Social and family circumstances should also be weighed into the evaluation alongside the impact that any future deterioration or lack of improvement in the patient's condition would have on their children, other relatives or carers.[35]

5.27 Both the MHA 1983, ss 2 and 3 go on to require an assessment of the necessity of the detention for the health or safety of the patient or for the protection of others. The criteria at s 2 asks for consideration of whether the person 'ought to be so detained in the interests of his own health or safety or with a view to the protection of other persons' and s 3 requires that it is concluded as 'necessary for the health or safety of the patient or for the protection of other persons that he should receive such treatment and it cannot be provided unless he is detained under this section'.

5.28 When assessing necessity in relation to the patient's own health or safety, the Code of Practice requires consideration of:

(a) Evidence suggesting patients are at risk of suicide, self-harm, self-neglect, jeopardising their own health or safety accidentally, or that their mental disorder is putting their health or safety at risk;

(b) Evidence suggesting the patient's mental health will deteriorate if they do not receive treatment, including the views of the patient or carers and relatives about the likely course of the disorder;

(c) The patient's own ability to manage their condition;

(d) The patient's capacity to consent to or refuse admission to hospital and treatment, and whether the patient does object to treatment or is likely to;

34 Code of Practice: Mental Health Act 1983, Department of Health and Social Care (2015), para 14.6.

35 Code of Practice: Mental Health Act 1983, Department of Health and Social Care (2015), para 14.8.

(e) The reliability of the evidence including the history of the patient's mental disorder and the possibility of their condition improving;

(f) The potential benefits of treatment weighed against any adverse effects that being detained may have on the patient's wellbeing; and

(g) Whether any other methods of managing risk are available.[36]

5.29 The criteria for detention under both sections also requires consideration of whether the detention is necessary to protect others. This part of the assessment focuses on the nature of the risks to others which arise from the patient's mental disorder, the likelihood of harm to others and the severity of the potential harm. Harm in this instance includes psychological and physical harm.[37] These factors must be weighed up to determine if they present a risk to others sufficient to deem detention in hospital a necessary and proportionate step. The Code of Practice requires assessors to consider the ability of those living with or caring for the patient to manage the presenting risks, other available methods of managing risk aside from detention in hospital, and the patient's history of behaviours including any criminal behaviour.[38]

5.30 Finally, detention under the MHA 1983, ss 2 or 3 must be for the specified purpose. For s 2, the detention must facilitate an assessment of the person detained. The assessment can be of the person's mental disorder, its type, severity and presentation, or an assessment relating to the future treatment of the patient. Section 3 requires that appropriate medical treatment must be available. Medical treatment is defined later in the MHA 1983 as including 'nursing, psychological intervention and specialist mental health habilitation, rehabilitation and care.'[39] It goes on to confirm at s 145(4) that '[a]ny reference in this Act to medical treatment, in relation to mental disorder, shall be construed as a reference to medical treatment the purpose of which is to alleviate, or prevent a worsening of, the disorder or one or more of its symptoms or manifestations.'

5.31 The court has summarised what may fall within this definition of medical treatment for the purposes of detention in hospital. Charles J provided an outline of the principles arising from the case law in the judgment of *GJ v The Foundation Trust & Anor*.[40] The key principles underpinning the consideration of medical treatment were set down as follows:

> '(a) the core, or the primary purpose, of the medical treatment referred to in s.3(2) (and s.2(2)) MHA 1983 is for the mental disorder referred to in s.3(2)(a) (and s.2(2)(a)), namely in s.3 to mental disorder of a nature or degree that makes it appropriate for the person to receive medical treatment in a hospital, and
>
> (b) under s.3 it has to be considered whether it is necessary for the health and safety of the patient that he should receive that treatment and whether it can only be

[36] Code of Practice: Mental Health Act 1983, Department of Health and Social Care (2015), para 14.9.
[37] Code of Practice: Mental Health Act 1983, Department of Health and Social Care (2015), para 14.10.
[38] Code of Practice: Mental Health Act 1983, Department of Health and Social Care (2015), para 14.10.
[39] MHA 1983, s 145(1).
[40] *GJ v The Foundation Trust & Anor* [2009] EWHC 2972 (Fam).

provided if he is detained in hospital (there are differences in the wording of the equivalent test in s.2).'

5.32 Charles J goes on to distil the guidance from the relevant case law put before the court as follows:

'(a) A range of acts ancillary to the core treatment of the mental disorder may be considered to fall within the s.145 definition of medical treatment for mental disorder…

(b) Treatment for mental disorder may include treatment for the symptoms of a mental disorder…

(c) Treatment for mental disorder may also include treatment for the physical consequences of a mental disorder…

(d) If there is no proposed treatment for the core mental disorder it will not be lawful to detain a patient to treat the physical consequences of his disorder…

(e) Treatment for a physical disorder will not be treatment for mental disorder where the physical disorder is unconnected with the mental disorder…

(f) If the physical disorder is unconnected with the mental disorder then treatment of the physical disorder can only be considered 'treatment for mental disorder' if such treatment is likely to directly affect the mental disorder.'[41]

5.33 The Code of Practice to the MHA 1983 provides a number of important provisions to be considered when the Act is being applied to children. One overarching principle is that the best interests of the child must always be a significant consideration when decisions are being made, including deciding whether or not to detain the person.[42] The child's views, wishes and feelings should always be sought and should be taken seriously by the professionals working with the child.[43] All those working with children have a responsibility for keeping them safe and taking prompt action if welfare needs or safeguarding concerns are identified. What action is to be taken will depend on the circumstances of the child, their presentation, and their needs. If any intervention, including detention, is deemed necessary for a child, the least restrictive option should be taken. Any intervention should be the option least likely to expose the child to the risk of stigmatisation, so far as is consistent with effective care and treatment, and resulting in the least possible separations from family, carers, friends and community or interruption in their education.[44]

5.34 If, following assessment, the detention of a child in hospital is deemed necessary, it should be within a hospital or facility as close as possible to their home.[45] The child should still receive the same access to education as their peers and their right to dignity and privacy should be respected in the same way as it would be for an adult.

---

41 *GJ v The Foundation Trust & Anor* [2009] EWHC 2972 (Fam), para 52.

42 Code of Practice: Mental Health Act 1983, Department of Health and Social Care (2015), para 19.5.

43 Code of Practice: Mental Health Act 1983, Department of Health and Social Care (2015), para 19.5.

44 Code of Practice: Mental Health Act 1983, Department of Health and Social Care (2015), para 19.5.

45 Code of Practice: Mental Health Act 1983, Department of Health and Social Care (2015), para 19.5.

5.35 There may be cases in which consideration is given to detaining a child in hospital under the MHA 1983 but that course of action is deemed inappropriate or not the least restrictive alternative available for achieving the desired outcome. Usually, this will occur when assessment or treatment in the community is appropriate, and the MHA 1983 does not extend to permit a deprivation of liberty in the community. When those circumstances arise, the MHA 1983 Code of Practice reminds practitioners that it may be necessary for a referral to be made to the relevant local authority's children's services who can support efforts to safeguard and promote the welfare of the child.[46] This will then require consideration of authorising any deprivation of liberty in the community under alternative statutory provisions or using the inherent jurisdiction of the High Court.

5.36 The Code of Practice gives further guidance on what factors to consider when making a decision about which statutory scheme to use, when alternatives to detention in hospital under the MHA 1983 may be available. The guiding principles can be summarised as follows:

(a) The choice of statutory regime should never be based on a general preference for one or the other, or because of familiarity with one regime;

(b) Practitioners should not proceed on the basis that one regime is generally seen to be less restrictive than the other. Both regimes should be adopted in the least restrictive way;

(c) The two regimes provide different safeguards which must be considered in respect of the young person to determine which safeguards are likely to best protect the interests of the young person;

(d) Each decision about which statutory regime to use should be made based upon the individual circumstances at play.[47]

5.37 His Honour Judge Burrows grappled succinctly with the interplay between the MHA 1983 and the MCA 2005 for young people within *Manchester University Hospitals NHS Foundation Trust v JS & Anor*.[48] In this case, the court was tasked with analysing in detail the ineligibility provisions of the MCA 2005 to determine under which statute the young person, JS, may be lawfully deprived of her liberty in hospital. The ineligibility provisions remove the availability of the MCA 2005 to authorise a deprivation of liberty for certain people in circumstances specified within the MCA 2005, Sch 1A, para 2. The court determined on the facts of that case that JS was ineligible to be deprived of her liberty under the MCA 2005 as she fell within 'Case E' of the table at the MCA 2005, Sch 1A.[49] Falling within 'Case E' consisted of three factors. Firstly, JS was a mental health patient and fell within the scope of the MHA 1983. She was provided with a care plan akin to the care plan in place

---

46 Code of Practice: Mental Health Act 1983, Department of Health and Social Care (2015), paras 19.17-19.18.

47 Code of Practice: Mental Health Act 1983, Department of Health and Social Care, 2015, paras 13.57-13.61.

48 *Manchester University Hospitals NHS Foundation Trust v JS & Anor* [2023] EWCOP 12.

49 MCA 2005, Sch 1A, Pt 1, para 2.

when detained under the MHA 1983, s 2 with the focus being JS's mental health.[50] Secondly, JS was deemed detainable under the MHA 1983. Thirdly, JS satisfied the criteria of 'Case E' because she objected to her medical treatment.[51] In determining whether or not JS objected to being a mental health patient or being given some or all of the mental health treatment, the court had to consider her behaviour; her wishes and feelings; and her views, beliefs and values.[52] Having concluded that JS was detainable under the MHA 1983 and that she objected to the medical treatment, the court found that the MCA 2005 could not be used in these circumstances to authorise a deprivation of her liberty and the only available statutory route to detain JS in hospital was under the MHA 1983.

5.38 That judgment was the subject of an appeal before Theis J within which the court distilled the factors of Case E very neatly into three questions:

(a) Is P a mental health patient?'

(b) Is P an objecting mental health patient?;

(c) Could P be detained under the MHA 1983, s 3.[53]

5.39 Whilst the court dismissed the appeal and upheld the decision of His Honour Judge Burrows, Theis J went on to provide comment on the wider issues that had arisen in the case.[54] The court recognised that the statutory provisions, and the ability for a patient to be deemed ineligible for the provisions of the MCA 2005, could create a stalemate between statutory bodies when determining the appropriate regime to govern a person's deprivation of liberty. The court suggested as follows:

> '(1) In any application seeking authorisation to deprive the liberty of a 16 or 17 year old, the applicant should carefully consider whether the application should be made in the Court of Protection and, if not, why not.
>
> (2) If a Schedule 1A Case E issue is likely to arise any evidence filed in support of an application should address that issue, so the relevant evidence is available for the court, thereby reducing any delay.
>
> (3) In the event that the Court of Protection determines that P is ineligible the professionals should urgently liaise in the way outlined above' [at paragraph 118 of the judgment].[55]

5.40 The judgments relating to JS provides helpful insight into how the two statutory provisions interact. They also serve to emphasise that the purpose of both statutory schemes is to ensure proper safeguards are in place so that the young

---

50 *Manchester University Hospitals NHS Foundation Trust v JS & Anor* [2023] EWCOP 12, para 22.

51 MCA 2005, Sch 1A, Pt 1, para 5.

52 *Manchester University Hospitals NHS Foundation Trust v JS & Anor* [2023] EWCOP 12, para 72.

53 *Manchester University Hospitals NHS Foundation Trust v JS & Anor (Schedule 1A Mental Capacity Act 2005)* [2023] EWCOP 33, para 48.

54 *Manchester University Hospitals NHS Foundation Trust v JS & Anor (Schedule 1A Mental Capacity Act 2005)* [2023] EWCOP 33, paras 114 – 124.

55 *Manchester University Hospitals NHS Foundation Trust v JS & Anor (Schedule 1A Mental Capacity Act 2005)* [2023] EWCOP 33, para 123.

person concerned is not arbitrarily deprived of their liberty and has proper recourse to challenge any such deprivation.

Mental Capacity Act 2005

5.41 The MCA 2005 provides the third and final statutory framework considered in this chapter under which young people may be lawfully deprived of their liberty. The MCA 2005 applies to everyone aged 16 and older and its provisions may be used to make decisions in the best interests of young people and to authorise measures which amount to their deprivation of liberty. Before turning to the criteria required by the MCA 2005 to bring about a lawful deprivation of liberty, it is helpful to start by looking into the arena in which it operates: the Court of Protection.

5.42 The Court of Protection was established in 2007 when the MCA 2005 came into force. It is governed by the Court of Protection Rules 2017.[56] Within the Court of Protection, the person at the centre of the case is often referred to as 'P'. The court is governed by an overriding objective which requires all cases to be dealt with justly and proportionately, ensuring that P's interests and position are properly considered, and ensuring that the parties to proceedings are on an equal footing.[57] The rules place an emphasis on involving P within the proceedings.[58] The court must consider if P should be joined as a party to proceedings and whether P should have the opportunity to address the judge, either directly or indirectly.[59] The Court of Protection Rules 2017 are supplemented by practice directions which also govern how the Court of Protection operates. Practice Direction 1A focuses on ensuring P's participation within proceedings when that is required.

5.43 Practice Direction 11A relates to applications that are made to the court to authorise a person's deprivation of liberty. It is the second half of that practice direction which is relevant to young people. The first covers applications under the MCA 2005, s 21A which relate to urgent and standard authorisations. These are authorisations granted by a supervisory body (usually a local authority) permitting the deprivation of an adult's liberty in a care home or hospital. Those provisions cannot be implemented for a young person and so are not relevant here. However, the second half of the practice direction deals with deprivation of liberty applications that may be made to authorise the deprivation of liberty of a young person. These are applications made under the MCA 2005, s 16(2)(a) to authorise a deprivation of liberty pursuant to the MCA 2005, s 4A(3), (4). It is these types of applications which may constitute a lawful procedure by which to deprive a 16 or 17 year old of their liberty, in accordance with Article 5 of the ECHR.

5.44 For the Court of Protection to make any decisions for or about a person, that person must be unable to make those decisions themselves. This includes the decision

56 Court of Protection Rules 2017.

57 Court of Protection Rules 2017, r 1.1.

58 Court of Protection Rules 2017, rr 1.2 and 7.6.

59 Court of Protection Rules 2017, r 1.2.

to reside within arrangements that meet the objective criteria for a deprivation of liberty. This is the 'capacity' requirement. In order to make an interim order, to last for a short time within or for the duration of proceedings, the court must be satisfied that there is reason to believe that P lacks capacity in relation to the matter which the court is being asked to decide.[60] In order to make a final order, the court must be satisfied on the balance of probabilities that P lacks capacity to make a decision themselves in the specific subject area.[61]

5.45 Capacity is, therefore, the first area which must be explored when practitioners are considering whether the Court of Protection may be available to authorise a young person's deprivation of liberty. The starting point is the presumption of capacity at s 1(2). All persons to whom the MCA 2005 applies are first presumed to have capacity to make a decision for themselves, unless or until evidence is presented to rebut that presumption. Assessing capacity comprises two elements, the functional element and the diagnostic element. Both must be simultaneously satisfied for a person to be assessed as lacking capacity in the relevant subject area, and then opening up the court's jurisdiction. The MCA 2005 defines lacking capacity at s 2(1):

> '[A] person lacks capacity in relation to a matter if at the material time he is unable to make a decision for himself in relation to the matter because of an impairment of, or disturbance in the functioning of, the mind or the brain.'

5.46 This phrase can be broken down into a three-stage test which is used to determine if a person has capacity to make a decision or not:

(a) Is the person able to make a decision? If they cannot;

(b) Is there an impairment or disturbance in the functioning of the person's mind or brain? If so;

(c) Is the person's inability to make the decision because of the identified disturbance?[62]

5.47 The first question requires consideration of four functional tasks, and it is often referred to as the functional element of a capacity assessment. The tasks are whether the person is able to: understand the information relevant to the decision; retain that information; use or weigh that information as part of the process of making the decision; and, communicate a decision.[63] If the person is unable to complete one or more of those tasks, subject to satisfying the second two questions, they lack capacity in the relevant area. The focus of the functional assessment must be on P's ability to complete the tasks in relation to the information that is relevant to the specific decision that needs to be made. This is because capacity is a decision-specific concept. A person may have capacity to make a decision in one area of their life, but lack capacity to make a decision about something else. Capacity must be broken

---

60 MCA 2005, s 48.

61 MCA 2005, ss 15 and 16.

62 *A Local Authority v JB* [2021] UKSC 52.

63 MCA 2005, s 3(1).

down in this way to promote a person's autonomy and ability to make decisions in areas in which they can understand and employ the relevant information.

5.48 In assessing whether a person can conduct the functional tasks, the relevant information should be provided to them. For the purposes of a young person's capacity to consent to their deprivation of liberty, the relevant information relates to their living and care arrangements which constitute their confinement, including all of the available living and care arrangements for them and the consequences if they were to live or not live within particular arrangements.[64] A capacity assessment is not designed to test what knowledge a person already has, but to assess their ability to understand and use information when given to them.[65] This should include information about the reasonably foreseeable consequences of deciding one way or another.[66] The person does not need to be able to use and weigh all of the information provided to them, but they must be able to use and weigh the salient information sufficiently in order to make a capacitous decision.[67]

5.49 If a person cannot undertake the functional tasks required, practitioners must then consider if they have an impairment of or disturbance in the functioning of their mind or brain. This is the diagnostic element of the capacity assessment, and it can be particularly tricky in relation to young people whose brains are still developing. Although titled the 'diagnostic' element, a precise diagnosis is not required in order to establish a causal link between the person's functional abilities and an impairment of their brain. Hayden J provided the following comment to assist in understanding how this element should be approached:

> '… clear therefore that there are a number of identified pathologies which separately or in combination are likely to explain the disturbance or functioning in TM's mind or brain. It might well have been possible to be more precise if TM had been able to cooperate with the MRI scan. It is a misunderstanding of section 3 MCA 2005 to read it as requiring the identification of a precise causal link when there are various entirely viable causes. Insistence on identifying the precise pathology as necessary to establish the causal link is misconceived. Such an approach strikes me as inconsistent with the philosophy of the MCA 2005. What is clear, on the evidence, is that the Trust has established an impairment of the mind or brain and that has, in light of the consequences I have identified, rebutted the presumption of capacity.'[68]

5.50 The Code of Practice to the MCA 2005 provides some examples of impairments or disturbances in the functioning of the mind or brain.[69] These include conditions associated with mental illness, dementia, significant learning disabilities, the long-term effects of brain damage, delirium and concussion. It may be that the impairment or disturbance is temporary, although conducting a capacity assessment

---

64 *A PCT v LDV, CC & B Healthcare Group* [2013] EWHC 272 (Fam).
65 *CC v KK & STCC* [2012] EWHC 2136 (COP).
66 *A Local Authority v JB* [2021] UKSC 52, para 73.
67 *Kings College NHS Foundation Trust v C and V* [2015] EWCOP 80, para 37.
68 *Pennine Acute Hospitals NHS Trust v TM* [2021] EWCOP 8, para 37.
69 Mental Capacity Act 2005 Code of Practice, Department for Constitutional Affairs, 2007, chapter 4.

when a person is suffering a temporary impairment will require justification as to why the assessment could not wait until the young person was recovered.

5.51 The final element of a capacity assessment is establishing a causative nexus between the person's inability to make a decision and the impairment of their mind or brain.[70] The assessor must ask whether the young person's inability to make a decision is because of the impairment of or disturbance in the functioning of the mind or brain. It is not sufficient for an assessor to determine that the impairment or disturbance only impair a person's ability to make a decision, but that they render the person unable to make the decision.

5.52 The MCA 2005 itself provides a guiding framework on the approach to capacity. It stipulates that a person must be assumed to have capacity unless it is established that they lack capacity.[71] The MCA 2005 goes on to require that a person should not be deemed incapacitous unless all practicable steps have been taken to help them make a decision themselves, without success. Chapter 2 of the Code of Practice to the MCA 2005 provides some guidance on what support needs to be considered here.[72] It may include adapting the form of communication used, providing information in an accessible format such as via pictures, or using educational tools and a programme of education to support P's understanding of the relevant information.

5.53 Finally, a person is not to be treated as being unable to make a decision because the decision they make is unwise. Case law which followed the inception of the Court of Protection has made clear that a person making a decision opposed to the recommendations of professionals, or a decision which appears to others to be irresponsible, is not sufficient to establish that the person lacks capacity. The court recognises that people often make decisions that may seem unwise to others, for example smoking, but those are decisions that people are entitled to make if they understand the relevant information and can employ it in order to make their decision. In a 2020 judgment, Hayden J commented that at the core of the MCA 2005 was 'a central distinction between the inability to make a decision and the making of a decision which, objectively, would be regarded by others as unwise'.[73] The judgment goes on to surmise:

> 'Even where an individual fails to give appropriate weight to features of a decision that professionals might consider to be determinative, this will not in itself justify a conclusion that P lacks capacity. Smoking, for example, is demonstrably injurious to health and potentially a risk to life. Objectively, these facts would logically indicate that nobody should smoke. Nonetheless, many still do.'

5.54 Hayden J quoted a passage from MacDonald J's judgment in *Kings College NHS Foundation Trust v C and V* which included these comments:

---

70 *PC and NC v City of York Council* [2013] EWCA Civ 478, para 52.

71 MCA 2005, s 1(2).

72 Mental Capacity Act 2005 Code of Practice, Department for Constitutional Affairs (2007), chapter 2.

73 *London Borough of Tower Hamlets v PB* [2020] EWCOP 34, para 5.

> 'Where a court is satisfied that a person is able to use and weigh the relevant information, the weight to be attached to that information in the decision-making process is a matter for the decision maker. Thus, where a person is able to use and weigh the relevant information but chooses to give that information no weight when reaching the decision in question, the element of the functional test comprised by s 3(1)(c) will not be satisfied. Within this context, a person cannot be considered to be unable to use and weigh information simply on the basis that he or she has applied his or her own values or outlook to that information in making the decision in question and chosen to attach no weight to that information in the decision making process.'[74]

5.55 If the court is satisfied that either on an interim basis there is reason to believe the young person concerned lacks capacity to make a decision about their living and care arrangements, or on a final basis that the evidence establishes a lack of capacity on the balance of probabilities, the court has jurisdiction to make orders in respect of the young person which concern the areas in which the person lacks capacity. This includes a power of the court to authorise the deprivation of liberty of a young person under the MCA 2005, s 4A. The Court of Protection may only authorise a deprivation of a person's liberty if, in doing so, it is giving effect to an order under the MCA 2005, s 16(2)(a) – a decision made by the court in the person's best interests.[75]

5.56 All decisions made about a young person by the Court of Protection must be deemed to be within that young person's best interests.[76] What constitutes a person's best interests can be difficult to neatly define. The starting point for deciphering best interests is the MCA 2005, s 4 which sets down a list of things which must be considered and steps which must be taken to ascertain what is in a person's best interests. This includes looking at all of the relevant circumstances, considering the person's past and present wishes, their beliefs and values, and consulting with people involved in caring for the young person or interested in their welfare.[77] Assumptions should not be made on what is in a person's best interests based solely on their age, appearance, condition or behaviour.

5.57 Chapter 5 of the Code of Practice to the MCA 2005 adds flesh to the bones of best interests.[78] It makes clear that the concept of best interests is individual to every person, and what will be in one person's best interests may not be in the best interests of another. Whether a decision is in a person's best interests or not may also change over time. Anyone involved in making best interests decisions for a young person should be careful to consider the circumstances of that young person in their entirety, what their wishes and feelings are and what issues are relevant to this young person and so must be factored into the decision making. In respect of a proposed deprivation of liberty, this includes considering what the options are for the young person's residence and care, which arrangements are in line with the young person's wishes, and which is the least restrictive option for the young person. Practitioners

---

74 *Kings College NHS Foundation Trust v C and V* [2015] EWCOP 80, para 38.
75 MCA 2005, ss 4A and 16.
76 MCA 2005, s 1(5).
77 MCA 2005, s 4.
78 Mental Capacity Act 2005 Code of Practice, Department for Constitutional Affairs, 2007, chapter 5.

should consider what the risks are to each young person if they are deprived of their liberty and if they are not, and evaluate what measures are proportionate to meet those risks.

5.58 The process of making a decision in a young person's best interests where a deprivation of liberty will arise is complex and will often require the involvement of a number of professionals who can consider the social, emotional, physical and psychological impact of the proposed arrangements on the young person. Charles J provided some guidance on what the court must consider in these circumstances within *Re NRA & Ors*:

> 'I. … the determinative test on an application for a welfare order to authorise a deprivation of liberty is a best interests test, namely is the care package the least restrictive available option,
>
> ii. this test applies to care packages whether or not there is a deprivation of liberty,
>
> iii. the Article 5 deprivation of liberty or detention arising on the implementation of such a care package is a necessary consequence of the least restrictive available option that best promotes P's best interests,
>
> iv. so the test is not whether or not P should be deprived of liberty or detained.'[79]

5.59 When it has been established that a young person lacks capacity to consent to their living and care arrangements and a deprivation of liberty may be in a young person's best interests, an application must be made to the Court of Protection for authorisation of the arrangements. Any application must be accompanied by evidence which establishes firstly that the court has jurisdiction because the young person lacks capacity to consent to the arrangements, and secondly, that the proposed arrangements are in the young person's best interests. Practice Direction 11A requires that the person or body making the application (often a local authority responsible for arrangements for the young person) consults with the young person before the application is lodged with the court.[80] The duty of consultation also extends to informing any person interested in the young person's welfare of the intention to make an application to court.[81]

5.60 The Court of Protection will then be tasked with assessing the evidence before it and determining whether to authorise the deprivation of liberty of the young person. In some instances, this judicial assessment can be undertaken without a hearing and is referred to as the '*Re X*' process or 'streamlined procedure'. This process involves a judge reading the application and written evidence, and granting or refusing an order based upon the papers filed at court. However, case law has guided practitioners away from seeking this 'on paper' process in respect of young people. Within *KL (A Minor: deprivation of liberty)*, Senior Judge Hilder considered it likely to be inappropriate for cases concerning the deprivation of liberty of young

---

79 *Re NRA & Ors* [2015] EWCOP 59, para 41.

80 Court of Protection: Practice Directions, Court of Protection Rules 2017, Practice Direction 11A, para 35.

81 Court of Protection: Practice Directions, Court of Protection Rules 2017, Practice Direction 11A, para 39.

people to be dealt with by the court without a hearing.[82] The judgment set down some general guidance which included that the circumstances for young people who may need to be deprived of their liberty are likely to require a higher level of scrutiny by the court than is intended under the streamlined procedure. In that case, the judge was particularly concerned with the stage of development of the young person; the complexity of transitioning from children's services to adult services; the presence of a care order; the absence of any contact with family members for the young person; and the need for independent representation. It was based upon these factors that the judge determined the application could not be simply approved on the papers.

5.61 The case of *KL* highlights one factor of complexity which often arises when applications about young people are made to the Court of Protection, and that is previous proceedings having taken place under the CA 1989. It may also be the case that the child concerned has been involved in, or remains the subject of, proceedings or an order under the inherent jurisdiction of the High Court concerning their deprivation of liberty. Once that child turns 16, the MCA 2005 comes into force and the jurisdiction of the Court of Protection may be opened up. As explained above, the Court of Protection will only have jurisdiction if the young person concerned is deemed to lack capacity to make the relevant decision, being about their residence and care arrangements which amount to a deprivation of their liberty. If there is sufficient evidence before the court to rebut the presumption of capacity for the young person, consideration must be given to whether any existing proceedings in the High Court should be transferred to the Court of Protection once its jurisdiction is available. This conforms with the principle that the inherent jurisdiction of the High Court should only be invoked where there is no other statutory means of authorising a deprivation of liberty. Following this principle, if the MCA 2005 may be used, it should be used unless there is good reason not to.

5.62 The transfer of proceedings from the Family Division of the High Court to the Court of Protection is governed by the Mental Capacity Act 2005 Transfer of Proceedings Order, SI 2007/1899. Article 3 provides as follows:

> '1) This Article applies to any proceedings in a Court having jurisdiction under the Children Act which relate to a person under 18.
>
> 2) A court having jurisdiction under the Children Act may direct the transfer of the whole or part of the proceedings to the Court of Protection where it considers in all the circumstances it is just and convenient to transfer the proceedings.
>
> 3) In making a determination, the court having jurisdiction under the Children Act must have regards to-
>
> a) whether the proceedings should be heard together with other proceedings that are pending in the Court of Protection;
>
> b) whether any order that may be made by the Court of Protection is likely to be a more appropriate way of dealing with the proceedings;

82 *KL (A Minor: deprivation of liberty)* [2022] EWCOP 24.

c) the extent to which any order made as respects a person who lacks capacity is likely to continue to have effect when that person reaches 18; and

d) Any other matters that the court considers relevant.

4) A court having jurisdiction under the Children Act-

a) may exercise the power to make an order under paragraph (2) on an application or on its own initiative; and

b) where it orders a transfer, must give reasons for its decision.

5) Any proceedings transferred under this article-

a) are to be treated for all purposes as if they were proceedings under the Mental Capacity Act 2005 which had been started in the Court of Protection; and

b) are to be dealt with after the transfer in accordance with directions given by the Court of Protection.'

5.63 Although the Court of Protection and its powers may become available once a child turns 16, if they lack capacity to make decisions for themselves, the court will not automatically transfer cases to the Court of Protection when it has jurisdiction. This was an issue considered in detail by Munby J within *Re A-F No.2* in which he declined to transfer proceedings from the Family Division of the High Court to the Court of Protection.[83] In making that decision, the judge considered that the benefits to the young people of remaining subject to proceedings in the Family Division outweighed the benefits of transferring the case to be dealt with under the MCA 2005. The circumstances which led to that conclusion included the young people continuing to require the protection of the 'looked after children' provisions and the presence of an Independent Reviewing Officer to have oversight of their case, alongside the CAFCASS children's guardian allocated within proceedings. The judge also recognised that whilst the young people remained the subject of care orders, the Family Court may have cause to continue to intervene in their lives in a protective way, and so keeping the proceedings within the Family Division allowed all potential issues to be considered holistically by one judge who was familiar with the family. The judge also recognised the benefit of judicial continuity.

5.64 Whether or not existing cases should be transferred from the Family Division of the High Court to the Court of Protection will depend upon the specific facts of the case. Case law has provided examples of when the Court of Protection may be the appropriate arena in which to consider any deprivation of liberty of a young person. Within *B (A Local Authority) v RM & Others*, Hedley J provided a number of guiding principles to consider when determining which court is best placed to consider a young person's deprivation of liberty.[84] This included consideration of whether the young person's lack of capacity is likely to persist in the long-term; whether decisions and issues about the young person's welfare can be resolved during their minority; whether the powers of the Court of Protection are more appropriate to resolve the issues; and, whether the young person's welfare needs can be fully met within the scope of the Court of Protection's powers. Hedley

83 *Re A-F No.2* [2018] EWHC 2129.

84 *B (A Local Authority) v RM & Ors* [2010] EWHC 3802 (Fam).

J determined on the facts of the case before him that the powers of the Court of Protection were more appropriate for the young person, and her welfare would be better protected within the Court of Protection. His reasons for concluding that were because: there should be a court determination about the placement; the door of the court should remain open during the placement planning period; the issues before the court were unlikely to be resolved before the young person turned 18; the young person's disabilities and care needs were lifelong; the declarations which can be made by the Court of Protection avoid the negative consequences of a care order but provide a framework within which the young person's needs can be met; and the young person's lack of relevant capacity was manifest.

5.65 Practice Guidance was issued by the President of the Family Division in September 2023 dealing with the specific issue of transitioning proceedings from the High Court to the Court of Protection when a child turns 16 and the Court of Protection may be an appropriate arena in which to consider further issues.[85] Within the guidance, a number of steps are set down to facilitate a smooth transition between courts, with an emphasis on prompt applications being made and the Court of Protection being notified swiftly that an application is to be expected. The underlying theme of the guidance is that proper preparation and forethought is essential to ensure cases can be managed smoothly when a transition between courts is necessary.

THE INHERENT JURISDICTION

5.66 When none of the statutory schemes set out above are available, the inherent jurisdiction of the High Court is turned to as a means of authorising the deprivation of liberty of a child or young person. The statutory schemes may be unavailable for a number of reasons. A child or young person may not meet the criteria for detention under the MHA 1983; a young person may have capacity in the relevant domain and so the MCA 2005 is not available; or, there may be no secure accommodation placements available for the child or young person in order to pursue an application under the CA 1989, s 25.

5.67 The introduction to this book highlights the current state of crisis in respect of the provision of secure accommodation in England and Wales for children and young people. The extensive shortages of approved and regulated secure accommodation have given rise to an influx in deprivation of liberty applications to court for children who meet the criteria to be placed in secure accommodation but for whom there is no space in a registered provision. In November 2020, the Children's Commissioner for England produced two reports highlighting the scale of the shortages and their impact.[86] The reports describe a crisis in the provision of

---

85 Practice Guidance in respect of transition of matters from the National DOLs List to the Court of Protection, President of the Family Division, September 2023.

86 The Children Who No-one Knows What To Do With, The Children's Commissioner for England (11 November 2020); Who Are They? Where Are They?, The Children's Commissioner for England (27 November 2020).

secure accommodation for children which followed recognition from the High Court of this persisting issue, with Mr Justice MacDonald stating:

> 'It is plain that, despite the issue being highlighted in multiple court decisions since 2017, and by the Children's Commissioner, the shortage of clinical provision for placements of children and adolescents requiring assessment and treatment for mental health issues within a restrictive clinical environment, the shortage of secure placements and the shortage of regulated placements remains. In this context, children like G with highly complex needs and behaviour continue to fall through the gaps that exist between secure accommodation, regulated accommodation and detention under the mental health legislation.'[87]

5.68 There are similar challenges faced by NHS Trusts and health bodies in respect of secure units in which children and young people may be detained under the MHA 1983. The crisis in provision of appropriate inpatient beds for children and young people was highlighted before MacDonald J within *North Yorkshire County Council v M & Ors (Medium Secure Bed)*.[88] In this case, the court was concerned with the arrangements for a 15-year old girl, M. M was assessed as presenting in a way which required her placement under the provisions of the MHA 1983.[89] Despite that identified need, M was not placed within an NHS England placement equipped to meet her needs. The court was informed that there were only three services across the country able to admit young females and despite there being some empty beds, the services did not have capacity to accept M.

5.69 The court has since had the opportunity to consider in detail the process by which a child or young person may be accepted into a Tier 4 CAMHS unit and detained in hospital pursuant to the MHA 1983.[90] A child or young person may be assessed as meeting the criteria for detention under the MHA 1983, but the provision of a place for them in a suitable facility remains dependent on a national referral process which implements a separate criteria for a Tier 4 CAMHS service.[91] This imposes a further hurdle in the provision of placements for children and young people under the MHA 1983, and may result in a child or young person being refused a mental health inpatient placement. It is, invariably, at this stage that practitioners must consider the alternatives which may require authorisation under the High Court's inherent jurisdiction.

5.70 The High Court's inherent jurisdiction is a long-standing collection of powers which may be exercised by the High Court when statute does not provide for the decision or order that needs to be made. One of the earliest summaries defining the inherent jurisdiction was provided by Lord Denning MR in *Re L (An Infant)* when he said:

---

87 *Lancashire CC v G (Unavailability of Secure Accommodation)* [2020] EWHC 2828 (Fam).

88 *North Yorkshire County Council v M & Ors (Medium Secure Bed)* [2021] EWHC 2171 (Fam).

89 *North Yorkshire County Council v M & Ors (Medium Secure Bed)* [2021] EWHC 2171 (Fam), para 12.

90 *Blackpool Borough Council v HT (A Minor) & Ors* [2022] EWHC 1480 (Fam).

91 *Blackpool Borough Council v HT (A Minor) & Ors* [2022] EWHC 1480 (Fam), para 37-38 and 43-44.

> 'It derives from the right and duty of the Crown as parens patriae to take care of those who are not able to take care of themselves. The Crown delegated this power to the Lord Chancellor, who exercised it in his Court of Chancery... the Court of Chancery had power to interfere for the protection of the infant by making whatever order might be appropriate. ... The wide jurisdiction of the old Court of Chancery is now vested in the High Court of Justice and can be exercised by any judge of the High Court.'[92]

5.71 A more recent and well-known quote describing the inherent jurisdiction of the High Court came from Lord Donaldson MR in *Re F (Mental Patient: Sterilisation)* as follows:

> '[T]he common law is the great safety net which lies behind all statute law and is capable of filling gaps left by that law, if and in so far as those gaps have to be filled in the interests of society as a whole. This process of using the common law to fill gaps is one of the most important duties of the judges.'[93]

5.72 It is described by Lord Stephens in *Re T* as being the 'ultimate safety net'.[94] It may act as a valid 'procedure prescribed by law' for the purposes of Article 5 ECHR to bring about a lawful deprivation of liberty. This being so was clarified in *Re T* by Lady Black who confirmed:

> '89. The main thrust of the appellant's argument in this court in relation to article 5 is that use of the inherent jurisdiction to authorise the deprivation of liberty in cases like the present was not "in accordance with a procedure prescribed by law" as the article requires. This element of article 5 ties in with the requirement in article 5(1)(d) that the detention of a minor be "by lawful order". The appellant's case in this respect will be examined below, but there are some general points which can be set out concerning this element of article 5. ...
>
> 90. Article 5 imposes an obligation to conform to the substantive and procedural rules of national law. Accordingly, the detention must have a legal basis in domestic law, and the law must be of a quality which is compatible with the rule of law. This means that where the domestic law authorises deprivation of liberty, it must be sufficiently accessible, precise and foreseeable in its application to avoid the risk of arbitrariness. It must be attended by fair and proper procedures. An individual who is deprived of their liberty is entitled to have the lawfulness of that detention reviewed by a court.
>
> 91. There is nothing in article 5, or in the case law of the European Court of Human Rights, that requires the domestic law and procedure should be set out in statute and/or regulations, rather than being common law based.'[95]

5.73 For an order under the High Court's inherent jurisdiction to be made, a local authority needs to first seek leave of the court to invoke its inherent jurisdiction.[96] This process is governed by the CA 1989, s 100. The CA 1989, s 100(4) provides

---

92 *Re L (An Infant)* [1968] P 119.

93 *Re F (Mental Patient: Sterilisation)* [1990] 2 AC 1, para 13.

94 *Re T (A Child) (Appellant)* [2021] UKSC 35, para 168.

95 *Re T (A Child) (Appellant)* [2021] UKSC 35, paras 89-91 and 150-155.

96 CA 1989, s 100(3).

that the court may grant leave for an exercise of the inherent jurisdiction only if it is satisfied that:

(a) The result which the local authority wishes to achieve cannot be achieved through the making of another order which does not involve the inherent jurisdiction being exercised and which the local authority is entitled to apply for; and

(b) There is reasonable cause to believe that if the court's inherent jurisdiction is not exercised with respect to the child, they are likely to suffer significant harm.

5.74 To satisfy this test, the applicant local authority must establish that the result of the order they are seeking cannot be achieved in another way, and that if any order is not made, the child is likely to suffer significant harm. Significant harm is defined within chapter 6 and is harm (ill-treatment or impairment of health or development) which is considerable, noteworthy or important.

5.75 The CA 1989 also places limits on when the inherent jurisdiction can be exercised, providing that it must not be exercised in respect of children:

(a) To require a child to be placed in the care, or put under the supervision, of a local authority;

(b) To require a child to be accommodated by or on behalf of a local authority;

(c) To make a child who is the subject of a care order a ward of court; or

(d) For the purpose of conferring on any local authority power to determine any question which has arisen, or which may arise, in connection with any aspect of parental responsibility for a child.[97]

5.76 To assist practitioners approaching an application for leave to invoke the High Court's inherent jurisdiction, Keehan J has summarised some guiding principles within *Re AB (A Child) (Deprivation of Liberty: Consent)*:

> '(1) Local authorities are under a duty to consider whether any children in need, or looked-after children, are… subject to restrictions amounting to a deprivation of liberty.
>
> (2) The Cheshire West criteria must be rigorously applied to the individual circumstances of each case.
>
> …
>
> (4) A deprivation of liberty will be lawful if warranted under statute; for example, under s.25 of the Children Act 1989 or the Mental Health Act 1983 or under the remand provisions of LASPO 2012 or if a child has received a custodial sentence under the PCCSA 2000.
>
> …
>
> (8) The local authority must first consider whether s.25 of the Children Act is applicable or appropriate in the circumstances of the individual case. This will

97 CA 1989, s 100(2).

require an analysis of (1) whether any of the regulations disapply s.25, (2) whether the intended placement is accommodation provided for the purposes of restricting liberty and, thus, secure accommodation within s.25 and (3) whether the test set out in s.25.1(a) or (b) is met.

(9) If it is not, then the s.100(4) leave hurdle is likely to be crossed on the basis that any unlawful deprivation of liberty is likely to constitute significant harm.'[98]

5.77 There is no equivalent provision requiring leave to be sought for the inherent jurisdiction to be exercised when an application is made by a state body other than a local authority. The reason for this relates to the purpose of the CA 1989, s 100. It is summarised by Lady Black in *Re T* as:

> 'Both the material that we have about the lead up to section 100, and the wording of the section itself, suggest to me that the principal driving force behind section 100(2) was to ensure that the statutory scheme which the Act was establishing in relation to the intervention of local authorities in the lives of children and families would not be undermined, or evaded, by the use of the inherent jurisdiction.'[99]

5.78 The requirement of leave is, therefore, intended to prevent a local authority seeking to use the inherent jurisdiction as an alternative to the provisions and safeguards of the CA 1989, when the CA 1989 provides a framework for the type of order sought. It cannot be used as a 'back door' to seek an order for which statute has already made provision.

5.79 Once leave has been granted (if required) and an application is before the High Court to invoke its inherent jurisdiction, it is for the court to determine whether or not to exercise its inherent jurisdiction to authorise the deprivation of liberty of a child or young person. The court may make an order authorising a deprivation of liberty for any person under 18, irrespective of whether they have capacity or *Gillick* competence and whether the order is against their wishes or not.[100] The court's ability to make an order under the inherent jurisdiction also remains irrespective of the child's consent or absence of consent to the arrangements.[101] Within the 2018 decision in *Re T*, the court clarified that although an absence of valid consent is a necessary component of a deprivation of liberty, it is not a prerequisite for the court being able to exercise its powers under the inherent jurisdiction and grant a permissive order authorising a deprivation of liberty.

5.80 There are a number of factors which the court must consider when deciding whether or not to exercise its inherent jurisdiction and authorise the deprivation of liberty of a child or young person. MacDonald J summarised the position in *Blackpool Borough Council v HT (A Minor) & Ors*:

---

98 *Re AB (A Child) (Deprivation of Liberty: Consent)* [2015] EWHC 3125 (Fam), para 38.

99 *Re T (A Child) (Appellant)* [2021] UKSC 35, para 116.

100 *Re W (a minor) (medical treatment: court jurisdiction)* [1993] Fam 64; *An NHS Foundation Hospital Trust v P* [2014] EWHC 1650 (Fam); *Re T* [2021] UKSC 35; *re Z (A Minor) (Identification)* [1997] Fam 1; *A v A Health Authority* [2002] Fam 213.

101 *Re T (A Child)* [2018] EWCA Civ 2136, paras 68-69.

'Such a declaration may be made if the court is satisfied that the circumstances that will pertain for the child in the placement in question constitute a deprivation of liberty for the purposes of Art 5 of the ECHR and if it considers such an order to be in the subject child's best interests.'[102]

5.81 Lady Black also outlined what the court must consider before authorising any deprivation of liberty in *Re T* as follows:

'It is, of course, correct that the court will not itself regulate the detailed operation of the authorised deprivation of liberty, when it authorises a proposed placement and the regime that it is planned will be adopted there. However, it will not give the local authority the authorisation that they seek without considerable exploration of the circumstances, to ensure that the proposal is appropriate. By way of example, in addition to procedural matters that I have already mentioned, I would pick out that the procedure prescribed in the case law requires that the court be provided with evidence describing the nature of the proposed regime and justifying why the proposed arrangements are necessary and proportionate in meeting the child's welfare needs. The court will need to know the child's views on the matter. And the order will include express liberty to any party, including the child, to apply to the court for further directions on the shortest possible notice.'[103]

5.82 Case law has established three key principles which must be satisfied for the court to authorise the deprivation of liberty of a child or young person. Those are: that the order is necessary; it is proportionate; and it is in the welfare interests (or best interests, often used interchangeably in these cases) of the child or young person.[104] The concept of welfare is explored in chapter 6 and it encompasses the child or young person's physical, emotional, mental and psychological well-being. Welfare also includes specific social, cultural, ethnic and religious needs which the child or young person may have as part of their development. Necessity and proportionality are given their ordinary meaning. The necessity of an order will be determined by considering what the available options are, whether any alternative which is less restrictive or interventionist may achieve the desired outcome, and whether the risks or likelihood of risk is so great that no other option will suffice. Proportionality requires the court to consider the arrangement that is proposed in detail and evaluate whether that arrangement corresponds with the level of risk to the child or young person, including the risk they pose to others, if they are or are not deprived of their liberty. An arrangement or regime will only be deemed to be proportionate if it is the least restrictive regime that is capable of keeping the child safe and meeting their welfare needs. The court has been frank in accepting that there will rarely be an arrangement proposed for a child or young person that will perfectly meet all of the child's needs and suitably safeguard them. The court must, therefore, be alive to a 'degree of compromise' that is often required when assessing the suitability of

---

102 *Blackpool Borough Council v HT (A Minor) & Ors* [2022] EWHC 1480 (Fam), para 23.

103 *Re T (A Child)* [2021] UKSC 35, para 155.

104 *Tameside MBC v L (Unavailability of Regulated Therapeutic Placement)* [2021] EHC 1814 (Fam), para 57.

arrangements made for a child or young person whose safety requires their liberty to be deprived.[105]

5.83 Case law increasingly reiterates that any deprivation of liberty authorised by the court is just that: an authorisation. It is not a requirement to impose a regime but permission to do so if and when required. Keehan J summarised the approach neatly in concluding the judgment in *Re AB (A child: deprivation of liberty)* with '… the local authority should cease to impose such a deprivation as soon as…. the reasons justifying the deprivation of liberty no longer subsist. Authorisation is permissive and not prescriptive.'[106] It follows that even once an authorisation has been granted by the court, a child or young person may cease to be deprived of their liberty by removal of the restrictive measures once those measures are no longer necessary, proportionate and in their welfare interests.

5.84 Orders authorising the deprivation of liberty of a child or young person must expire when the young person turns 18 years old. The court's jurisdiction in this arena relates only to children and so ceases when a child reaches majority. There are limited means by which the inherent jurisdiction may be exercised in relation to adults. This is a separate process with different considerations not covered within the scope of this book. Orders made under the inherent jurisdiction should last for no more than 12-months at a time.[107] This time limit allows for regular judicial scrutiny in keeping with Article 5 and its requirement for a proper process to be in place to prevent arbitrary deprivations and to review the continued appropriateness of a deprivation of liberty over time.[108]

5.85 The court has also confirmed that it is within the scope of the inherent jurisdiction to authorise the deprivation of liberty of a child or young person when that regime is being imposed in an unregulated or unregistered placement. Unregulated and unregistered placements are explained at chapter 7. MacDonald J confirmed within *Tameside MBC v L (Unavailability of Regulated Therapeutic Placement)* that the inherent jurisdiction can be exercised in circumstances where the accommodation used is not a regulated provision, or it is unregistered with the relevant governing body.[109] In its judgment, the court reiterated that it was primarily concerned with the authorisation of the regime or restrictions imposed and not a strict authorisation of the accommodation in which those restrictions were implemented. The court emphasised that factoring into its decision to authorise the regime was the fact that there were no available alternative (and regulated or registered) placements in which the regime could be implemented. The court required, as a safeguard,

---

105 *Tameside MBC v L (Unavailability of Regulated Therapeutic Placement)* [2021] EHC 1814 (Fam), para 71.

106 *Re AB (A Child: deprivation of liberty)* [2015] EWHC 3125 (Fam), para 38.

107 *Re A-F (Children)* [2018] EWHC 138 (Fam), para 55.

108 Guidance on Article 5 of the European Convention on Human Rights: Right to liberty and security, Council of Europe (August 2022), para 45.

109 *Tameside MBC v L (Unavailability of Regulated Therapeutic Placement)* [2021] EHC 1814 (Fam).

that the matter return before the court frequently to review the availability of more appropriate accommodation.[110]

5.86 Within *Re T*, the court was also considering the circumstances of a child deprived of their liberty in an unregistered provision, being a placement that should be registered as a children's home with Ofsted but that was not so registered. The court confirmed that the inherent jurisdiction may be exercised in these circumstances to authorise a deprivation of liberty when a child or young person was placed in such a setting. In explaining the decision, Lady Black commented:

> 'I have been particularly concerned as to whether it is a permissible exercise of the inherent jurisdiction to authorise a local authority to place a child in an unregistered children's home in relation to which a criminal offence would be being committed. Ultimately, however, I recognise that there are cases in which there is absolutely no alternative, and where the child (or someone else) is likely to come to grave harm if the court does not act. I also have to recognise that there are other duties in play, in addition to those which prohibit carrying on or managing an unregistered children's home. I gave an idea earlier… of the duties placed upon local authorities to protect and support children. How can a local authority fulfil these duties in the problematic cases with which we are concerned if they cannot obtain authorisation from the High Court to place the child in the only placement that is available, and with the ability to impose such restrictions as are required on the child's liberty? It is such imperative considerations of necessity that have led me to conclude that the inherent jurisdiction must be available in these cases. There is presently no alternative that will safeguard the children who require its protection.'[111]

5.87 The court was cautious to be clear that authorisation in these circumstances was deemed necessary in light of the lack of any alternative provisions where the child could live. Sir Andrew McFarlane, President of the Family Division, subsequently considered the position following the implementation of the Care Planning, Placement and Case Review (England) (Amendment) Regulations 2021 which prohibit the placement of looked after children under the age of 16 in unregulated accommodation, including independent, semi-independent and supported living accommodation. In *A Mother v Derby City Council & Anor*, Sir Andrew McFarlane confirmed that the powers of the inherent jurisdiction continue to extend to the authorisation of a child's deprivation of liberty in an unregistered children's home, as the amendment regulations apply to issues around regulation and not registration, therefore not impacting the legal position for the placement of children in unregistered placements.[112] The court went on to confirm that even if the amending regulations applied in the circumstances of the accommodation in question, the inherent jurisdiction must be available by virtue of necessity to 'meet the overarching needs of the child'.[113]

---

110 *Tameside MBC v L (Unavailability of Regulated Therapeutic Placement)* [2021] EHC 1814 (Fam), para 84.

111 *Re T (A Child) (Appellant)* [2021] UKSC 35, para 145.

112 *A Mother v Derby City Council & Anor* [2021] EWCA Civ 1867, para 72-73.

113 *A Mother v Derby City Council & Anor* [2021] EWCA Civ 1867, para 74.

5.88 In September 2023, the President of the Family Division issued an updated practice guidance addressing the court's approach when children or young people are placed in unregistered placements.[114] This guidance was a revision of the previously implemented practice guidance which required close judicial scrutiny of cases wherein a child was living in an unregistered provision and deprived of their liberty.[115] In the revised guidance, the President recognises that the previous protocol placed a great burden on the court to oversee unregistered placements which is not at the core of the court's functions. The guidance emphasises that the limit of the court's function is to ensure that 'any deprivation of liberty is not itself unlawful' and that issues concerning the registration status of the placement should be referred to the governing body whose role it is to oversee those issues. Whilst the President did not expressly discourage continued judicial oversight of cases in which a child is living in an unregistered setting, he made clear that the burden should not be on the court to manage. The central concern of the court must remain on the child's best interests and whether they are being met or capable of being met in the proposed placement, even if that placement is unregistered. The President stipulated that it may still be appropriate for the court to order that a local authority informs the appropriate governing body of the placement.

5.89 Although the powers of the court under its inherent jurisdiction are wide reaching, they are not limitless. The court has been prudent to articulate where its boundaries lie. Within *A City Council v LS & Ors (Secure Accommodation Inherent Jurisdiction)*, MacDonald J made clear that the inherent jurisdiction cannot be used to authorise a young person's deprivation of liberty when the circumstances proposed would amount to the child being removed from the care of their parents and the parents objected to that.[116] In this case, the young person, KS, who was 17, was not looked after by the local authority and it was not open to the local authority to seek an order under the CA 1989, s 25 for a placement in secure accommodation. The local authority therefore sought an order under the court's inherent jurisdiction to permit KS to reside in accommodation in which he would be deprived of his liberty and kept safe. MacDonald J came to the clear conclusion that the remit of the inherent jurisdiction does not extend this far. KS was not the subject of a care order and, being 17, no application for a care order could be made by virtue of his age.[117] KS was also not looked after by the local authority in a consensual agreement. The judge summarised the position of the law as follows:

> 'Second, and within this context, in circumstances where KS is not and (in circumstances where his mother objects to his accommodation and where KS cannot be made the subject of a care order by reason of his age) cannot be a looked after child, the order the local authority seeks under the inherent jurisdiction is one which would not only authorise the accommodation of KS in a secure placement, but would, a priori, have the effect of

---

114 Revised Practice Guidance on the Court's approach to unregistered placements, President of the Family Division (September 2023).

115 Practice Guidance: Placements in unregistered children's homes in England or unregistered care home services in Wales (November 2019).

116 *A City Council v LS & Ors (Secure Accommodation Inherent Jurisdiction)* [2019] EWHC 1384 (Fam).

117 CA 1989, s 31(3).

authorising his removal from his mother's care without her consent for this purpose in circumstances where his mother, who retains exclusive parental responsibility for him, objects to this course of action. In the circumstances, I am satisfied that the effect of the order sought by the local authority under the inherent jurisdiction would be to require KS to be removed from his mother's care and be accommodated by the local authority. This course of action is prohibited by s 100(2)(b) of the Children Act 1989.'[118]

5.90 The procedure for making applications to the High Court for an order under its inherent jurisdiction is now governed by the Revised National Listing Protocol for Applications that seek Deprivation of Liberty Orders Relating to Children under the Inherent Jurisdiction.[119] This sits alongside the Family Procedure Rules 2010, PD12D which governs applications made for the exercise of the inherent jurisdiction. The listing protocol establishes a 'National DoL List' working within the Family Division of the High Court to manage applications relating to the deprivation of liberty of children and young people. The protocol sets down a procedure by which applications will be 'gatekept' in the national list and consideration will be given at the earliest opportunity to transferring the proceedings to be dealt with by the court which is local to the child and family. The protocol establishes a presumption that where the child or young person is the subject of ongoing care proceedings (as explained in chapter 6) or there have recently been proceedings in the local court about the child or young person, the application about their deprivation of liberty should be dealt with in the local court, rather than in the central court in London. The protocol also sets out a framework for local authorities to follow when making applications to the National DoL List, including what information should be contained within the initial statement of evidence produced by the local authority.

5.91 Alongside administrative structures being implemented, the court has also provided guidance as to the procedure to be followed when an application is made under the inherent jurisdiction. Within *Re A-F,* Sir James Munby distilled the key elements into the following guidance for practitioners:

(a) An application to the court for authorisation 'should be made where the circumstances in which the child is, or will be, living constitute, at least arguably (taking a realistic rather than fanciful view), a deprivation of liberty';

(b) 'The key elements of an Article 5 compliant process can be summarised as follows:

 (i) If a substantive order (interim or final) is to be made authorising a deprivation of liberty, there must be an oral hearing in the Family Division… A substantive order must not be made on paper, but directions can, in an appropriate case, be given on paper without an oral hearing.

 (ii) The child must be a party to the proceedings and have a guardian [referring to a children's guardian appointed for court proceedings]…

118 *A City Council v LS & Ors (Secure Accommodation Inherent Jurisdiction)* [2019] EWHC 1384 (Fam) para 48.

119 Revised National Listing Protocol for applications that seek Deprivation of Liberty Orders relating to children under the inherent jurisdiction, President of the Family Division (October 2023).

The child, if of an age to express wishes and feelings, should be permitted to do so to the judge in person if that is what the child wants.'

(c) Evidence should be provided in support of an application and it should address: the nature of the regime in which the child is to be placed including a description of the features of the child's confinement; the child's circumstances including why it is proposed that they be deprived of their liberty; why the proposed regime is considered to be necessary and proportionate in meeting the child's welfare needs, and that no less restrictive regime will do; and, the views of the child, parents and Independent Reviewing Officer. The child's care plan, minutes of any looked after child review and any recent reports relevant to the application should also be provided.[120]

5.92 The court has emphasised the need for a local authority, or other state body responsible for implementing or proposing the deprivation of liberty of a child or young person, to apply promptly to the court for authorisation. His Honour Judge Dias KC emphasised the gravity of this requirement in *AB (A Child: Human Rights)*.[121] In this case, the court was concerned with AB, a 13-year old girl, who had been deprived of her liberty in a privately run care home for four months without lawful basis. The judge stressed that the lack of authorisation of the provisions constituted a 'fundamental interference with the child's rights under the European Convention on Human Rights and the UN Convention on the Rights of the Child.'[122] The court was concerned that not only had such a fundamental right of the child been interfered with without lawful authority, but that the absence of this rendered there no effective safeguards in place surrounding her confinement. The court emphasised the important role of the children's guardian within court proceedings, being one of the safeguards which rendered a deprivation of liberty under the inherent jurisdiction lawful under the terms of Article 5 of the ECHR. The judge went further in reminding that the CA 1989, s 41(2)(b) includes within the duties of the guardian to safeguard the interests of the child.[123] The Family Procedure Rules 2010, PD16A, Pt 3 requires children's guardians to take proactive steps as part of their safeguarding role.[124] The combination of these duties placed significant weight on the role of the children's guardian which not only emphasised the need for proceedings to be brought promptly, but for the children's guardian to be active (not only reactive) within those proceedings. This may include referring matters to the court when its attention is required and the local authority has failed to do so.

5.93 When no application is forthcoming from a local authority in respect of a child or young person living in circumstances which may amount to a deprivation of their liberty, the court has confirmed that it remains open to the child's parents to seek a writ of habeas corpus.[125] A writ of habeas corpus is governed by the Civil

---

120 *Re A-F (Children)* [2018] EWHC 138 (Fam), paras 45-53.

121 *AB (A Child: Human Rights)* [2021] EWFC B100.

122 *AB (A Child: Human Rights)* [2021] EWFC B100, para 4.

123 *AB (A Child: Human Rights)* [2021] EWFC B100, para 178.

124 *LR v Local Authority & Ors* [2019] EWFC 49; Practice Direction 16A, Family Procedure Rules 2010.

125 *CGM v Luton Council* [2021] EWHC 709 (Admin).

Procedure Rules 1998, Pt 87. It is a remedy which may be sought by a third party in connection with a person who is unlawfully detained.[126] In *CGM v Luton Council*, Mostyn J confirmed that on an application for a writ of habeas corpus, it is within the court's power to make initial directions to allow a finding of fact as to whether a deprivation of liberty has arisen and if appropriate, to authorise that.[127]

5.94 In concluding this section, it is important to recognise that although the powers of the court to authorise a deprivation of liberty of a child or young person are far-reaching, the court is not required to grant authorisation when faced with an application seeking it. Increasingly, the court's scrutiny is resulting in applications for authorisation being dismissed, either because a statutory scheme is available and should be used or because the court is not satisfied that the regime is necessary, proportionate and in the child's welfare interests.

5.95 A widely-publicised occasion on which the court refused to authorise a deprivation of liberty was the case of *Wigan Metropolitan Borough Council v Y (Refusal to Authorise Deprivation of Liberty)*.[128] MacDonald J was concerned with a 12-year old boy, Y, who was suspected of suffering from attention deficit hyperactivity disorder and autism spectrum disorder, and was diagnosed with epilepsy. Y displayed challenging and violent behaviour. He was assessed as not suffering a mental disorder and therefore was not detainable under the MHA 1983. Y was placed on a clinical ward in hospital where he had been subjected to physical and chemical restraint. There were five adult staff members with Y at all times to try and control his behaviour. There were no available placements for Y in a specialist therapeutic treatment facility that may have been appropriate for him. The court was provided with evidence of Y's circumstances as follows:

> 'The situation on [the ward] is described by staff as harrowing, Y feels like he is being 'caged' and is frightened when Police are called by the ward who require assistance when his behaviour becomes a safety risk to himself and others. At all times Y still requires an incredibly high level of supervision, he is restrained often and is controlled by chemical sedation.'[129]

5.96 There was no alternative available for Y. The court was tasked with considering whether to authorise his deprivation of liberty in circumstances where there was no alternative which could offer any 'lesser degree of restriction'.[130] MacDonald J also made clear that as part of this evaluation, he must determine 'whether the placement is so unsuitable as to breach Y's rights under Art 5 of the ECHR, in which case the court would be unable to authorise it as being lawful.'[131]

---

126 *Justice for Families Ltd v Secretary of State for Justice* [2014] EWCA Civ 1477.

127 *CGM v Luton Council* [2021] EWHC 709 (Admin), para 29.

128 *Wigan Metropolitan Borough Council v Y (Refusal to Authorise Deprivation of Liberty)* [2021] EWHC 1982 (Fam).

129 *Wigan Metropolitan Borough Council v Y (Refusal to Authorise Deprivation of Liberty)* [2021] EWHC 1982 (Fam), para 28.

130 *Wigan Metropolitan Borough Council v Y (Refusal to Authorise Deprivation of Liberty)* [2021] EWHC 1982 (Fam), para 36.

131 *Wigan Metropolitan Borough Council v Y (Refusal to Authorise Deprivation of Liberty)* [2021] EWHC 1982 (Fam), para 36.

The court ultimately concluded that it was not appropriate for the deprivation of Y's liberty on the ward to be authorised, providing the following reasons:

(a) Y's welfare was the court's paramount consideration when determining if it was in Y's best interests for the deprivation of liberty to be authorised. Given the description provided to the court about the state of Y's welfare when living on the ward, the court was not satisfied that granting authorisation was in his best interests. The judge described the situation as 'an inappropriate, demeaning and, quite frankly, brutal one for a 12-year old child';

(b) Y was medically fit for discharge and there was no clinical basis for him to remain on a hospital ward which was ill-equipped to meet his needs and implement the restrictive measures;

(c) Y had no privacy at all on the ward: the door to the shower he was using had been removed. The situation in which he was living was 'grossly humiliating';

(d) The placement of Y on a hospital ward gave rise to an increased risk that the restrictions authorised by the court may be exceeded in an attempt to manage Y's behaviours;

(e) The medical staff were being required to act outside of the usual safeguards that would be implemented in a hospital in order to manage a patient's behaviour;

(f) The evidence displayed no positive outcomes with regard to Y's situation and there was no evidence of any improvements in his behaviours, relationships or in any other area.[132]

5.97 Poole J arrived at a similar conclusion in the case of *Nottinghamshire County Council v LH, PT and LT* which concerned a 12-year old girl, LT, deprived of her liberty in an acute psychiatric unit.[133] The local authority in this case similarly explained to the court that there was no alternative place for the child to be accommodated other than to remain in a hospital[134]. However, despite the court accepting its jurisdiction could be exercised in circumstances where a child is residing on a hospital ward with no clinical need to be there, the judge refused to grant the authorisation sought. The judge described the continued accommodation of LT on the ward as being impossible as a means of properly safeguarding her.[135] By the time of the second reported judgment in the matter, five days after the first, the local authority had devised a plan to create a bespoke unit for LT in which she would be deprived of her liberty by virtue of a care package managed by agency nurses and NHS staff.[136] The court did consider that proposal to be capable of authorisation by the court and so authorised LT to be deprived of her liberty in a bespoke setting with supervision from three staff members. Poole J was cautious to comment that the inherent jurisdiction should not be seen as a means to 'rubber stamp' deprivations of

---

132 *Wigan Metropolitan Borough Council v Y (Refusal to Authorise Deprivation of Liberty)* [2021] EWHC 1982 (Fam), paras 51-60.

133 *Nottinghamshire County Council v LH, PT and LT* [2021] EWHC 2584 (Fam); *Nottinghamshire County Council v LH, PT and LT (No.2)* [2021] EWHC 2593 (Fam).

134 *Nottinghamshire County Council v LH, PT and LT* [2021] EWHC 2584 (Fam), para 2.

135 *Nottinghamshire County Council v LH, PT and LT* [2021] EWHC 2584 (Fam), para 14.

136 *Nottinghamshire County Council v LH, PT and LT (No.2)* [2021] EWHC 2593 (Fam), para 4.

liberty, making them lawful, in wholly unsuitable circumstances just because there is no alternative.[137]

5.98 Shortly thereafter, Holman J similarly refused to grant authorisation of the deprivation of liberty of a child who was placed in hospital in *A County Council v A Mother & Ors (Refusal to make a DOLs Order)*.[138] This case concerned a young girl of 14 who entered hospital on an emergency basis after running away from care staff. She was subsequently assessed as being medically fit for discharge but there was no available placement willing to accept her or that could meet her needs, and so she remained in hospital. The court had initially granted authorisation of the deprivation of liberty on an out-of-hours urgent application. However, on reconsidering the matter and the child's circumstances, the court refused to renew the authorisation. The court was concerned by the description that the arrangements for the child were beyond being simply not in her best interests, but were 'damaging for her and her future'.[139] The judge was not satisfied that the arrangements constituting a deprivation of liberty met the criteria of being necessary, proportionate and in the best interests of the child. Holamn J commented 'I am simply not willing myself to apply a rubber stamp and to give a bogus veneer of lawfulness to a situation which everybody in the court room knows perfectly well is not justifiable and is not lawful.'[140]

5.99 These examples are a stark reminder of why the framework of the ECHR and the safeguards which fall within the exercise of the inherent jurisdiction are so fundamentally important. They are essential components of ensuring that children and young people have their needs met in proportionate and appropriate ways, putting their welfare at the forefront. It is crucial for practitioners and all those involved in the lives of children and young people who are deprived of their liberty to be proactive in ensuring any deprivation of liberty is lawful and is authorised. That authorisation should be sought and granted before the child or young person is confined. Consideration should always be given to the statutory routes available to govern a deprivation of liberty, before the inherent jurisdiction of the High Court is turned to. And, when the inherent jurisdiction is called upon, the court must be satisfied that the arrangements for the child or young person are necessary, proportionate and in their best interests.

CONCLUSION

5.100 This chapter has explored the different routes to a lawful deprivation of liberty, and the different procedures prescribed by law within England and Wales which can be utilised to ensure any deprivation of liberty is compliant with Article 5 of the ECHR. Unfortunately, at the time of writing, the inherent jurisdiction of the High Court continues to be frequently relied upon as a means of authorising deprivations

137 *Nottinghamshire County Council v LH, PT and LT (No.2)* [2021] EWHC 2593 (Fam), para 11.

138 *A County Council v A Mother & Ors (Refusal to make a DOLs Order)* [2021] EWHC 3303.

139 *A County Council v A Mother & Ors (Refusal to make a DOLs Order)* [2021] EWHC 3303, para 29.

140 *A County Council v A Mother & Ors (Refusal to make a DOLs Order)* [2021] EWHC 3303, para 37.

of liberty because there is simply not enough appropriate accommodation for children and young people in order to follow the statutory routes to authorisation. Alongside exploring the various procedures prescribed by law which are available in England and Wales, this chapter (and chapter 3) also emphasise the importance of any deprivation of liberty according with the permitted exceptions set out in Article 5.

Chapter 6

LOCAL AUTHORITY DUTIES AND THE INTERSECTION WITH CARE PROCEEDINGS

INTRODUCTION

6.01 For a child or young person to be deprived of their liberty, there must be some involvement of the state. This may be direct involvement in the restrictive regime, commissioning a restrictive care package or an awareness of the arrangements which restrict the child or young person's liberty. This is the third of the *Storck* limbs: attribution of responsibility to the state. This third limb may also be satisfied when a local authority ought to be aware of the arrangements for the child or young person, because of its duties to certain children and young people in its area. It is therefore helpful, when considering deprivations of liberty, to look more widely at the role of the state in the lives of children and young people and what duties local authorities have as state bodies to keep children safe and secure their welfare. This chapter focuses on local authorities, the state body with the widest scope of responsibilities for children, prescribed largely by the Children Act 1989 (CA 1989). There are other state bodies, including NHS Trusts and Integrated Care Boards, that also owe duties to children and young people, and may be involved in proceedings concerning deprivations of liberty, but the remit of their involvement is narrower.

6.02 Local authorities are divided into different departments dealing with different categories of people and issues. For the purposes of children and young people, the relevant local authority department is the children's services team, also referred to as children's social care. These teams are made up of social workers, advanced practitioners and supporting professionals who deliver children's services to families in their area.

6.03 A local authority's children's social care team will usually be involved in the lives of children and young people who are deprived of their liberty. However, it is often the case that local authorities are aware of a child or young person's circumstances long before a deprivation of liberty arises. This may be because it is providing support services to a disabled child or accommodation to a child displaying challenging behaviours who cannot be cared for by their parents. There may also be circumstances where a local authority has significant child protection concerns in relation to a child and has issued court proceedings seeking to remove the child from their birth family before any deprivation of liberty is being considered.

6.04 In order to understand a local authority's role in the lives of the children and young people in its area, it is important to first consider what a local authority's duties to those children and young people are. This chapter will then explore the role of a local authority when significant child protection concerns arise and when they may lead to court proceedings separate from any deprivation of liberty proceedings. Local authorities have a wide range of duties to children, all of which it is not possible to cover in detail in one chapter. The focus of this chapter is the duties and powers of a local authority insofar as they are relevant to children and young people who may be deprived of their liberty. Save where specified, the statutory duties and principles set out herein apply equally to local authorities in England and Wales, and to children and young people.

THE WELFARE OF THE CHILD

6.05 Statute imposes a wide range of duties on each local authority to ensure that children living within its area are safe and their needs are met. The foundation of these duties in relation to local authorities in England is contained within the CA 1989 which states at s 17 that:

> '(1) It shall be the general duty of every local authority (in addition to the other duties imposed on them by this Part)-
>
> (a) to safeguard and promote the welfare of children within their area who are in need; and
>
> (b) so far as is consistent with that duty, to promote the upbringing of such children by their families,
>
> by providing a range and level of services appropriate to those children's needs.'

6.06 For local authorities in Wales, the duties they owe to children are contained within the Social Services and Well-being (Wales) Act 2014 (SSWWA 2014) which requires local authorities to seek to promote the well-being of children who need care and support.[1] Well-being in relation to children is defined within the SSWWA 2014, s 2 and relates to any of the following: physical and mental health and emotional well-being; protection from abuse and neglect; education, training and recreation; domestic, family and personal relationships; contribution made to society; securing rights and entitlements; social and economic well-being; suitability of living accommodation; physical, intellectual, emotional, social and behavioural development; and welfare insofar as it is interpreted for the purposes of the CA 1989.

6.07 The welfare of children as a concept is not defined within statute but has been the subject of discussion within case law. One of the earliest definitions came in the late 19th century when the court stated '...the welfare of the child is not to be measured by money only, nor by physical comfort only. The word welfare must be taken in its widest sense. The moral and religious welfare of the child must be considered as well as its physical well-being. Nor can the ties of affection be

---

1 SSWWA 2014, s 5.

disregarded.'[2] This summary was reaffirmed by the court over a century later when Munby LJ said:

> 'Evaluating a child's best interests involves welfare appraisal in the widest sense, taking into account, where appropriate, a wide range of ethical, social, moral, religious, cultural, emotional and welfare conditions. Everything that conduces to a child's welfare and happiness or relates to the child's development and present and future life as a human being, including the child's familial, education and social environment, and the child's social, cultural, ethnic and religious community, is potentially relevant and has, where appropriate, to be taken into account.'[3]

6.08 The CA 1989 requires that a child's welfare is the paramount consideration when determining any question in respect of the upbringing of the child or the administration of the child's property or application of any income.[4] This requirement is often termed the 'paramountcy principle' and means that a child's holistic welfare must be the priority in all decisions made concerning that child. Whilst the CA 1989 sets down that the paramountcy principle must apply to all decisions made by the court, welfare must also be at the forefront of decisions made by local authorities in respect of children living in its area, including decisions about what support is needed and whether to initiate court proceedings.

IDENTIFYING CHILDREN AND FAMILIES

6.09 A local authority's first challenge in securing the welfare or well-being of children in its area is identifying who requires support or intervention. Some children and families may come to the attention of a local authority by a formal referral being made to children's services. A referral can be made by any person who is involved with or aware of the child's circumstances and who has concerns about the child's safety or believes that local authority support may be required. The Working Together to Safeguard Children 2023 guidance produced by the government encourages all agencies involved with children to have procedures in place to allow them to identify children who need support and provide swift referrals to local authority children's services who can then investigate the concerns.[5]

6.10 A multi-agency approach should be adopted to identify children and families who need the support or services of a local authority. The framework brought in by the Children Act 2004 (CA 2004) served to facilitate local authorities working closely with other bodies and agencies in their area to secure the welfare and well-being of children. The CA 2004 requires local authorities in England to work collaboratively with other bodies with a view to improving the well-being of children. Specifically, the aime is to improve their physical and mental health; emotional well-being; protection from harm and neglect; education, training and recreation; the contribution made by them to society, and their social and economic

---

2 *Re McGrath (Infants)* [1893] 1 Ch 143, 148.

3 *Re G (Children)* [2012] EWCA Civ 1233.

4 CA 1989, s 1.

5 HM Government, *Working Together to Safeguard Children*, December 2023.

wellbeing.[6] This extends to local authorities in Wales who are required to cooperate with their relevant partners to improve the well-being of children including the quality of care and support provided to children in each local authority's area, and to protect children who are experiencing or are at risk of abuse, neglect or other kinds of harm as defined in the CA 1989.[7]

6.11 In England, local authorities must work alongside their safeguarding partners and relevant agencies to promote and safeguard the welfare of children in their area.[8] A safeguarding partner to a local authority in England is the local Integrated Care Board (ICB) and local police. The organisations which are considered to be 'relevant agencies' are set out within the Child Safeguarding Practice Review and Relevant Agency (England) Regulations 2018. They include education providers, NHS bodies and health services, CAFCASS (the Children and Family Court Advisory and Support Service) and youth offending teams.[9] In Wales, relevant partners of a local authority also include local police, youth offending teams, health boards and NHS trusts. In practice, this requires a children's services team to have a framework in place for liaison with other public bodies to ensure that children who need support are identified quickly and referred to the local authority for the appropriate intervention. Families may also self-refer to the local authority to request an assessment for support under the CA 1989, s 17 and the SSWWA 2014, s 21.

6.12 There are also children, either born within or who move into a local authority's area, who require support or safeguarding but formal referrals to the local authority are not made and so the child is not brought to the attention of children's services. This may occur because the child is not visible to professionals, such as teachers or doctors, who may raise a referral with the local authority. In order to prevent children who need support flying under a local authority's radar, the statutory framework is extended to include duties upon local authorities themselves to work to identify children and families who need their support, rather than being reliant on referrals alone. The CA 1989, Sch 2 provides that every local authority in England shall take reasonable steps to identify the extent to which there are 'children in need' within its area. In Wales, the principle of identifying children who need support is encapsulated in s 21 of the SSWWA 2014 which requires a local authority to assess a child's need for care and support when it appears to a local authority that the child may need care and support.

6.13 Local authorities also have duties to conduct investigations into a child's circumstances when they are directed to do so by the Family Court, pursuant to the CA 1989, s 37. A judge may direct this type of investigation when the court is determining a question concerning the child's welfare and the court considers it may be appropriate for an order to be made in favour of the local authority. The CA 1989, s 47 places a further duty on local authorities to conduct investigations into a child's welfare when they are informed that a child in their area is subject to an emergency

---

6 CA 2004, s 10.

7 CA 2004, s 25.

8 CA 2004, s 16E.

9 The Child Safeguarding Practice Review and Relevant Agency (England) Regulations 2018, Sch.

protection order or is in police protection, or when a local authority has reasonable cause to suspect that a child in its area has suffered significant harm or is likely to do so. These are all other routes by which a local authority may identify a child or family in its area who requires support.

6.14 The collection of these statutory provisions place clear duties on local authorities to the children and families living in its area. Local authorities must work collaboratively with other bodies to identify children living within its area who are in need of support. Once those children and families have been identified, the work of children's services must then move to consider what support a family or child may need.

LOCAL AUTHORITY INTERVENTION

6.15 In order to determine the correct level of support and intervention for a child, local authorities must assess the circumstances of the child as a whole, including their individual needs. There are different types of assessments that can be undertaken depending on the type of referral made to the local authority and the concerns which are raised. This includes education-focussed assessments, social care assessments and child protection assessments. This section will consider the assessments that are undertaken by local authorities and the support or intervention which may flow from that.

Education needs

6.16 When children have or may have additional needs in respect of their education, health and social care, the parents, the child or their school may request an assessment by the local authority to determine if the child is eligible for special support.[10] This is referred to in England as an 'EHC needs assessment'. It often takes place for children with special educational needs (including potential special educational needs), learning difficulties or a learning disability. An EHC needs assessment determines whether the child has any needs which require an Education, Health and Care Plan (EHCP) to be implemented to meet those needs. EHCPs are used to ensure children with special educational needs are provided the right support to engage successfully in education, and that their health and social care needs connected to their special educational needs are identified and met.[11] Special education needs are defined within the Children and Families Act 2014 (CFA 2014) as being a learning difficulty or disability which calls for special educational provision to be made.[12] A learning difficulty or disability is established when a child of school age or a young person has significantly greater difficulty in learning than the majority of others of the same age, or has a disability which prevents or hinders them from making use of facilities of a kind generally provided for others of the

---

10 CFA 2014, s 36.
11 CFA 2014, s 37.
12 CFA 2014, s 20.

same age in schools. Once an EHCP is in place for a child, a local authority must ensure any specified special education provision is secured and that any appropriate health care provision specified is also arranged.[13]

6.17 In Wales, this area of assessment and planning for children is encapsulated within the Individual Development Plan (IDP). The IDP is governed by the statutory framework of the Additional Learning Needs and Education Tribunal (Wales) Act 2018 (ALNETWA 2018). The ALNETWA 2018 defines a person, including children, as having additional learning needs if they have a learning difficulty or disability which requires additional learning provision.[14] A child is considered to have a learning difficulty or disability if they have a significantly greater difficulty in learning than the majority of others of the same age, or have a disability for the purposes of the Equality Act 2010 which prevents or hinders them from making use of facilities for education or training of a kind generally provided for others of the same age.[15] An IDP is implemented when a local authority establishes that a child has additional learning needs and the circumstances do not fall within the exemptions set out within the ALNETWA 2018, s 12(2). An IDP will set out the additional learning provision required for the child, imposing a duty upon the relevant local authority to secure that provision.[16]

Disabled children

6.18 The statutory duties and guidance set out in this chapter apply to disabled children equally as they do to children without disabilities. Disabled children are, by virtue of their disability, children in need in England.[17] There are further provisions made within statute and guidance to ensure that a disabled child's needs are met and that the support they receive is reflective of their level of need. The United Nations Convention on the Rights of Persons with Disabilities provides an overarching framework in which national legislation falls. Article 7 of the Convention requires all necessary measures to be taken by signatories to ensure the full enjoyment by children with disabilities of all human rights and fundamental freedoms on an equal basis with other children. It goes on to set down that the best interests of the child shall be the primary consideration when any action is taken regarding a child with disabilities. In a similar vein, the United Nations Convention on the Rights of the Child protects disabled children against discrimination on the grounds of their disability, prescribing that the rights within that Convention apply equally to disabled and non-disabled children.[18]

6.19 Every local authority in England must exercise its functions with a view to identifying and keeping a register of all children in its area who have a

---

13 CFA 2014, s 42.
14 Additional Learning Needs and Education Tribunal (Wales) Act 2018, s 2.
15 Additional Learning Needs and Education Tribunal (Wales) Act 2018, s 2.
16 Additional Learning Needs and Education Tribunal (Wales) Act 2018, s 14.
17 CA 1989, s 17(10).
18 The United Nations, *The Convention on the Rights of the Child,* Article 2.

disability.[19] The CA 1989, Sch 2, Pt 1 also requires local authorities in England to provide services which are designed to minimise the effect on disabled children of their disabilities; to give disabled children the opportunity to lead lives which are as normal as possible, and to assist those providing care for disabled children by giving them breaks from caring.[20] Local authorities in England must also ensure that disabled children in receipt of services must be informed of any other services which are provided by the local authority relevant to their needs.[21] The Chronically Sick and Disabled Persons Act 1970 further requires local authorities in England to make arrangements necessary to meet the needs of the disabled child living in their area. This includes providing practical assistance at home; the provision of, or assistance in obtaining, recreational facilities; assistance in arranging travel for the purposes of obtaining support; providing or assisting in adapting the home to secure the safety, comfort or convenience of the child, and facilitating holidays.[22] The provision of education, training and social care services must be kept under review to ensure its suitability to meet the needs of disabled children in a local authority's area.[23]

6.20 A child in Wales is considered to be disabled if they have a disability for the purposes of the Equality Act 2010.[24] In Wales, a local authority's duty to assess the needs of a child is enhanced in respect of disabled children. The local authorities are to presume that a disabled child needs care and support in addition to, or instead of, the care and support provided by their family.[25] This therefore triggers a needs assessment for disabled children in Wales, which will identify the specific support they require.

6.21 The Community Care, Services for Carers and Children's Services (Direct Payments) (England) Regulations 2009 is designed to support those caring for children with disabilities. It includes provision for direct payments from local authorities in England in order to purchase services for a child with disabilities directly, rather than relying upon a local authority to mediate the provision. Whilst there are some limits on the use of direct payments, they may be used to purchase services which are identified to assist a disabled child. The SSWWA 2014, s 51 also provides for direct payments to be arranged by local authorities in Wales in order to meet the needs of an eligible child. The applicable regulations in Wales for the use of direct payments are the Care and Support (Direct Payments) (Wales) Regulations 2015.

Social care needs

6.22 Alongside special educational provision and support tailored for disabled children, local authorities also work with children and families to ensure that

19 CFA 2014, s 22; The CA 1989, Sch 2, para 2.
20 CA 1989, Sch 2, para 6.
21 Chronically Sick and Disabled Persons Act 1970, s 1.
22 Chronically Sick and Disabled Persons Act 1970, s 2.
23 CFA 2014, s 27.
24 SSWWA 2014, s 3.
25 SSWWA 2014, s 21(7).

children's holistic social care needs are met throughout their childhood. Social care needs include education, housing, parenting, stimulation, protection from harm and development. Local authorities can identify what social care needs a child or family has by undertaking an assessment of them. This assessment should consider the child's circumstances as a whole and the child's wishes themselves.[26] In England, this form of assessment is often referred to as a 'section 17 assessment' in reference to that provision of the CA 1989. It requires a local authority to consider what the child's support needs are, whether the child meets the criteria to be considered a 'child in need' and to then ascertain what types of support may be suitable for the child. The criteria for a 'child in need' and what this means is discussed in detail later in this chapter. In Wales, the equivalent provision requiring an assessment of the child's circumstances in order to identify the right support is contained within the SSWWA 2014, s 21. The following sections explore the different types of local authority support and intervention that may be provided to meet a child's social care needs.

Early help

6.23 The first category of local authority involvement is 'early help'. This title is used to describe services provided to children and families who have a low level of need, not reaching the threshold to be considered 'children in need', but who nonetheless require local authority support. Local authorities are not under a statutory duty to provide early help services for families, but these services can play a pivotal role in assisting families before their circumstances develop and require more formal and intensive support. The Working Together to Safeguard Children guidance, published by the government in 2018 and updated in 2023, describes early help services as an effective avenue to promote the welfare of children before a situation deteriorates.[27] The guidance defines this type of support as being for children of all ages. It aims to improve a family's resilience and outcomes or reduce the chance of a problem getting worse. Early help is designed to be a system of support, rather than one specific service, which can include education and health services. The process of providing early help services should involve the identification at an early stage of children and families who would benefit from it by undertaking an assessment of their need for help; ensuring communication and regular meetings throughout the process; and coordinating a plan of support to improve outcomes for the child and family.

6.24 Early help support may take the form of assistance with education, housing, health including mental health, and criminal offending. It encompasses a wide range of services including community support work and advisory schemes. The Department for Levelling Up, Housing and Communities and the Department for Education have produced an 'Early Help System Guide' which identifies the target

---

26 CA 1989, ss 17 and 47; SSWWA 2014, s 21.

27 HM Government, *Working Together to Safeguard Children*, July 2018, p 16; HM Government, *Working Together to Safeguard Children*, December 2023, p 118.

aims of early help services and what they may include.[28] The guide makes clear that early help services are designed to be collaborative and multi-agency, drawing upon support from a range of professionals in different areas to provide the right package of support for each family. These services work with children and families by consent and are not imposed upon them.

Children in need or with identified needs

6.25 A local authority assessment may identify that early help support is not sufficient for a child or young person because their needs are greater. This often occurs when a local authority's assessment in England identifies that a child meets the criteria to be considered a 'child in need', under the CA 1989, s 17. A child who is considered to be 'in need' for the purposes of the CA 1989 is any child who is unlikely to achieve or maintain a reasonable level of health or development, or whose health and development is likely to be significantly or further impaired, without the provision of services, or a child who is disabled.[29] A disabled child for the purposes of the CA 1989 is a child who is blind, deaf, dumb or suffers from a mental disorder of any kind or is substantially and permanently handicapped by illness, injury or congenital deformity or such other disability as may be prescribed. A child in need under the CA 1989 includes children with special educational needs, young carers, children who have committed criminal offences and asylum seeking children. The scope of the CA 1989 is purposefully broad to ensure children who may need different types of support are not missed out.

6.26 When children are identified as being in need, or as having eligible care and support needs, local authorities are under a duty to take steps to meet those needs. In England, this duty is contained within the CA 1989, s 17. It is a broad duty which requires local authorities to safeguard and promote the welfare of children identified as being in need. They are required to promote the upbringing of those children within their families where that is consistent with the child's welfare.

6.27 In Wales, the CA 1989 definition of a 'child in need' under s 17 does not apply, but a child who is in need of local authority support is identified by an assessment under the SSWWA 2014, s 21. The SSWWA 2014, s 37 requires local authorities in Wales to meet the child's identified needs if the child is living in the local authority's area and meets the eligibility criteria or the intervention is required to protect the child from abuse, neglect or other harm or a risk of abuse, neglect or harm. The eligibility criteria referred to in the SSWWA 2014 is set out within the Care and Support (Eligibility) (Wales) Regulations 2015. Regulation 4 dictates that a need meets the eligibility criteria if it falls within the following: it arises from the child's physical or mental ill-health, age, disability, dependence on alcohol or drugs or similar; or, the need is one that if unmet is likely to have an adverse effect on the child's development. In order to be eligible, the need must relate to: the ability to carry out self-care or domestic routines; the ability to communicate;

---

28 HM Government, *Supporting Families: Early help system guide,* April 2022.

29 CA 1989, s 17.

protection from abuse or neglect; involvement in work, education, learning or leisure activities; maintenance or development of family or other significant personal relationships; development and maintenance of social relationships and involvement in the community; or, achieving developmental goals. The identified need must be unmet by the child, their parents, the support of others and community services, and the child must be deemed to be unlikely to achieve one or more of their personal outcomes without local authority support. When considering the needs of the child, local authorities in Wales must assess the developmental needs of the child and identify the appropriate outcomes for the child by the provision of support services.[30]

6.28 Determining whether or not a child is 'in need' or that the criteria of the SSWWA 2014, s 37 is met is at the discretion of the local authority and is determined by a social work assessment of the child and family. In England, the duty to conduct an assessment of whether a child is 'in need' is triggered when a local authority receives information that a child may be in need, no matter how vague that information is.[31] The Department of Health has published a Framework for the Assessment of Children in Need and their Families giving guidance as to how to assess a child and their family who may be in need.[32] The framework places at the centre of the assessment the child being safeguarded and their welfare promoted. Other factors which should be considered are the child's basic care provision, the stimulation and stability they experience, their education, development and relationships alongside environmental factors such as housing, community resources and household income.

6.29 Once the scope and intensity of a child's needs are identified, the focus then turns to how to meet those needs. Appropriate provision must be made by local authorities for children in need who remain living with their family to access advice, guidance and counselling related to their social care needs alongside opportunities for occupational, social, cultural and recreational activities. Local authorities must also have available to children in need assistance in managing home life, facilities for and assistance with travel in order to access services, and to enable the child and their family to have a holiday.[33] Information about the services available to children in need should be published and accessible to those who may benefit from them.[34]

6.30 Meeting the needs of these children is achieved by devising a child in need plan in England. A child in need plan is a document created by the local authority's social work team which identifies the needs of the relevant child and the plan to meet those needs. It should be created in conjunction with the child's parents or people with parental responsibility for the child and other key agencies which are involved with the child, including education and health services.[35] The process often begins with a child in need meeting at which discussions are held about what the identified needs are and what the relevant available services may be. The plan and its

30 SSWWA 2014, s 21(4).

31 *R v LB Lewisham ex parte MM* [2009] EWHC 416 (Admin).

32 The Department of Health, *Framework for the Assessment of Children in Need and their Families*, 2000.

33 CA 1989, Sch 2, part 1, para 8.

34 CA 1989, Sch 2, part 1, para 1.

35 HM Government, *Working Together to Safeguard Children*, December 2023.

aims should be specific to the relevant child, including goals which are achievable for the child and their family and realistic strategies which can be implemented to address any identified concerns. Timescales are also usually found within child in need plans, providing a structure for the work proposed and junctures at which it will be reviewed. A report published in March 2024 by the Children's Commissioner confirms that 12 months prior, in England, 106,000 children were on child in need plans.[36]

6.31 In Wales, local authorities are under a duty to assess the needs of children in their area when it appears to them that a child may need care and support in addition to, or instead of, that which is being provided by their family.[37] When a need has been identified and is considered eligible under the Care and Support (Eligibility) (Wales) Regulations 2015, the SSWWA 2014, s 37 places a duty on local authorities in Wales to meet that need by the provision of care and support. That duty also arises for needs which fall outside of the eligibility criteria but a local authority considers it necessary to meet that need to protect the child from abuse, neglect or harm or a risk of abuse, neglect or harm. The SSWWA 2014 requires a care and support plan or support plan to be devised when an eligible need is identified for a child.[38] This process and the related regulations are adopted in a similar way to that of child in need planning in England.

Child protection

6.32 During the child in need process in England, and the process of identifying needs in Wales, some concerns may be identified which present a more significant safeguarding risk to the child. These are risks which would lead a local authority to have reasonable cause to suspect that a child who lives, or is found, in its area is suffering or is likely to suffer significant harm. This triggers child protection planning and considerations of a local authority's duty to investigate under the CA 1989, s 47. The CA 1989, s 47 requires a local authority to make such enquiries as are necessary to allow a decision to be made on what action, if any, needs to be taken to safeguard or promote the welfare of a child for whom there are child protection concerns. It also brings into play a local authority in England's duty to take reasonable steps to prevent children in their area suffering ill-treatment or neglect.[39]

6.33 Significant harm is not itself defined within the CA 1989, but harm is. At s 31(9), the CA 1989 defines harm as being ill-treatment or impairment of health or development including, for example, impairment suffered from seeing or hearing the ill-treatment of another. Development is defined as physical, intellectual, emotional, social or behavioural development. Health means physical or mental health and ill-treatment includes sexual abuse and forms of ill-treatment which are not physical. Where a child's health or development is concerned, the question of whether

---

36 Children's Commissioner, *Children on child in need plans*, March 2024.

37 SSWWA 2014, s 21.

38 SSWWA 2014, s 54.

39 CA 1989, Sch 2, Part 1, para 4.

the harm suffered is significant is assessed by comparing the child's health or development with that which could reasonably be expected of a similar child.[40] The meaning of 'significant' has been discussed at length within case law, with a helpful definition being provided by Lady Hale, in a 2013 Supreme Court judgment which reads: 'Significant harm is harm which is "considerable, noteworthy or important". The court should identify why and in what respects the harm is significant. Again, this may be particularly important where the harm in question is the impairment of intellectual, emotional, social or behavioural development which has not yet happened'.[41]

6.34 The Working Together to Safeguard Children Guidance 2023 recommends that practitioners assessing the presence or likelihood of significant harm consider the following: the severity, duration and frequency of any abuse; the degree of threat, coercion or cruelty; the significance of others in the child's world including all adults and children in contact with the child; and, the cumulative impact of adverse events.[42]

6.35 When a local authority has reasonable cause to suspect the presence or likelihood of such harm to a child, its duties to investigate under the CA 1989, s 47 are triggered. This duty is also triggered when a local authority is informed that a child in its area is the subject of an emergency protection order or is in police protection. Once the investigative process begins, it must include steps being taken to access the child unless sufficient information can be obtained from other avenues.[43] A local authority's enquiries will also include liaison with other professionals involved with the child and family, similar to the process of assessing the needs of a child. There are duties upon other relevant organisations, including the NHS, to cooperate with enquiries made by a local authority under section 47 of the CA 1989 unless unreasonable to do so.[44] Strategy discussions should be convened between the local authority, the police, health services and any other relevant bodies to identify and share information about any child protection concerns.

6.36 Once a local authority has concluded its investigation under the CA 1989, s 47, it must make a decision about what, if any, action must be taken to safeguard the child and promote their welfare. If the investigation concludes that action must be taken, the local authority has a duty to take that action so far as is practicable and not simply walk away.[45] The action identified as necessary by a local authority is often reduced into a child protection plan. This plan is, similarly to a child in need plan, devised on a multi-agency approach working alongside all relevant bodies involved with the child. Child protection plans should be specific, achievable and relevant to the significant harm or likelihood of significant harm identified and the context in which it is occurring or likely to occur. The aim of all child protection plans is to ensure the child is safe from harm, to promote their health and development,

40 CA 1989, s 31(10).
41 *Re B (A Child)* [2013] UKSC 33.
42 HM Government, *Working Together to Safeguard Children*, December 2023, p 82.
43 CA 1989, s 47(4).
44 CA 1989, s 47(9)-(11).
45 CA 1989, s 47(8).

to support the family and to set out the support and resources available to them.[46] A child protection conference should also be arranged as part of the overarching process, to discuss what the concerns are and explore how the plan is capable of addressing the issues for the child. The Working Together to Safeguard Children Guidance recommends that parents are involved in the child protection planning process as much as is possible to allow their engagement with the strategies to be implemented.[47]

6.37 If a child protection plan is successful, it can be stepped-down to a child in need plan, or discharged. The process of stepping-down to a child in need plan generally reduces the level of local authority involvement and is reflective of a child having identified support needs but no longer being considered to be suffering or likely to suffer significant harm. All plans in place for children should be regularly reviewed to ensure they remain appropriate and achievable, and to give consideration to whether the plan should be stepped-down or discharged. When a plan is not successful following the child protection process, and the presence or likelihood of significant harm remains, the local authority must consider whether or not to initiate the pre-proceedings process. This process is described in the Working Together to Safeguard Children Guidance as a final opportunity for parents to avoid care proceedings.[48]

6.38 Specific guidance has been issued in respect of the pre-proceedings process which accompanies the Public Law Outline (PLO) implemented by the Ministry of Justice as a framework to be adopted by local authorities in advance of and during care proceedings.[49] The process of care proceedings will be explored later; however, the PLO and accompanying guidance also discuss what should happen before an application is made to court, when child protection work has not been successful in securing the child's welfare. The aim of the pre-proceedings process is to bring about positive change for the child and secure their welfare without an application to court. The PLO in particular sets out its aims as assisting families to make necessary changes and avoid court proceedings; to create better-informed resolutions by ensuring all safe and appropriate alternatives to court proceedings are explored; to prepare for proceedings, and to improve the management of proceedings and working relationships.

6.39 The pre-proceedings process includes specific expectations of local authorities in furtherance of their overall duty to promote the welfare of children in their area. This includes an emphasis on the involvement of a child's family and ensuring they are supported to engage with the local authority's processes. For some parents, this may include bringing in advocacy services who can support parents who struggle to understand the local authority's concerns and the complexity of their work by virtue of their own needs or difficulties.[50] The Department for Education

---

46 HM Government, *Working Together to Safeguard Children*, December 2023, p 96.

47 HM Government, *Working Together to Safeguard Children*, December 2023, p 83.

48 HM Government, *Working Together to Safeguard Children*, December 2023, p 101.

49 Department for Education, *Court Orders and Pre-Proceedings for Local Authorities*, April 2014.

50 Department for Education, *Court Orders and Pre-Proceedings for Local Authorities*, April 2014, p 15.

guidance also encourages the use of family group conferences prior to proceedings to ensure the wider family is aware of the child's circumstances and their support can be drawn upon if appropriate. The process should ensure that all necessary assessments are undertaken before a decision is made to issue court proceedings and that all available and appropriate support is attempted with a family before court intervention is sought. The PLO process can be successful in bringing families together with the local authority to address the concerns about the child's welfare. In those instances, the PLO process would not lead to court proceedings being issued. However, if the pre-proceedings process does not adequately address the identified concerns, it will progress to the issuing of court proceedings which is considered further below.

6.40 Best practice guidance in respect of the pre-proceedings process has most recently been issued by the Public Law Working Group in March 2021. The importance of the process was reiterated by the President of the Family Division in his 're-launch of the Public Law Outline' guidance given in January 2023.[51] The President emphasised the need for robust and thorough assessments to be undertaken before court proceedings are issued in respect of a child. This ensures the support that a child and family need is properly explored before any steps are taken to bring the matter to court, and it helps to reduce the length of time a child is subject to court proceedings. The Public Law Working Group's guidance stresses that court proceedings should only be issued as a last resort, and that the pre-proceedings process is an opportunity to work closely with families to negate the need to issue proceedings. The safety of the child should be at the forefront of decisions made during the child protection and pre-proceedings processes.

Children looked after

6.41 Children who require accommodation to be provided by a local authority and are so accommodated are considered 'children looked after' (previously 'looked after children'). This term is defined in the CA 1989, s 22, and the SSWWA 2014, s 74 as any child who is in the care of the local authority or provided with accommodation by the local authority for a continuous period of more than 24 hours.

6.42 There are a number of ways in which a child may become 'looked after'. This may happen when a child is placed in the local authority's care by their parents, by a court order, or by the protective powers of the police. When a child is relinquished by their parents and placed in local authority care with their consent, this is termed a 'section 20' arrangement in reference to that provision of the CA 1989. Alternatively, the Family Court may make an order which grants parental responsibility to a local authority and endorses a plan for the child to be removed from the care of their parents and to live in arrangements made by the local authority. Practitioners often refer to this as 'removal' from family care and into local authority

---

[51] Public Law Working Group, *Recommendations to achieve best practice in the child protection and family justice systems,* March 2021; HM Courts and Tribunals Service, *Re-Launch of the Public Law Outline,* January 2023.

accommodation. The process of the Family Court in this respect will be considered later in this chapter.

6.43 It is important to note that children will also be considered 'looked after' if they are provided with respite care or 'short breaks' under the CA 1989, as this arrangement meets the definition under the CA 1989, s 22, and the SSWWA 2014, s 74, even if it is not permanent. Children who are provided with accommodation by a local authority's housing department but who are not known to children's services will not be considered looked after children even if that is a long-term arrangement.[52]

6.44 There may also be instances in which children are living within residential schools but are still considered to be 'looked after', triggering the local authority's applicable duties.[53] This is due to the wide span of the duties contained within the CA 1989 Act, to consider the holistic needs of children, which includes their educational needs. A placement in a school for a child with holistic care and support needs is not necessarily a placement governed by the Education Act 1996. Consideration must be given to whether that placement in fact forms part of the local authority's duties under the CA 1989 and therefore opens the child up to the further support available for children looked after by a local authority.

6.45 The court has provided guidance on what needs to be considered when determining if a child is 'looked after' in England.[54] Mr Justice MacDonald set out the following relevant questions:

> 'i) In determining whether a child was or is "looked after" for the purposes of the CA 1989 the court must consider the following questions asked by s.20(1) of the Act:
>
> a) Is the child "a child in need"?
>
> b) Is the child in the relevant local authority's area?
>
> c) Does the child appear to the local authority to require accommodation by reason of:
>
> A: there being no person who has parental responsibility for him or her;
>
> B: he or she being lost or having been abandoned;
>
> C: the person who has been caring for him or her being prevented (whether or not permanently, and for whatever reason) from providing him with suitable accommodation or care.
>
> ii) The words "for whatever reason" in s.20(1)(c) indicate that the widest possible scope must be given to the term 'prevented' in order to ensure children do not suffer for the shortcomings of their parents or carers. The guiding principle is the need to safeguard and promote the child's welfare.
>
> iii) The duty under s.20(1) arises as soon as it appears to the local authority that the child requires accommodation for one of the reasons specified in s.20(1). Within

52 *R (M) v Hammersmith and Fulham London Borough Council* [2008] UKHL 14.

53 *R(O) v East Riding of Yorkshire Council* [2011] EWCA Civ 196.

54 *Salford City Council v W* [2021] EWHC 1689 (Fam).

this context, the duty under s.20(1) can arise prior to any steps having been taken to accommodate the child.

iv) Once a duty under s.20(1) has arisen, the child is being "looked after" by the local authority for the purposes of the CA 1989.

v) Once the duty under s.20(1) has arisen the obligation on the local authority to provide accommodation for a looked after child is a mandatory one and the authority must take steps to ensure that accommodation is provided in accordance with s.22C of the CA 1989. Once it has arisen, the duty under s.20(1) cannot be sidestepped or finessed away by reliance on the general duty under s.17 of the Act.

vi) In circumstances where the duty under s.20(1) can arise prior to any steps having been taken to accommodate the child and where, pursuant to s.22C(5) and (6) the local authority must consider for a looked after child a placement with a relative or friend, an offer or action by a relative or friend to care for the child after the duty has arisen will not prevent the child being "looked after" for the purposes of the CA 1989.

vii) Whether and when the duty under s.20(1) has arisen is a question of fact to be answered having regard to all the circumstances of the case.

viii) A distinction can be drawn between a child who does not have a home to go to, and a child who has a home to go to, whether of his or her own or with family or friends, but who requires assistance getting to or into that accommodation.

ix) Where a local authority takes a major role in making arrangements for a child to be accommodated, it is more likely to be concluded that, in doing so, it is exercising its powers and duties as a public authority pursuant to s.20(1).

x) If the local authority is facilitating a private arrangement, it must make it plain to the proposed foster parent that she or he must look to the parents or person with parental responsibility for financial support. If such matters are left unclear, the court may conclude that the local authority was acting under its statutory powers and duties and that the arrangement was not a private one at all.

xi) Whilst the absence of compliance with the proper formalities applicable to the provision of accommodation pursuant to s.20(1) of the CA 1989 may point away from the duty under that section having arisen, the absence of compliance does not prevent the court from concluding that the child is nonetheless accommodated under s.20(1) of the 1989 Act.'

6.46 The duty is as set out at i) c) of the above quote and for children who fall within that criteria, a local authority must provide accommodation. A parallel provision is made for local authorities in Wales under the SSWWA 2014, Pt 6. The sections within that Part place a duty on local authorities to take steps as far as is reasonably practicable to provide children with accommodation which meets their needs when those children are in the local authority's care, and when circumstances arise which mean it would be consistent with the child's well-being to be provided with accommodation in the authority's area.[55]

[55] SSWWA 2014, ss 75 – 77, s 79 and s 81.

6.47 The duty to provide accommodation in England includes at the CA 1989, s 20(3) that a local authority shall also provide accommodation for any child in need who has reached the age of 16 and whose welfare is likely to be seriously prejudiced if accommodation is not provided.[56] In addition, a local authority may decide to provide accommodation for any child within its area if the local authority considers that to do so would promote the child's welfare, although it is not mandatory.[57]

6.48 There are also categories of children in England who are not considered children in need but for whom a local authority is under a duty to provide accommodation. This includes children in police protection when a local authority is requested to accommodate them; children who are arrested and a custody officer makes arrangements for local authority accommodation, or children who have been remanded to local authority accommodation awaiting trial or sentence for a criminal offence.[58] A local authority is not absolved of its duty to provide accommodation in circumstances where other authorities or bodies may be able to assist in providing the accommodation.[59] The duty to provide accommodation under the CA 1989, s 20 ends when a child arrangements order is made setting out where the child is to live and granting parental responsibility to that person or people.[60]

6.49 There is no limit on the duration for which a child may be accommodated by a local authority in England.[61] Under the provisions of the CA 1989, s 20 and the SSWWA 2014, s 76, a person with parental responsibility may remove the child from local authority accommodation at any time, provided the child is not subsequently placed there pursuant to a court order.[62] A person with parental responsibility may not remove a young person from local authority accommodation if that young person agrees to being provided with accommodation under the CA 1989, s 20.[63] Local authorities must consider whether the provision of accommodation is meeting the child's long-term welfare needs, and if so, the accommodation may be maintained for a longer than short-term period without court order, provided it is subject to regular review.[64]

6.50 When obtaining a parent's consent to a child being accommodated by the local authority, the court has provided guidance on what would amount to good practice by a local authority. Sir James Munby P held that good practice includes:

(a) Wherever possible, parental agreement to accommodation under the CA 1989, s 20 must be properly recorded and evidenced by the parent's signature;

---

56 CA 1989, s 20(3).

57 CA 1989, s 20(4).

58 CA 1989, ss 21 and 46; Police and Criminal Evidence Act 1984, s 38(6) as amended by CA 1989, Sch 13, para 53; Children and Young Persons Act 1969, s 23 and CA 1989 s 21; SSWWA 2014, s 77.

59 *R (G) v London Borough of Southwark* [2009] UKHL 26.

60 *GC v LC and Others* [2009] EWHC 1942 (Fam); *Re B (Looked After Child)* [2013] EWCA Civ 964.

61 *Williams v Hackney LBC* [2018] UKSC 37.

62 *Re S and W (s.20 Accommodation)* [2023] EWCA Civ 1.

63 CA 1989, s 20(11).

64 *Williams v Hackney LBC* [2018] UKSC 37; *Re S and W (s.20 Accommodation)* [2023] EWCA Civ 1.

(b) The written document should be clear and precise, using simple and straightforward language;

(c) The document should include that the parent can remove the child from local authority accommodation at any time;

(d) The document should not seek to impose any restraints on the exercise of a parent's rights under the CA 1989, s 20(8); and

(e) The document should be translated into the parent's first language when required.[65]

6.51 The above paragraphs explore the ways in which a child may be considered 'looked after' and what the duties of local authorities are to provide accommodation to children within its area. Before a local authority provides accommodation to a child pursuant to its duties, it must first, as far as is possible and consistent with the child's welfare, ascertain the child's wishes and feelings about being provided with local authority accommodation, and give consideration to those wishes.[66]

6.52 For children who are 'looked after', local authorities have specific additional duties to safeguard them and promote their welfare.[67] The duty to promote the welfare of the child includes promoting their educational achievement. When making any arrangements for the placement of a child who a local authority proposes to look after, the Care Planning, Placement and Case Review (England) Regulations 2010 (CPPCER 2010) are applicable in England, and in Wales, the Placement of Children (Wales) Regulations 2007 (PCWR 2007) and the Care and Support (Care Planning) (Wales) Regulations 2015 (CSCPWR 2015) apply.

6.53 The CPPCER 2010 requires local authorities to prepare a care plan for children which is aimed at promoting their welfare.[68] The SSWWA 2014 also requires care plans to be prepared for children in Wales with eligible needs which are to be met by the local authority (whether they are looked after or not).[69] Care plans are designed to identify the background and experience of the child and set out the ways in which their holistic needs will be met.[70] Care plans should be agreed, where possible, with the parent or any person with parental responsibility, and with the child if they are over 16.[71]

6.54 Once a duty to provide accommodation has been established, there are different types of accommodation in which a child may be placed. The type of accommodation provided to a child should be determined by evaluating the child or young person's welfare needs, and considering which type of accommodation can

---

65 *Re N (Adoption: Jurisdiction)* [2015] EWCA Civ 1112.

66 CA 1989, s 20(6); SSWWA 2014, s 78.

67 CA 1989, s 22(3).

68 Care Planning, Placement and Case Review (England) Regulations 2010, reg 4.

69 SSWWA 2014, s 54 and s 83.

70 Care Planning, Placement and Case Review (England) Regulations 2010, reg 5; Care and Support (Care Planning) (Wales) Regulations 2015, reg 3.

71 Care Planning, Placement and Case Review (England) Regulations 2010, reg 4.

best provide for them. The accommodation should also be near to the child's home, as far as is practicable and consistent with their welfare.[72]

6.55 When a local authority is considering the type of accommodation to be provided to a child or young person, the first consideration must be whether the child can live with their parent or other person with parental responsibility. If that can be arranged and the child's welfare maintained, it should be. However, a child should not be placed with a parent or person with parental responsibility if to do so would not be consistent with the child's welfare or it is not reasonably practical.[73] If a child cannot be placed with a parent or person with parental responsibility, the CA 1989 requires the child to be placed in a placement which is, in the local authority's opinion, the most appropriate placement available. This includes with local authority foster parents, adults who are connected to the child, or in a children's home which is registered as such under the Care Standards Act 2000, Pt 2 or the Regulation and Inspection of Social Care (Wales) Act 2016, Pt 1, for placements in Wales.

6.56 There is further provision within the CA 1989 for children to be placed in 'other arrangements' when required and subject to their compliance with regulations. The placement of a child or young person in 'other arrangements' is governed by the Care Planning, Placement and Case Review (England) Regulations 2010 and the provisions added by the Care Planning, Placement and Case Review (England) (Amendment) Regulations 2021. These regulations prevent the placement of children under 16 in settings which are unregulated, and require a local authority to be satisfied when placing a child or young person in other arrangements that the accommodation is suitable and there is regular oversight. The 2021 Regulations clarify that permissible 'other arrangements' for children under 16 include placement in a care home, hospital, residential family centre, school or an establishment providing care and accommodation for children as a holiday scheme for disabled children.[74] Chapter 7 deals in detail with the different types of placements for children and their governance.

6.57 In Wales, the statutory provisions are similar and are set out within the SSWWA 2014, s 81. Local authorities in Wales must place a child with their parent, a person with parental responsibility or a person with whom a child was previously living under a child arrangements order, unless: to do so would be inconsistent with the child's well-being; it is not reasonably practical, or the local authority is satisfied that the child ought to be placed for adoption and there are suitable arrangements in place. Children in Wales may also be placed in 'other arrangements' for which provisions are made for its assessment and review under the SSWWA 2014, s 82.

6.58 Local authorities in both England and Wales may place children in accommodation which restricts their liberty under the provisions of statute. This type of accommodation is labelled secure accommodation. It is defined as 'any accommodation designed for, or having as its primary purpose, the restriction of

72 CA 1989, section 22C; The Placement of Children (Wales) Regulations 2007, reg 5.

73 CA 1989, s 22C.

74 Care Planning, Placement and Case Review (England) (Amendment) Regulations 2021, reg 4.

liberty'.[75] Secure accommodation under the CA 1989 must be authorised by the court and can only be provided for under the statutory scheme in placements which are approved to provide secure accommodation. Secure accommodation is governed by the CA 1989, s 25 in England and the SSWWA 2014, s 119, in Wales. These statutory provisions permit the use of secure accommodation but place limitations on its use, requiring it not to be used as a routine provision for children looked after by a local authority. There is an essential criteria in the use of secure accommodation, being that the child to be placed in secure accommodation must either have a history of absconding and be likely to abscond from any other accommodation and if absconding, be likely to suffer significant harm, or that the child if kept in any other type of accommodation is likely to injure themselves or others. The criteria which must be satisfied before a secure accommodation order can be granted is explored in more detail in chapter 5.

CHILD PROTECTION PROCEEDINGS

6.59 When the child protection process outside of court is unsuccessful, or an urgent and significant issue arises which requires immediate action, local authorities will turn to the power of the court to assist in securing the welfare of children and young people. Cases involving the deprivation of liberty of a child frequently accompany or follow child protection proceedings under the CA 1989, and they can be either heard together by the same judge or heard alongside one another at linked hearings. Alternatively, the cases may also be kept separate despite relating to the same child if that is considered to be the right approach in the circumstances. This section will provide an overview of child protection proceedings and how they link with deprivation of liberty proceedings under the High Court's inherent jurisdiction.

6.60 The presence of simultaneous care and deprivation of liberty proceedings is often due to the interlinked nature of the issues which require two types of court intervention. When a child requires a regime which amounts to their deprivation of liberty, it can sometimes stem from events which arose in the child protection arena and led to behaviours by the child which require their deprivation of liberty. One example which features in reported judgments and investigative reports alike is of children who suffer abuse during their childhood and as such an application is made to remove them from the care of their parents and place them in local authority accommodation. As those children grow up, they begin to suffer trauma which prompts dysregulated behaviour and can only be managed by a plan which includes restricting their physical liberty. Whilst this is an extreme example of the impact of abuse and childhood experiences, it is one which is regularly seen in deprivation of liberty cases. This example is one instance where a child may be subject to both care proceedings and deprivation of liberty proceedings at the same time or in close proximity.

6.61 Proceedings under the CA 1989 involving a local authority (as the applicant) and concerning the protection of a child or young person, where they live and who

---

75 *Re B (Secure Accommodation)* [2019] EWCA Civ 2025.

cares for them are termed 'care proceedings'. Care proceedings are governed by the CA 1989, applicable case law, and the Family Procedure Rules 2010. The relevant provisions of each will be explored in this section.

6.62 The CA 1989 places a duty on every local authority to take reasonable steps designed to reduce the need to bring care proceedings and proceedings under the inherent jurisdiction in relation to the deprivation of liberty of a child or young person.[76] In practice, this involves identifying families who need support at an early stage and attempting to engage them in the provision of services to address any difficulties they may have before the situation escalates to requiring the intervention of the court. The duties and support provisions set out above in relation to children in need and children looked after are designed in part to achieve this.

6.63 There will, however, be circumstances in which the child in need and pre-proceedings processes are unsuccessful and a child remains suffering or likely to suffer significant harm. If all available avenues of support have been attempted and are unsuccessful, local authorities will turn to the court to seek measures which can secure a child or young person's welfare. In some instances, there may also be unexpected or sudden events which occur and cause the child such significant harm or create a significant likelihood of harm that the court is turned to for immediate safeguarding orders before pre-proceedings work can take place (although these cases with no advance local authority involvement are rare). Care proceedings cover a wide range of issues and can take a number of different courses. This section is not an exhaustive explanation of care proceedings in their entirety, but a helpful guide to the issues which may arise for children who may also become involved in deprivation of liberty proceedings.

6.64 Care proceedings are proceedings in which a local authority has issued an application under the CA 1989, s 31 seeking a care order or a supervision order in respect of a child. A care order is an order which grants parental responsibility to the local authority to act as a corporate parent and make decisions about where the child lives, the contact they have with their parents and other day to day decisions.[77] The parental responsibility granted to a local authority under a care order is enhanced from that which parents or others may have in that a local authority is able to determine the extent to which a person with parental responsibility may meet their responsibility for the child.[78] The scope of parental responsibility is considered further in chapter 4. The effects of a care order are defined in the CA 1989, s 33, and include a duty on a local authority to receive the relevant (or 'subject') child into their care. A supervision order does not grant parental responsibility to a local authority but requires it to advise, assist and befriend the child.[79]

6.65 In order to grant a care order or a supervision order, a court must be satisfied that the circumstances set out within the CA 1989, s 31(2) are met.

76 CA 1989, Sch 2, Part 1, para 7; SSWWA 2014, s 15.

77 CA 1989, s 33; The Children and Social Work Act 2017, s 1.

78 CA 1989, 33(3).

79 CA 1989, section 35(1).

Those circumstances are that the child concerned is suffering or is likely to suffer significant harm, and that the harm or likelihood of harm is attributable to the care given to the child, or likely to be given, if the order were not made not being what it would be reasonable to expect a parent to give, or because the child is beyond the parents' control. This criteria is often called the 'threshold criteria' as it creates a threshold which must be crossed before the court can consider making orders under the CA 1989, Pt 4. Because this criteria, or threshold, is in place, when making an application a local authority will set out for the court why it says the child is suffering or is likely to suffer significant harm if an order were not made, and how that links to the parents' care or the child being beyond parental control. This will be set out by the local authority within a document colloquially termed the 'threshold' document, and it is the role of the local authority during the course of proceedings to establish that the facts relied upon within their threshold document are proven to the requisite standard, on the balance of probabilities.[80]

6.66 Before the proceedings have run their course and all of the evidence required to substantiate the threshold criteria is produced, the court may still make orders on an interim basis. Interim orders can be essential to safeguard children who are at immediate risk of harm and whose safety requires immediate action which can only be sanctioned by the court. This may be, for example, an immediate risk that the child will suffer physical harm if they remain living with their parents. In circumstances like this, a local authority will seek an interim order before it has been able to provide sufficient evidence to prove, or attempt to prove, the facts within its threshold document.

6.67 The court's power to make interim orders is contained within the CA 1989, s 38. Section 38 contains the court's power to make interim orders subject to the court being satisfied that there are reasonable grounds to believe that the criteria as set out in the CA 1989, s 31(2) is met. This requires a judge to be satisfied that at the time protective measures were taken by a local authority, there were reasonable grounds to believe that the subject child was suffering or likely to suffer significant harm attributable to the care being given or likely to be given to them not being what would be reasonable to expect a parent to give, or being beyond parental control. If the court is so satisfied, it may make an interim care or supervision order. Interim care orders also grant parental responsibility to a local authority and allow it to make decisions about where the child lives, but these orders only exist whilst court proceedings are ongoing and there is oversight of a judge. Interim supervision orders similarly place the same duties on a local authority as a supervision order, but only persist within or for the duration of proceedings.

6.68 If, as part of its application, a local authority seeks to remove a child from the care of their parents as a protective measure, this may also be sought as an interim order pending the filing of evidence which will feed into the court's final decision. This application is labelled an application for interim removal or interim separation, and accompanies or follows an application for an interim care order. The law in relation to an interim removal application was summarised most recently within *Re*

80 *Re BR (Proof of Facts)* [2015] EWFC 41; *Re B (Children)* [2008] UKHR 35.

C (A Child: Interim Separation).[81] In this case, the court reiterated the long-standing principle that the interim removal of a child from the care of their parents must only be sanctioned by a court when it is both necessary and proportionate, and when the child's physical safety or psychological or emotional welfare demands it. This must include consideration of whether the length and likely consequences of the separation are a proportionate response to the risks that would arise if the child was not removed. The test, as set down in an earlier judgment concerning the same child, was summarised as being: 'whether the child's safety is at risk and, if so, any removal should be proportionate to the actual risks faced and in the knowledge of alternative arrangements which would not require separation'.[82] Prior to this judgment, the phrase often used in respect of the test for interim removal was set down by Thorpe LJ within *Re H (A Child) (Interim Care Order)*, being that 'separation was only to be contemplated if the child's safety demanded immediate separation'.[83]

6.69 The meaning of 'significant harm' is set out at **6.33** and requires the harm to be considerable, noteworthy or important. Ward LJ provided further description in the context of proceedings in saying: 'the harm must, in my judgment, be significant enough to justify the intervention of the State and disturb the autonomy of the parents to bring up their children by themselves in the way they choose.'[84] When considering the likelihood of harm, the court has defined likely as meaning a real possibility that could not sensibly be ignored having regard to the nature and gravity of the feared harm in the particular case.[85]

6.70 When a local authority issues proceedings and seeks an interim care order, interim supervision order or both an interim care order and interim removal, it must provide to the court a number of documents in support of its application.[86] This includes a chronology of the events relevant to the application, a statement from the social worker providing evidence relating to the application, the assessment undertaken by the local authority which underpins the orders it seeks, and a care plan setting out how it is proposed that the child or young person's welfare needs will be met. These documents are necessary so a judge can undertake an initial evaluation of the child's circumstances and what steps are required on an interim basis, during proceedings, to safeguard the child's welfare and protect them from harm.

6.71 Once an application has been made, it will be listed for an initial hearing. This may be an urgent hearing, listed within a matter of hours or days, if there is an urgent need for a decision to be made by the court to secure the child's safety and welfare. If an urgent hearing is not necessary, an initial case management hearing will be listed 12 to 18 days following the application being issued.[87] At this first hearing, the court will consider whether any interim orders are required to keep the child safe whilst the proceedings are ongoing and before final decisions can be made.

81 *Re C (A Child: Interim Separation)* [2020] EWCA Civ 257.
82 *Re C (A Child: Interim Separation)* [2020] EWCA Civ 257, p 7.
83 *Re H (A Child) (Interim Care Order)* [2003] 1 FCR 350.
84 *Re A (Children) (Care Proceedings: Threshold Criteria)* [2009] EWCA Civ 853.
85 *Re R (A Minor)* [2009] EWCA Civ 942.
86 Family Procedure Rules 2010, PD 12A.
87 Family Procedure Rules 2010, PD12A.

6.72 The first and overarching principle guiding decisions of the Family Court in respect of children and young people is the 'no order' principle.[88] This is set out at the CA 1989, s 1(5) and requires the court to not make any order unless to do so would be better for the child than making no order. This principle is well-established in the Family Court. Judges must always consider whether the child can be safeguarded and their welfare needs met without a court order, and if that can be done then no order should be made. This principle is furthered by the 'least interventionist approach' which also guides the Family Court. The least interventionist approach was summarised in case law within *Re O (Minors) (Care or Supervision Order)* when the court stated:

> 'The question of the children's interests should be approached from the point of view exemplified by s.1(5) of the 1989 Act that, when considering whether to make any order, the court was not to make an order unless it considered that doing so would be better for the child than making no order at all. The court should begin with a preference for the less interventionist rather than the more interventionist approach.'[89]

6.73 The court's approach should be to take the course which constitutes the least state involvement in a child's life that is possible in order to secure their welfare. There are many circumstances in which the court will be required, by virtue of the child's welfare needs, to take very interventionist measures; however, such measures should only be adopted where necessary and proportionate and where there is no alternative that would involve less disruption for the child with the same outcome.

6.74 When making an initial order, a case management order or any final order which involves decisions about the upbringing of the child, the court must have as its paramount consideration the welfare of the child.[90] This is the 'paramountcy principle' and it applies to decisions made by the High Court under its inherent jurisdiction as well as the Family Court in care proceedings. Upbringing in this context includes the care of the child but not their maintenance and financial support.[91] Statute has imposed a list of factors which must be taken into account when the court is considering making, varying or discharging an interim or final care or supervision order. These factors are set out at the CA 1989, s 1(3) which reads:

> '(3) In the circumstances mentioned within subsection (4), a court shall have regard in particular to-
>
> (a) the ascertainable wishes and feelings of the child concerned (considered in light of his age and understanding);
>
> (b) his physical, emotional and educational needs;
>
> (c) the likely effect on him of any change in his circumstances;
>
> (d) his age, sex, background and any characteristics of his which the court considers relevant;
>
> (e) any harm which he has suffered or is at risk of suffering;

---

88 CA 1989, s 1(5).

89 *Re O (Minors) (Care or Supervision Order)* [1997] 2 FCR 17.

90 CA 1989, s 1(1).

91 CA 1989, s 105.

(f) how capable each of his parents, and any other person in relation to whom the court considers the question to be relevant, is of meeting his needs;

(g) the range of powers available to the court under this Act in the proceedings in question.'

6.75 The court must also factor into any decision making the general principle set down in the CA 1989, s 1(2) that any delay in determining the question before the court is likely to prejudice the welfare of the child. This principle applies to ensure that decisions are made promptly for children and young people so they are not 'in limbo' or left lingering within temporary arrangements that do not provide security or longevity. This 'no delay' principle is enshrined within the PLO too which requires proceedings to be determined within 26 weeks from issue.[92] The President of the Family Division sought to reinforce the importance of this principle in his 're-launch of the Public Law Outline' guidance in January 2023.[93] The guidance emphasises the need for proceedings to be focussed, structured and with clear aims in order to progress without unnecessary delay.

6.76 The President of the Family Division's January 2023 guidance also reiterates what the structure of care proceedings should be, as set down within the Family Procedure Rules 2010, PD12A. Proceedings should begin with an initial hearing, where interim orders may be made, followed by focussed case management hearings which are used to make orders gathering the evidence necessary for a final decision. Once the evidence-gathering stage is complete, the court will list the case for an Issues Resolution Hearing (IRH). An IRH is designed to identify the key issues which remain in relation to the child's welfare, to narrow those issues where possible, and to work out how the remaining issues should be dealt with.[94] An IRH may be used as a final hearing if there is sufficient court time and the issues can be appropriately resolved at that stage. When an IRH cannot be used as a final hearing, the court will then list the case for a final hearing at which final orders will be made and the case will conclude. A final hearing may involve hearing oral evidence from witnesses, hearing submissions from lawyers and hearing directly from parties who are not legally represented. It must be noted that although oral evidence is most commonly a feature of final hearings, the court may also require oral evidence at earlier hearings too, when interim issues within proceedings are contested. At a final hearing which involves a dispute between the parties, the judge will deliver a judgment after hearing all of the evidence and hearing from each party. This may be delivered orally during the hearing or in writing after the hearing. The judgment will set out what order, if any, the court makes and the reasons for the same. Once a judgment has been delivered, the parties then have the opportunity to consider the judge's decision and reasons and whether they may seek to appeal that. Appeal processes are complex and are governed by the Family Procedure Rules 2010, Pt 30. This chapter will not deal with the process of appealing a decision of the Family Court.

---

92 Family Procedure Rules 2010, PD12A.

93 HM Courts and Tribunals Service, *Re-Launch of the Public Law Outline,* January 2023.

94 Family Procedure Rules 2010, r 12.25.

6.77 The principles and statutory provisions set out above guide judges in the Family Court when they are making decisions about the welfare of a child. In many cases where a child is being deprived of their liberty, or a deprivation of liberty is proposed, there will be imminent, ongoing or recently concluded care proceedings. This is because the issues at play in deprivation of liberty cases are sometimes intertwined with the issues dealt with by the Family Court in care proceedings. In many cases before the High Court concerning a deprivation of liberty, the child or young person at the centre of proceedings is being deprived of their liberty because they exhibit extreme and challenging behaviours and they can only be kept safe by measures which restrict their physical liberty. Often these children display extreme behaviours as a result of things that happened during their childhood which may have caused trauma or other psychological difficulties. These events or circumstances experienced by the child can often be events or circumstances which also prompt a local authority's involvement in a child protection capacity, sometimes leading to care proceedings.

6.78 The Family Procedure Rules 2010 dictate that where both the Family Court and the High Court have jurisdiction to deal with a case, the proceedings must first be issued in the Family Court unless there are existing proceedings involving the same parties in the High Court, or the court directs otherwise.[95] This means that if a child is the subject of deprivation of liberty proceedings in the High Court before care proceedings are issued, the care proceedings may be issued to be dealt with by the same judge, ensuring judicial continuity. However, an application in respect of a deprivation of liberty cannot be issued in the Family Court if there are existing care proceedings, as these applications must go to the High Court, and not all judges dealing with care proceedings are able to hear applications within the High Court. Further guidance around issuing deprivation of liberty applications in the High Court is provided in chapter 5.

6.79 Judicial continuity is important for cases involving a deprivation of liberty which are often complex. It is helpful if the same judge deals with all hearings in a deprivation of liberty case as it allows the judge to become familiar with the issues and the circumstances of the child to assist prompt decision-making, and for parents and other family members involved to feel more comfortable if the judge is known to them. The importance of judicial continuity is highlighted by the President of the Family Division in the 'Revised National Listing Protocol for Applications that seek Deprivation of Liberty Orders Relating to Children under the Inherent Jurisdiction' provided in September 2023.[96] This protocol expects that where care proceedings have been heard or are ongoing in relation to a child for whom an application for a deprivation of liberty authorisation is made, the deprivation of liberty application will be dealt with in the local court which heard or is hearing the care proceedings. If the care proceedings are ongoing, the court may also consolidate the applications, bringing them together as one case. Whether or not this is appropriate will depend upon the circumstances of each case. Frequently, cases are kept as separate distinct

95 Family Procedure Rules 2010, r 5.4.

96 HM Courts and Tribunals Service, *Revised National Listing Protocol for Applications that seek Deprivation of Liberty Orders Relating to Children under the Inherent Jurisdiction*, September 2023.

proceedings but are heard by the same judge at the same time, to allow the live issues to be considered holistically at one hearing but whilst not binding the proceedings together which can cause logistical complications if one application can be concluded before another.

CONCLUSION

6.80 This chapter has explored the role of a local authority in the lives of children, young people and families who require its input and support. This ranges from voluntary early help support to the removal of children from the care of their family by way of a court order. It is crucial that families who are involved in circumstances where a deprivation of liberty arises are alive to the framework of support which can be provided to them by a local authority, ensuring that their child's needs are met. What the support may look like is explored within this chapter and can range from advisory sessions to providing accommodation or respite care for children. When local authority support is not sufficient to address the concerns arising for a child or young person, a local authority may issue proceedings within the family court and seek orders which it considers are necessary to secure the welfare of the child or young person. The framework surrounding child protection and care proceedings is designed with the welfare of the child at the forefront, and with a view to all those involved working together to secure the best outcome for the child.

Chapter 7

PLACEMENTS

INTRODUCTION

7.01 An important element of the arrangements for a child or young person who is deprived of their liberty is the placement in which the restrictive regime is implemented. The type of placement or setting in which a child or young person is deprived of their liberty can vary greatly. It depends on a number of factors, including the child or young person's individual needs and what is available to them at the time a placement is required. This chapter will explore the different types of placements available to children and young people, ranging from their family home to secure accommodation and inpatient hospital settings. It will explain why the different settings may be more appropriate for some children and young people than others. The chapter will delve into what the gaps are in availability of the different types of placements and why some children end up living in unregistered or unregulated settings.

7.02 The number of applications for deprivation of liberty orders has grown significantly in recent years. This suggests a simultaneous increase in the demand for local authorities and NHS bodies to accommodate children and young people in specialist placements that can meet their needs. However, the number of placements actually available for these children and young people has not proportionately increased. The number of children requiring placements outweighs the number of placements available. Consequently, many orders that are now made by the court include orders to deprive children of their liberty in unconventional placements which are often not registered under the relevant statutory regimes and regulations. This is recognised by the court and those working within it as a crisis that needs to be urgently addressed. It is leaving some of our most vulnerable children and young people in society without appropriate placements and, significantly, without the clinical, therapeutic or educational resources necessary to enable them to transition safely into adulthood.

ENGLAND AND WALES

Accommodating children

7.03 When children and young people are deemed unable to safely reside with their parents, a local authority may accommodate the child or young person. Children may also become accommodated by their parents or carers relinquishing care of them. Chapter 6 explores the circumstances which may lead to a local authority accommodating a child or young person and the duties which local authorities have to children and young people looked after by them.

7.04 The Children Act 1989 (CA 1989), ss 22A–22D make provision for the accommodation and maintenance of looked after children in England (or 'children looked after' which is now accepted as the more appropriate title). These sections provide a framework within which decisions about accommodating and maintaining a child must be made by local authorities in England:

(a) the CA 1989, s 22A imposes a duty on the responsible authority when a child is in its care to provide the child with accommodation;

(b) the CA 1989, s 22B sets out the duty of the responsible authority to maintain a child looked after in other respects apart from providing accommodation;

(c) the CA 1989, s 22C sets out the different ways in which a child looked after is to be accommodated and includes placement with their parents or a person with parental responsibility; placement with a relative or person connected to the child; placement in foster care, or placement within a registered children's home.

7.05 When making decisions about where a child or young person should be placed, local authorities should first consider if it is consistent with the child's welfare to place them with a parent. Where a placement with the child's parent is not possible, the CA 1989, s 22C(5) states that the responsible authority should place the child in 'the most appropriate placement available', that is, the one that it considers will best promote and safeguard the child's welfare.[1]

7.06 In Wales, the statutory provisions are found within the Social Services and Well-being (Wales) Act 2014 (SSWWA 2014). The duty for local authorities in Wales to accommodate children falls within the SSWWA 2014, ss 76 and 79. The wider duty of Welsh local authorities to children who are looked after by them is set out within the SSWWA 2014, s 78. The SSWWA 2014, s 81 provides mirroring provisions for local authorities in Wales to those set out for English local authorities at the CA 1989, s 22C.

7.07 Where none of the placement types named within the legislation are available, or appropriate, a local authority may place a child in 'other arrangements' in accordance with the CA 1989, ss 22C(6)(d) and 22D and the SSWWA 2014, ss 81(6)(d) and 82. 'Other arrangements' means outside of an approved family or connected carers placement, not within foster care and not within a registered children's home.

7.08 The duty upon local authorities to provide accommodation to some children and young people comes with great responsibility. Accommodating a child brings with it a need to ensure that the accommodation is suitable, that it is the right fit for the child or young person, and that it is capable of meeting the child or

---

1 CA 1989, ss 22A–22D.

young person's needs. To ensure registered placements can meet those requirements, regulations are in place to govern the different types of accommodation which may lawfully be used by local authorities to accommodate children and young people.

7.09 In England, the central regulation governing placements for children and young people is the Care Planning, Placement and Case Review (England) Regulations 2010. These regulations are designed to ensure that children and young people are accommodated in appropriate settings which are fit to meet their needs. By way of example, the regulations mandate that local authorities must:

(a) Devise a placement plan for the child which considers how the proposed accommodation will contribute to meeting their needs;[2]

(b) Conduct suitability assessments of different types of placements before a child or young person is placed there;

(c) Ensure children and young people who are living within accommodation arranged by the local authority are visited at regular intervals by professionals who can oversee the continued suitability of the placement.[3]

7.10 The regulations also govern what type of placements may not lawfully be used for some children. The Care Planning, Placement and Case Review (England) Regulations 2010, reg 27A (incorporated by the Care Planning, Placement and Case Review (England) (Amendment) Regulations 2021)[4] provides that a responsible authority may only place a child under 16 in accommodation which constitutes 'other arrangements' under the CA 1989, s 22C(6)(d) where the accommodation is:

(a) A care home as defined in the CA 1989, s 105(1);

(b) A hospital as defined in the National Health Service Act 2006, s 275(1);

(c) A residential family centre as defined in the Care Standards Act 2000, s 4(2);

(d) A school within the meaning of the Education Act 1996, s 4 providing accommodation that is not registered as a children's home as defined in of the CA 1989, s 105(1);

(e) An establishment that provides care and accommodation for children as a holiday scheme for disabled children as defined in the Residential Holiday Schemes for Disabled Children (England) Regulations 2013, reg 2(1).

7.11 This, in effect, creates a prohibition on placing children under 16 within supported living, semi-independent and independent living settings which fall within the definition of 'other arrangements' (sometimes also referred to as 'unregulated accommodation' which is explored in further detail later in this chapter). The change was implemented following national concern that a number of 'other arrangements' settings were not required to register with Ofsted (the Office for Standards in

---

2 Care Planning, Placement and Case Review (England) Regulations 2010, reg 9.

3 Care Planning, Placement and Case Review (England) Regulations 2010, reg 28.

4 Care Planning, Placement and Case Review (England) Regulations 2010 (added by Care Planning, Placement and Case Review (England) (Amendment) Regulations 2021), reg 27A .

Education, Children's Services and Skills) and therefore lacked regulatory oversight. As the children who often require placement in 'other arrangements' settings are vulnerable and in need of skilled support, some 'other arrangements' settings were not suitably equipped to meet their needs. This underpinned the amended regulations which sought to prevent the placement of children in settings which are not regulated.

7.12 For children aged 16 and older, the amended regulations do not place a prohibition on the use of 'other arrangements', as 16 and 17-year olds may still be placed in 'other arrangements' settings which includes supported living, semi-independent and independent living accommodation. However, before placing a young person in an 'other arrangements' setting, Schedule 6 to the 2010 Regulations requires a number of factors to be considered to determine the suitability of the accommodation. This includes the facilities and state of repair; the safety of the accommodation; its location; the support provision; tenancy status, and the affordability of the placement.[5] There are, therefore, different types of placements available for local authorities to consider depending upon the age of the child or young person. For children, under 16, local authorities are limited to considering regulated placements including those listed in the 2021 amendment regulations, whereas the potential placement options for young people is broader and may include placements that do not reguire registration with Ofsted.

Secure accommodation

7.13 In some cases when a child or young person is deprived of their liberty, they are placed in secure accommodation. Secure accommodation placements are only available for children and young people that meet the criteria set out in the CA 1989, s 25, for children and young people in England, or in the SSWWA 2014, s 119, for children and young people in Wales. The criteria for placing a child in secure accommodation and the definition of secure accommodation is explored in-depth within chapter 5.

7.14 Secure accommodation settings are approved to implement restrictive regimes and so to deprive children and young people of their liberty. They are placements for children and young people aged between 10 and 17 and they provide full residential care, educational facilitates and healthcare provisions. Secure children's homes should also provide trauma aware and psychologically informed integrated services.[6] Within a secure accommodation setting, the placement provider is able to implement a restrictive care regime which constitutes the confinement of a child or young person, in accordance with the definition explained in chapter 3. This may include measures such as locked doors, supervision of the child or young person and monitoring of their whereabouts. The granting of a secure accommodation order

5 Care Planning, Placement and Case Review (England) Regulations 2010 (added by Care Planning, Placement and Case Review (England) (Amendment) Regulations 2021, Sch 6).

6 Details of the secure children's homes in England and Wales can be found on https://www.securechildrenshomes.org.uk/.

permits a child or young person's placement withing a secure children's home, therefore authorising their deprivation of liberty therein.

7.15 In England, secure children's homes require registration under the Care Standards Act 2000 (CSA 2000) and in Wales, under the Regulation and Inspection of Social Care Act (Wales) 2016 (RISCA 2016). To make a secure welfare referral for a child under the age of 13 to be placed in a secure accommodation setting, approval by the Secretary of State under the Children (Secure Accommodation) Regulations 1991 for local authorities in England, or approval from Welsh Ministers for local authorities in Wales, is required. Beds within secure children's homes are either contracted to the Youth Custody Service or are available to local authorities for welfare or criminal justice placements.

7.16 Secure accommodation has been the subject of increased discussion within court judgments and in relation to government policy owing to a perceived crisis in the provision of such specialist placements. The most recent statistics published by the government in May 2024 show some improvement in the availability of secure placements since 2023.[7] There are 14 secure children's homes in England and Wales, which now carry 237 approved places. This is an increase of seven approved places since 2023. However, there remains an overall decrease in the number of available placements, which stood at around 250 prior to 2023.

7.17 The availability of places can be affected by secure homes being temporarily closed to make improvements, a bed being out of use due to damage or refurbishment, or a lack of staffing meaning placements cannot accept more children or young people into their care. The occupancy rate of secure children's homes in 2024 sits at 66%, up from 60% the previous year, and with 156 children reported to be accommodated. However, an occupancy rate below 100% does not always mean that there are available spaces or empty beds. Some spaces within secure accommodation are contracted to youth offending services, meaning those places are not available to local authorities and children looked after by them. Some placements caring for children with particularly complex needs are required to reduce their occupancy rates to ensure the children and young people within the placement are properly cared for.[8] Both of these factors impact hugely upon the actual number of secure accommodation placements open to local authorities.

7.18 The Secure Welfare Coordination Unit (SWCU) is a single point of contact for local authorities in England and Wales to streamline the process of identifying the most suitable placements for children and young people by matching their individual needs to available placements. The SWCU has been collecting data on welfare placements in secure children's homes since 2016. Their annual report from 2023 highlights that 366 referrals were made for children to be placed in secure accommodation during 2023, with 58 referrals open daily. The data shows that the

---

7 HM Government, Children accommodated in secure children's homes, 16 May 2024 (https://explore-education-statistics.service.gov.uk/find-statistics/children-accommodated-in-secure-childrens-homes).

8 HM Government, Children accommodated in secure children's homes (16 May 2024).

majority of young people referred had been accommodated by a local authority for over five years before the referral to a secure setting had been made. The data also identifies that a high volume of individuals (35.52%) are placed in 'other' settings such as unregulated or unregistered placements as their first placement. Some young people are reported as having had over 35 placement moves at the point of the secure welfare referral being submitted.[9]

7.19 For a long time, there has not been enough secure accommodation places for children and young people who need them. The court recognises the lack of placements and inadequate resources as a nationwide problem. Practitioners regularly involved in deprivation of liberty cases will have the depressingly familiar experience of being told that there is no secure bed available for a child who desperately needs one. In 2019, in the case of *Re B*, Baker LJ spoke of the 'crisis in the provision of secure accommodation in England and Wales' which appears to have worsened over the past few years.[10]

7.20 This crisis in provision leads to a regular reliance on the inherent jurisdiction of the High Court to authorise a deprivation of liberty outside of the statutory scheme. The inherent jurisdiction is often turned to either because the criteria for an order under the CA 1989, s 25 is not met or, more commonly, because no registered secure placement can be identified for a child.[11] Therefore, the inherent jurisdiction is being used in part to cover the lack of resources and placements and 'plug the gap'. HHJ Moradifar has also recently referred to this as the 'silent crisis'[12] and many courts have expressed grave concern about the frequent use of the inherent jurisdiction in such a way.[13] It is against this backdrop that a growing number of children are now placed in unregistered and often unsuitable settings that struggle to meet their needs.

Unregistered provisions

7.21 England and Wales operate separate legal regimes in relation to the regulation and registration of children's homes. A residential unit for children and young people is registered as a children's home in England or a care home service in Wales. Once registered, the placement will be regulated and inspected by Ofsted or the Care Inspectorate Wales (CIW).

7.22 In England, the definition of a children's home is set out at the CSA 2000, s 1(2), as follows: 'an establishment in England is a children's home (subject to the following provisions of this section) if it provides care and accommodation wholly or mainly for children.'[14] It follows that establishments such as hospitals, residential

---

9 SWCU Annual Report, England, (January 2023-December 2023).
10 *Re B (A Child)* [2020] Fam 221.
11 *Re T (A Child)* [2021] UKSC 35.
12 *Re X (Child: Deprivation of Liberty: Lack of Placement)* [2023] EWHC 3416 (Fam).
13 See obiter of Lady Black in *Re T (A Child)* [2021] UKSC 35, [2021] 3 FCR 780, [2021] 2 FLR 1041.
14 CSA 2000, s 1(2).

family centres and most schools do not qualify as children's homes.[15] However, children's homes providing short break care and residential schools accommodating children for more than 295 days per year will fall within the definition. In accordance with the guidance provided by Ofsted, settings which accommodate young people may be considered as children's homes if the young person is unable to choose to stay away overnight; if the young person cannot go out without staff permission; and if the young person is not responsible for meeting all of their health needs independently.[16] These factors contribute to an assessment of whether the placement provides care alongside accommodation to the young person, over and above simply providing accommodation with support.

7.23 The CSA 2000, s 11 includes a requirement that any person providing or managing a children's home in England must be registered in respect of that home. The body with which a children's home in England must be registered is Ofsted. Any person who carries on or manages a home without registration shall be guilty of a criminal offence.[17]

7.24 The regulations made under the CSA 2000, s 22, namely the Children's Homes (England) Regulations 2015, prescribe objectives and standards for children's homes. These are designed to ensure that the regulated placements are fit to meet the needs of the children and young people residing within them. Regulation 20 specifically addresses restraint of children and young people. It includes that the restraint of a child is only permitted for the purpose of preventing injury to any person (including the child), serious damage to property, or to prevent a child within a secure children's home from absconding. The regulation goes on to confirm that the use of any restraint must be necessary and proportionate. No other form of restraint is permitted under the regulations and to be carried out within a children's home, unless separately authorised by the court.

7.25 In Wales, the RISCA 2016 is the applicable statute. Schedule 1 defines a care home service as being a service for 'the provision of accommodation, together with nursing or care at a place in Wales, to persons because of their vulnerability or need'. It expressly excludes a hospital, school (in accordance with subparagraph (3)), residential family centre or secure accommodation service from the definition of a care home service. The Regulated Services (Service Providers and Responsible Individuals) (Wales) Regulations 2017, reg 2 provides further clarity on types of settings which do not fall within the definition of a care home service in Wales.[18]

7.26 The requirement for registration of a care home service is with the CIW and once registered, will be inspected by the CIW and subject to extensive requirements by virtue of the RISCA 2016. The RISCA 2016 , s 5 provides that it is an offence for a person to provide a regulated service without being registered and that a provider

---

15 CSA 2000, s 1(4).

16 Ofsted Annex A, Supported Accommodation Checklist.

17 CSA 2000, s 11.

18 Regulation and Inspection of Social Care (Wales) Act 2016.

of a care home service that is not properly registered would be liable to prosecution by the CIW.

7.27 Registration ensures that the regulatory bodies, Ofsted and the CIW, are aware of all placements providing care and accommodation to children and young people within their area. This allows for oversight and scrutiny of each placement, both as part of the registration process and thereafter. Once registered, Ofsted and the CIW are responsible for inspecting the placements, ensuring their continued suitability and acting in response to any shortfalls within the provision of the accommodated children and young people.

7.28 Once registration is obtained, these settings are deemed to be 'registered placements'. However, not all placements which provide care and accommodation seek the necessary registration. This can be due to several factors, including disputes as to whether the placement does fall within the relevant definition; issues with meeting the requirements of the regulatory body in order to become registered; or due to the placement not intending to act as a children's home but operating as one in an emergency situation where there are simply no other alternatives. When this situation occurs, and a child is placed in a setting where they are provided with accommodation and care but the placement is not registered with Ofsted or the CIW, the child is living within an unregistered placement.

7.29 Although a placement may be unregistered, it is still open to the court to authorise a child to be deprived of their liberty when residing in that placement.[19] Even in circumstances where the court has authorised a child or young person's deprivation of liberty whilst they are living within an unregistered placement, the requirement to register remains, and the onus is on the providers and managers of the children's home or care home service to progress an application for registration.

7.30 The Nuffield Family Justice Observatory data published in June 2023 uncovers that between 4 July and 31 August 2022, in over half of the cases reviewed (53.8%), children and young people were placed in at least one unregistered placement during the study period.[20] This data confirms the perceived crisis in registered accommodation provision with a majority of the children considered having had some experience of a placement not registered with a regulatory body to ensure its suitability for them.

7.31 The President of the Family Division issued Revised Practice Guidance on the court's approach to unregistered placements in September 2023.[21] This

---

19 *Re T (a child)* [2021] UKSC 35.

20 Roe, A., Ryan, M., Saied-Tessier, A. and Edney, C. (2023). Legal outcomes of cases at the national deprivation of liberty court, Nuffield Family Justice Observatory; https://www.nuffieldfjo.org.uk/resource/legal-outcomes-of-cases-at-the-national-deprivation-of- liberty-court.

21 Practice Guidance: Revised practice guidance on the courts approach to unregistered placements guidance, Sir Andrew McFarlane, 11 October 2023 (https://www.judiciary.uk/guidance-and-resources/revised-practice-guidance-on-the-courts-approach-to-unregistered-placements/).

guidance replaces the 2019 Practice Guidance[22] and 2020 Addendum Guidance,[23] which set out the steps that judges were encouraged to take in respect of establishing whether a placement was registered, which included the court having oversight of the registration process. The revised guidance acknowledges that it is not part of the court's functions to have oversight of the registration process and instead recognised that is the function of Ofsted and the CIW as the regulatory bodies:

> '5. It is not for the Court to become a regulatory body or the overseer of the regulatory process. The Court's role in deprivation of liberty applications, is to exercise its inherent jurisdiction to ensure that any deprivation of liberty is not itself unlawful, whether as an unlawful detention under the common law, or a breach of Article 5 of the ECHR. That is the extent of the Court's powers, and the Court's role should not go beyond those powers.'

7.32 The revised guidance goes on to state that the withdrawal of the 2019 guidance, which placed a burden on the court to monitor a placement's registration status, does not mean that there are not usually benefits for the child or young person in being placed in a registered rather than unregistered placement. Although the burden on the court is alleviated within the revised guidance, the President acknowledged that the court should still be enquiring as to whether the proposed placement is registered, and if not, question why such placement is in the best interests of the child. In circumstances where the local authority is placing a child in an unregistered placement, the court may also order the local authority to inform Ofsted or the CIW within seven days.

7.33 The registration process with Ofsted and CIW can be onerous and requires that the providers have a solid understanding of the service-specific regulations and quality standards in place for the establishment. Both Ofsted and the CIW provide detailed guides on how to register which can be accessed online.[24] Ofsted also offers a fast-track registration process to prioritise applications to register children's homes in an emergency. These can only be made:

(a) by providers who are accommodating a child who is the subject of a deprivation of liberty order from the court;

(b) for a provision that is being specifically opened as part of the response to accommodate unaccompanied asylum-seeking children who are being transferred under the national transfer scheme; or

---

22 Practice Guidance: Placement in unregistered children's homes in England or unregistered care home services in Wales, Sir Andrew McFarlane, 12 November 2019 (https://www.judiciary.uk/wp-content/uploads/2022/07/PG-Placements-in-unregistered-childrens-homes-in-Eng-or-unregistered-care-home-services-in-Wales-NOV-2019..pdf).

23 Addendum to Practice Guidance: Placements in unregistered children's homes in England or unregistered care home services in Wales, Sir Andrew McFarlane, 1 December 2020 (https://www.judiciary.uk/guidance-and-resources/addendum-to-practice-guidance-placements-in-unregistered-childrens-homes-in-england-or-unregistered-care-home-services-in-wales/).

24 Ofsted: Registration guide for children's social care services, 14 April 2023 (https://www.gov.uk/government/publications/guide-to-registration-for-childrens-social-care-services/registration-guide-for-childrens-social-care-services) CIW : Guide to Registration Regulation and Inspection of Social Care (Wales) Act 2016, March 2024 (https://www.careinspectorate.wales/sites/default/files/2024-04/240409-Guide-to-Registration-RISCA-en.pdf).

(c) for a provision that is needed in exceptional circumstances in response to an emergency situation – the Ofsted Senior His Majesty's Inspector (SHMI) in region will determine if the application can be prioritised.[25]

7.34 The Supreme Court considered the issue of unregistered placements in the case of *Re T*, and whether the High Court's inherent jurisdiction could still be exercised in circumstances where a child was being deprived of their liberty whilst residing in an unregistered setting.[26] In her judgment, Lady Black deliberated on the questions of what would happen if the inherent jurisdiction was unavailable to authorise arrangements for children in unregistered settings, and how that would impact local authorities trying to comply with their statutory duties towards children. Lady Black expressed her concern about the use of the inherent jurisdiction to authorise arrangements enacted in an unregistered setting, but ultimately recognised that sometimes there is simply no alternative, and a child would come to harm if the court did not act. In summarising this issue, the court stated:

> '143. It has to be recognised that when the local authority applies under the inherent jurisdiction for the court to authorise a secure placement which is either not in a registered children's home or is in a children's home that has not been approved for secure accommodation, those placements will not satisfy all the requirements of the regulatory framework. If the placement is in an unregistered children's home, a criminal offence will be committed by any person who carries on or manages the home. The important safeguards that come with registration will be absent. If the placement is in an unregulated setting, it will equally escape these safeguards, and it is noted that the Children's Commissioner expresses particular concern about children being deprived of their liberty in unregulated placements, to the point of questioning whether such placements, for example in caravans and outward bound centres, could ever be classed as sufficiently appropriate for article 5 purposes.
>
> 144. The courts have put in place such safeguards as they can to overcome the shortcomings of the present arrangements, and I will come to these in due course. But whatever the courts devise cannot replicate the official safety net that the regulatory framework provides when it is applicable. To take an obvious example, the court is not able to carry out the sort of inspections and checks that Ofsted and the Care Inspectorate Wales are obliged to carry out.
>
> 145. I have been particularly concerned as to whether it is a permissible exercise of the inherent jurisdiction to authorise a local authority to place a child in an unregistered children's home in relation to which a criminal offence would be being committed. Ultimately, however, I recognise that there are cases in which there is absolutely no alternative, and where the child (or someone else) is likely to come to grave harm if the court does not act. I also have to recognise that there are other duties in play, in addition to those which prohibit carrying on or managing an unregistered children's home. I gave an idea earlier (see para 30 et seq) of the duties placed upon local authorities to protect and support children. How can a local authority fulfil these duties in the problematic cases with which we are concerned if they cannot obtain authorisation from the High Court to place

---

25 Ofsted Guidance: Registering children's homes in an emergency: priority applications, 14 August 2024 (https://www.gov.uk/guidance/registering-childrens-homes-in-an-emergency).

26 *Re T (A Child) (Appellant)* [2021] UKSC 35.

> the child in the only placement that is available, and with the ability to impose such restrictions as are required on the child's liberty? It is such imperative considerations of necessity that have led me to conclude that the inherent jurisdiction must be available in these cases. There is presently no alternative that will safeguard the children who require its protection.'[27]

7.35 Lord Stephens, agreeing with Lady Black's judgment, went on to emphasise that where there is no alternative, it is a 'permissible exercise of the inherent jurisdiction to authorise a local authority to place a child in an unregistered children's home' but that this must only be done in circumstances where there are 'imperative considerations of necessity'.[28] It can be drawn from this judgment that whilst the court is able to authorise a regime of confinement which is implemented in an unregistered setting, this should only be authorised by the court when absolutely necessary: when there is no alternative option.

7.36 The registration process is there for a reason. It offers children important safeguards to ensure that accommodation providers comply with the regulations designed to ensure that the welfare of children and young people is prioritised within their accommodation. Although the court has now confirmed that deprivation of liberty authorisations may be granted for children residing in unregistered accommodation, the accommodation itself remains unlawful. The court has expressed on multiple occasions the grave reservations it has in authorising placements in unregistered provisions which cannot guarantee the standards offered by placements within the regulatory framework.[29] As published judgments continue to deal with this issue, it is evident that the crisis in provision of registered and suitable accommodation for children and young people continues.

7.37 When dealing with the registration of placements, it is important to also touch upon the requirement on some care providers to register with the Care Quality Comission (CQC). The CQC regulates certain activities undertaken in relation to children and young people (and adults, but that falls outside of the scope of this book). It is different from Ofsted in that its focus is regulating activities rather than settings. The CQC regulates health and social care in England. This includes most health care services provided for children and care homes and domiciliary care agencies. What the CQC must regulate is dictated by the Health and Social Care Act 2008 (HSCA 2008). Anyone deemed to be a service provider of a regulated activity must register with the CQC. This includes individuals, organisations, charities, NHS trusts and local authorities. A regulated activity is defined in the HSCA 2008, s 8(1), as being 'an activity involving or connected with, the provision of health or social care'. A list of activities is then provided at Sch 1 to the Act. They include personal care for those who by reason of old age, illness or disability cannot provide it for themselves, and the provision of treatment for a disease, disorder or injury by, or supervised by, a health care processional or a social worker. The regulated activities

---

27 *Re T (A Child) (Appellant)* [2021] UKSC 35, paras 143-145.

28 *Re T (A Child) (Appellant)* [2021] UKSC 35, para 170.

29 See also *Z (A Child: DOLS: Lack of Secure Placement)* [2020] EWHC 1827 (Fam) at [23]; *Dorset Council v E (Unregulated placement: Lack of secure placements)* [2020] EWHC 1098 (Fam); *Re B (Secure Accommodation Order)* [2019] EWCA Civ 2025 at para 6.

do extend to the provision of accommodation in certain circumstances, such as when that is provided with nursing or personal care. However, the CQC cannot regulate the accommodation element of a placement registered with Ofsted in England. This maintains the requirement for services acting as a children's home to register as such with Ofsted, and that cannot be bypassed by CQC registration for the provision of regulated activities. If health care is also being offered within a placement which meets the definition of a children's home, the provider will also need to register with the CQC for the health care element of their service. If a service provider is providing a regulated activity to a child outside of an Ofsted-registered setting, for example providing personal care to disabled a child in their own home, they must register with the CQC. Ofsted and the CQC cannot both regulate the same activity, and so those activities cannot be dual registered. If a provider must register with Ofsted for part of its service, Ofsted will be the regulator for that service and it will be exempt from registering that activity with the CQC.

Unregulated provisions

7.38 When considering accommodation for children and young people in England and Wales, there is not only a distinction between registered and unregistered settings. There are also settings which either fall within the regulatory schemes, which are regulated placements, and placements which fall outside of them: unregulated placements. The types of placements which fall to be considered when looking at unregulated provisions are those which fall within the definition of 'other arrangements', discussed at **7.4–7.12**. This is because some of the placement types which fall within the list of 'other arrangements' do not fall to be regulated by a regulatory body, and are so 'unregulated'.

7.39 Unregulated provisions, generally, are those which do not cross the boundary into providing care for children, which would require their registration as a children's home or care home service. They must only provide support and accommodation. Unregulated accommodation is traditionally settings described as supported accommodation, independent or semi-independent living provisions. Supported accommodation is the most common form of placement in England used under the 'other arrangements' provisions. This type of setting is aimed at providing support to young people as they move towards adulthood, without straying into directly providing care to the young people living there. It is expressly provided for as a suitable option for 16 and 17-year olds who require a placement in 'other arrangements' by virtue of regulation 36 of the Supported Accommodation (England) Regulations 2023. These regulations, brought in to place from October 2023, implemented a requirement on supported accommodation providers to register with Ofsted if they are accommodating a young person who has been placed there by a local authority under the CA 1989, s 22C(6)(d) or 23B(8)(b). This covers the placement of a looked after child there in 'other arrangements' or placement of a care leaver in 'suitable accommodation'. These new regulations therefore brought about a regulatory scheme which now governs placements that fall within the definition of supported accommodation. The government describe the new regulations as: 'the measures mean that from October 2023, all providers of accommodation for children in care or care leavers up to the age of 18 will be regulated by Ofsted, putting an end to children living in poor quality homes with no meaningful oversight'.[30]

7.40 The Care Planning, Placement and Case Review (England) (Amendment) Regulations 2021 made the placement of children under 16 years old in unregulated settings in England illegal. This prohibits the placement of under 16s in settings which do not fall within the list of regulated placements at the CA 1989, s 22C(6)(a)–(c) or placements made under the CA 1989, s 38(6). In England, unregulated provisions are allowed in law for young people aged 16 and 17 provided that they are used for accommodation purposes only and not for the provision of care. If an unregulated provision is being used, against the regulations, as a placement caring for a child under 16, it will also be an unregistered placement. If, once that child reaches 16, the placement continues to provide care to the young person, it will be a legal unregulated placement but it will continue to be unregistered whilst it is acting within the definition of a children's home and is not registered with Ofsted. The Welsh Government has made no similar moves to ban unregulated accommodation in any form, and so unregulated provisions may still be used for children aged below 16 in Wales.

7.41 Ofsted estimated that there were as many as 7,000 looked after children and care leavers living in unregulated accommodation, before the new regulations were brought into place. Their research suggests that a lack of suitable care provision was one of the main drivers for the growing reliance on these types of settings.[31] Due to increased concerns about the suitability of such placements for young people, and a lack of safeguards which comes with an unregulated provision, a public consultation was launched in July 2023 to address the issue. It was following this consultation that the mandatory national standards and Ofsted registration and inspection were introduced for providers of unregulated provisions that accommodate 16 and 17-year old children looked after by a local authority and care leavers in October 2023.[32]

7.42 The report into the consultation's findings highlighted a strong support for the recommendation of implementing inspections of unregulated placements. Notably, Ofsted stated that they would not expect supported accommodation settings to be suitable for children and young people who are deprived of their liberty, with the report commenting that:

> 'Not all looked-after children and care leavers aged 16 and 17 are ready for supported accommodation. We would not, for example, expect to see children who are deprived

---

[30] HM Government, 'Government bans unregulated accommodation for young people in care', 23 March 2023 https://www.gov.uk/government/news/government-bans-unregulated-accommodation-for-young-people-in-care.

[31] Ofsted: Social care: 'Getting ready to regulate supported accommodation', 6 January 2023 https://socialcareinspection.blog.gov.uk/2023/01/06/getting-ready-to-regulate-supported-accommodation/.

[32] Ofsted Consultation: 'Proposals for inspecting supported accommodation', July 2023, https://www.gov.uk/government/consultations/proposals-for-inspecting-supported-accommodation.

of their liberty, or need ongoing high levels of supervision or personal care, in this type of provision.'[33]

7.43 Guidance on how Ofsted inspects supported accommodation for looked after children and care leavers was published in February 2024.[34] The aim of the inspections is to assess whether the support being provided to young people within the setting is effective and to determine the impact of that support on the young person's experiences and progress. It extends to all placements that fall within the definition of supported accommodation, as set out at the Care Standards Act 2000 (Extension of the Application of Part 2 to Supported Accommodation) (England) Regulations 2022, reg 2. It includes placements which fall within 'other arrangements' but are not care homes, education institutions or hospitals.

7.44 In Wales, it remains legal to place children and young people under the age of 18, including those under 16, in unregulated settings. Concerns have been raised about the divergence in law between England and Wales in this respect, with Welsh ministers describing the practice to be placing children potentially at risk[35] and the National Youth Advocacy Service Cymru calling for a ban on placing children in unregulated settings.[36]

Detention or placement in hospital

7.45 An individual of any age can be lawfully detained in hospital for assessment or treatment, if they fall within the criteria set out within the Mental Health 1983 (MHA 1983), s 2 or 3. There are other sections of the MHA 1983 under which a person may be lawfully detained but they are not explored within the confines of this book and are rarely used in relation to children and young people. The criteria for detention under the MHA 1983 is explained at chapter 5 and is one route by which a child or young person may come to be living in a hospital setting.

7.46 By virtue of the Care Planning, Placement and Case Review (England) Regulations 2010, reg 27A, as amended in 2021, it can be lawful for a responsible

33 Ofsted Consultation Outcome: Supported accommodation for looked-after children and care leavers aged 16 and 17: a report on the responses to the consultation on our inspection proposals, February 2024 https://www.gov.uk/government/consultations/proposals-for-inspecting-supported-accommodation/outcome/supported-accommodation-for-looked-after-children-and-care-leavers-aged-16-and-17-a-report-on-the-responses-to-the-consultation-on-our-inspection-pro#the-consultation-findings-in-full.

34 Ofsted Guidance: 'Social Care Common Inspection Framework (SCCIF): supported accommodation for looked after children and care leavers ages 16 and 17', updated April 2024, https://www.gov.uk/government/publications/social-care-common-inspection-framework-sccif-supported-accommodation/social-care-common-inspection-framework-sccif-supported-accommodation-for-looked-after-children-and-care-leavers-aged-16-and-17.

35 Over half of Welsh councils breaking the law over looked-after children (2023), Senedd News, 5 April 2023; Available at https://www.conservatives.wales/news/over-half-welsh-councils-breaking-law-over-looked-after-children.

36 *Regulate!, Unregulated Accommodation, NYAS* (no date); https://www.nyas.net/support-us/policy-and-research/current campaigns/regulate!/#:~:text=In%20our%20response%20to%20the,%2Dyear%2Dolds%20in%20care.

authority in England to place a child in a hospital. A hospital setting is included within the definition of acceptable 'other arrangements' for children looked after who are under 16. The definition of a 'hospital' is wide, and refers to:

(a) any institution for the reception and treatment of persons suffering from illness;

(b) any maternity home; and

(c) any institution for the reception and treatment of persons during convalescence or persons requiring medical rehabilitation, and includes clinics, dispensaries and out-patient departments maintained in connection with any such home or institution, and "hospital accommodation" must be construed accordingly.[37]

7.47 In Wales, other accommodation is considered under the SSWWA 2014, s 81(6)(d) and the principles on exercising the use of those powers are contained in the Care Planning, Placement and Case Review (Wales) Regulations 2015 (CPPCWR 2015), reg 30, Sch 7.

7.48 With resources across the public sector already stretched, and regulated placements limited, it is not uncommon for children and young people to be accommodated in hospital after being deemed fit for discharge pending the identification of a more suitable placement. When a child is placed on a hospital ward, Integrated Care Boards (ICBs) have duties to arrange healthcare services to meet reasonable requirements for the people for whom it is responsible, pursuant to the National Health Service Act 2006, s 3. In commissioning services, ICBs must act consistently with the NHS Mandate, which includes a wide duty to promote a comprehensive health service.[38]

7.49 When a request is made by a local authority to the health services to consider the accommodation of a child or young person in an inpatient hospital setting, ICBs and NHS Trusts are entitled to refuse to place a child in such a setting in circumstances where a child does not have a clinical need for that admission. Whilst remaining in an acute hospital setting without clinical need is not likely to be in a child's best interests, this type of setting is frequently relied upon when there is no other alternative in the community available. When a child or young person does become placed in a hospital, it is imperative that the relevant local authority, ICB and NHS Trust work together to ensure the child's holistic needs are being met within that setting. A local authority is not absolved of its duties to that child or young person in relation to their social care needs simply because the child or young person is accommodated in a clinical setting.

7.50 Where children or young people are placed on hospital wards inappropriately, families can challenge their detention or seek a review of any deprivation of liberty order that has been granted. This can be done through a number of avenues depending upon the framework regulating their admission, including: applying to the Mental

37 National Health Service Act 2006 (NHS Act 2006), s 275(1).

38 National Health Service Act 2006 (NHS Act 2006), ss 3 and 3(A).

Health Tribunal; seeking resolution via the Court of Protection, or seeking a review of an order granted under the inherent jurisdiction of the High Court.

7.51 The decision in *An NHS Trust v ST (Refusal of a Deprivation of Liberty Order)*[39] highlights the increasing issue with paediatric hospital wards inappropriately being used as settings in which to deprive children of their liberty when that is not the purpose of the ward and there is no clinical basis for a child to be there. In *ST*, the court refused to authorise the child's deprivation of liberty due to the setting being manifestly unsuitable and not designed to meet the child's needs. It is evident from this case that whilst hospitals are continually being turned to as options of last resort, they will not necessarily be acceptable, and the focus must still be on whether the placement is capable of meeting the child's welfare needs and best interests.

7.52 Hospital beds being utilised inappropriately for this purpose is also having an impact on the health and welfare of other children, young people and families who are being denied the opportunity of being cared for on such wards when there is a clinical need.[40] This consequence again stems from the lack of suitable placements for children and young people who require specialist types of care and accommodation.

SCOTLAND

Secure accommodation

7.53 Children in England and Wales can be placed in secure accommodation units in Scotland. Due to the shortage of accommodation for children and young people within England and Wales, many local authorities resort to seeking out placements in Scotland. When placing a child or young person outside of England and Wales, the responsible local authority must take steps to ensure that the requirements equivalent to the Care Planning, Placement and Case Review (England) Regulations 2010 have been met. In England, before approving a decision, the director of children's services must be satisfied that:

(a) The requirements of the CPPCR 2010, reg 9(1)(b)(i) have been complied with, namely that the child's wishes and feelings have been ascertained and given due consideration and the IRO informed;

(b) The placement is the most appropriate placement and consistent with their care plan;

(c) The child's relatives have been consulted, where appropriate;

(d) The area authority notified, or the area authority consulted and provided with a copy of the care plan; and

(e) The IRO has been consulted.

---

39 *An NHS Trust v ST (Refusal of Deprivation of Liberty Order)* [2022] EWHC 719 (Fam).

40 *Wigan BC v Y (Refusal to Authorise Deprivation of Liberty)* [2021] EWHC 1982 (Fam), para 72.

7.54 Sir James Munby handed down a series of judgments in 2016 and 2017 in the case of *Re X* which touched upon this issue.[41] This included a judgment in the linked cases of *Re X (a child) and Y (A child)* in September 2016, involving two sets of proceedings brought by English local authorities concerning children placed outside of the jurisdiction, in Scotland. The court considered the question of whether an English court could make secure accommodations orders, either under the CA 1989, s 25 or under the inherent jurisdiction of the High Court, for a child to be placed in a unit in Scotland, and whether such orders would be enforceable in Scotland. These issues arose because of the shortage of places in secure accommodation in England and Wales which led to a need to make use of any available places in Scotland.

7.55 The judgment clarified the lawful mechanism for the placement of English children in secure accommodation settings in Scotland. It was determined that a judge in England cannot make a secure accommodation order under the CA 1989, s 25 if the child is to be placed in Scotland. Firstly, the statutory mechanism of the CA 1989 only applies to secure accommodation in England and Wales. Secondly, the order could not be made because secure accommodation in Scotland is not approved by the Secretary of State in accordance with the Children (Secure Accommodation) Regulations 1991, reg 3. This means that the placement in which the child was to be placed would not fall within the definition of secure accommodation which must be satisfied for an order to be made in England.

7.56 In this situation, the High Court in England and Wales would need to be invited to exercise its inherent jurisdiction to place a child in a secure accommodation setting in Scotland. This would allow for a lawful placement from the perspective of the law in England and Wales; however, the only way to provide for the recognition of that order in Scotland would be for an application to be made by the local authority to the Court of Session in Scotland, seeking to invoke the *nobile officium*.[42] Sir James Munby observed this to be a 'serious lacunae in the law' which required urgent attention.[43] Without this recognition, Scottish officials would not be in a position to enforce the order.

7.57 Following Munby J's judgment, recognition and enforcement was sought by three local authorities in England, by way of a petition to the Inner House of the Court of Session under the *nobile officium* in Scotland in October 2016, in the case *Cumbria County Council and Others*.[44] Orders were sought to declare that the secure accommodation orders granted by the High Court of England and Wales to place the children in Scotland should be treated as if they were made by the Scottish Court, making them recognisable and, crucially, enforceable in Scotland. Lord Drummond Young delivered the opinion of the Court in Scotland, recognising and enforcing the orders made by the High Court in England in respect of each child. Lord Drummond Young went on to express that urgent consideration needed to be given to joining

41 *X (A Child) and Y (A Child) [2016]* EWHC 2271 (Fam), *X (A Child) (No 2)* [2017] EWHC 1585 (Fam), *X (A Child) (No 3) [2017]* EWHC 2036 (Fam).

42 *X (A Child) and Y (A Child)* [2016] EWHC 2271 (Fam) para 70.

43 *X (A Child) and Y (A Child)* [2016] EWHC 2271 (Fam) para 3.

44 *Cumbria County Council and Others* [2016] CSIH 92.

up the legislation, and for action to be taken in both Scottish and United Kingdom Parliaments at the earliest possible opportunity to address this issue.[45]

7.58 These two judgments ultimately led to amendments to both English and Scottish legislation that followed shortly after. The Children and Social Work Act 2017 (CSWA 2017) came into force on 27 April 2017.[46] This amended the CA 1989, s 25 to allow for the placement of children from England and Wales in Scotland and the enforceability of orders.[47]

Non-secure accommodation in Scotland

7.59 The CSWA 2017 did not change the position on the recognition of English orders made under the inherent jurisdiction in Scotland. For a number of years following the CSWA 2017, the only way for an order to be recognised by the Scottish Court was if English or Welsh local authorities took affirmative action to have such order recognised as outlined above, again requiring the English and Welsh local authorities to petition the Scottish Court of Session to invoke the *nobile officium* to recognise the order.[48]

7.60 What followed instead was the Supreme Court judgment of *Re T (A Child)* [49] which raised important questions of law about the use of the inherent jurisdiction to authorise a local authority to deprive a child or young person of his or her liberty in non-secure accommodation. The Supreme Court in *Re T* dismissed the appeal and held that the use of the inherent jurisdiction to authorise a deprivation of liberty is permissible in accommodation which is not registered as secure accommodation. Notably, within the case of *Re T*, the Children's Commissioner for Scotland raised concerns in relation to the placement of children in Scotland pursuant to the exercise of the inherent jurisdiction of a court in England and Wales.

7.61 The Cross-Border Placements (Effect of Deprivation of Liberty Orders) (Scotland) Regulations 2022 came into force in Scotland on 24 June 2022 and is said to have been introduced in response to *Re T*. The regulations provide that any deprivation of liberty order (either a fresh order or an extension of an existing order) made on or after 24 June 2022 will have effect and be treated in Scotland as if it were a Compulsory Supervision Order (CSO) for up to three months, for specified purposes and subject to certain conditions.[50] However, the placing local authority must have complied with the notification and undertaking requirements before the order is recognised.[51] The placement notice and undertaking template is provided at

45 *Cumbria County Council and Others* [2016] CSIH 92, para 32.

46 CSWA 2017, s 70(1)(a), Sch1, para 2(2)(b).

47 CA 1989, s 25 (1), Sch1, para (6), Sch 2, para 19(9)(a).

48 *Cumbria CC, Petitioner* [2016] CSIH 92 (19 October 2016).

49 *Re T (A Child) (Appellant)* [2021] UKSC 35.

50 Cross-Border Placements (Effect of Deprivation of Liberty Orders) (Scotland) Regulations 2022, reg 5(4)(b) and (5).

51 Cross-Border Placements (Effect of Deprivation of Liberty Orders) (Scotland) Regulations 2022, reg 5(3).

Annex A of the regulations, for use by the placing authority.[52] If the notification and undertaking requirements are met, then the order is enforceable in Scotland.

7.62 A CSO is made pursuant to the Children's Hearings (Scotland) Act 2011, s 83 at a Children's Hearing in Scotland. It provides that the relevant local authority to the application is responsible for looking after and helping the child or young person, similar to the provisions of a Supervision Order in England and Wales.

7.63 The notice and undertaking requirements are that the placing local authority must give written notifications, in accordance with the Cross-Border Placements (Effect of Deprivation of Liberty Orders) (Scotland) Regulations 2022, reg 9, as follows:

(a) The name of the placing local authority;

(b) The gender of the child who is the subject of the deprivation of liberty order;

(c) The age of the child who is the subject of the deprivation of liberty order;

(d) The name of the residential care setting in which the child is to be placed;

(e) The time that the deprivation of liberty order:

  (i) comes into effect; and

  (ii) expires (if it is not subsequently extended).[53]

7.64 The placing local authority is also required to give, in writing, an undertaking recognising its role and duties in respect of the child being placed in Scotland under a deprivation of liberty order. The undertaking remains in place for the duration of the placement. The content of the undertaking must be in accordance with reg 10, setting out that the placing local authority will:

(a) provide or secure the provision of all services required to support the child; and

(b) meet all the costs arising from, or in consequence of, the child's placement, other than the costs of advocacy provided to the child in accordance with reg 11 (meaning that the costs of advocacy offered to the child by Scottish Ministers will not need to be funded by the placing authority).[54]

---

52 Cross-Border Placements (Effect of Deprivation of Liberty Orders) (Scotland) Regulations 2022, Annex A. See: https://www.gov.scot/publications/cross-border-placements-effect-deprivation-liberty-orders-scotland-regulations-2022-practice-guidance-notice-undertaking-template/pages/10/.

53 Cross-Border Placements (Effect of Deprivation of Liberty Orders) (Scotland) Regulations 2022, reg 9.

54 Cross-Border Placements (Effect of Deprivation of Liberty Orders) (Scotland) Regulations 2022, , reg 10.

7.65 The Regulations replaced the previous practice of placing authorities having to petition to the Court of Session in Scotland for recognition of a deprivation of liberty order through use of the court's *nobile officium*.[55]

LACK OF PROVISION

7.66 What this chapter undoubtably highlights is the existing lack of suitable accommodation for children and young people in England and Wales, particularly those who have complex needs and require specialist placements. Sir James Munby, then President of the Family Division, when he was dealing with the case of *Re X* termed the issue 'a well-known scandal' stating:

> '37. What this case demonstrates, as if further demonstration is still required of what is a well-known scandal, is the disgraceful and utterly shaming lack of proper provision in this country of the clinical, residential and other support services so desperately needed by the increasing numbers of children and young people afflicted with the same kind of difficulties as X is burdened with. We are, even in these times of austerity, one of the richest countries in the world. Our children and young people are our future. X is part of our future. It is a disgrace to any country with pretensions to civilisation, compassion and, dare one say it, basic human decency, that a judge in 2017 should be faced with the problems thrown up by this case and should have to express himself in such terms.
>
> 38. … If this is the best we can do for X, and others in similar crisis, what right do we, what right do the system, our society and indeed the State itself, have to call ourselves civilised? The honest answer to this question should make us all feel ashamed. For my own part, acutely conscious of my powerlessness – of my inability to do more for X – I feel shame and embarrassment; shame, as a human being, as a citizen and as an agent of the State, embarrassment as President of the Family Division, and, as such, Head of Family Justice, that I can do no more for X.
>
> 39. If, when in eleven days' time she is released from ZX, we, the system, society, the State, are unable to provide X with the supportive and safe placement she so desperately needs, and if, in consequence, she is enabled to make another attempt on her life, then I can only say, with bleak emphasis: we will have blood on our hands.'[56]

7.67 Despite this issue being highlighted in multiple decisions by Munby J as early as 2017, and this problem being brought to the attention of the wider public after making national headlines, the lack of provision and resources available for our children and young people persists and remains widespread.

---

55 Scottish Government (2022) *Cross-Border Placements (Effect of Deprivation of Liberty Orders) (Scotland) Regulations 2022:* practice guidance, notice and undertaking template. https://www.gov.scot/publications/cross-border-placements-effect-deprivation-liberty-orders-scotland-regulations-2022-practice-guidance-notice-undertaking-template/pages/1/.

56 *Re X (A Child) (No 3)* [2017] EWHC 2036 (Fam).

CONCLUSION

7.68 This chapter has explored the placements that are available to children and young people throughout England, Wales and Scotland, including the different types of placements which may be available and their regulation. The scope of accommodation options for children and young people ranges from independent living settings with limited support provision, to hospital inpatient wards, to secure settings. Which type of placement is selected for a child or young person will be determined by their needs and presentation, and governed by what is available at the time. Throughout this chapter, reference has been made to the ongoing crisis in provision of suitable accommodation for children and young people which has resulted in many of the most vulnerable in society residing in settings which do not have regulatory body oversight, which are temporary and which cannot meet their holistic needs. However, it is also evident from the body of case law in this area that there are suitable and high quality placements available in England and Wales for children and young people with complex needs and behaviours that challenge. The placement of a child or young person in the right accommodation for them can have a huge impact on shaping their future and securing their welfare.

Chapter 8

TRANSITIONING INTO ADULTHOOD

Written by Jacqueline Thomas KC

THE MOVE FROM CHILDREN'S SERVICES TO ADULT SERVICES

8.01 The progression at age 18 from children's services to adult's social care and healthcare provisions has been described as a cliff edge for both young people and their parents alike.[1] The age of 18 should not be treated as a 'bright line' with one set of rules in place at age 17, only to be replaced wholesale and without transition, at the age of 18 years.[2] Yet all too often, families are faced with a change of team within the local authority, without proper transition planning, and find themselves in a new regime of social care approaches to issues such as the funding of placements and care, an emphasis on autonomy which can seem abrupt and exclusionary of parents, and a complex set of legal principles.

8.02 The NICE guidelines for the transition from children's to adult's services recommend that planning commence for young people from age 13 to –14 years.[3] Yet that is very rarely seen in practice and all too often planning is left until very close to a young person's 18th birthday. The situation has not improved despite repeated calls for change, for example by the CQC in their 2104 report, 'From the pond into the sea,' and the work of numerous charities trying to support young adults and their families.[4]

8.03 In Scotland, the 'Principles of Good Transitions 3' have been developed, providing a framework to encourage the continual improvement of support for young people with additional needs between the ages of 14 and 25 who are making the transition to young adult life.[5] In England and Wales, the 'Preparing for Adulthood'

---

1 Social Care Blog (2017). *Avoiding the cliff edge: making transitions work – Social care.* [online] Available at: https://socialcare.blog.gov.uk/2017/02/06/avoiding-the-cliff-edge-making-transitions-work/.

2 See for example the treatment of age within the Immigration Tribunal https://tribunalsdecisions.service.gov.uk/utiac/pa-02667-2016.

3 NICE Guideline (2016) *Transition from children's to adults' services for young people using health or social care services.* Available at: https://www.nice.org.uk/guidance/ng43.

4 CQC '*From the pond to the sea: Children's transition to adult health services*' (2014) https://www.cqc.org.uk/sites/default/files/CQC_Transition%20Report_Summary_lores.pdf; Also see Field Alice, Young Futures; '*Turning 18: Independence or Cliff Edge?*' (2018) Sheffield University.

5 Scottish Transitions Forum '*The Principles of Good Transitions 3*' (2017) https://scottishtransitions.org.uk/summary-download/.

website provides information and works to develop good practice across the country by sharing learning and delivering workshops to those in local authorities. Despite efforts to improve the system however, practitioners including the legal teams involved find themselves managing crises as a matter of urgency, without the proper planning and longer-term needs being fully considered.

8.04 One area in which parents often struggle is with the change in their status once their child turns 18 years old and they no longer have parental responsibility. In the years approaching the age of 18, as a young person reaches adulthood, the scope of parental responsibility is described as 'dwindling' as the young person's autonomy increases:

> '… the legal right of a parent to the custody of a child … is a dwindling right which the courts will hesitate to enforce against the wishes of the child, and the more so the older he is. It starts with a right of control and ends with little more than advice.' [6]

8.05 Whilst parents retain responsibility until the age of 18 years, society expects and allows teenagers to make an increasing number of decisions, which are given greater weight as they move closer to adulthood. However, if a child is significantly impaired by mental disorder or physical disability, parents have often played a much more significant role in advocating for their best interests during their teenage years and the transition to parenting an adult child can be more challenging.

8.06 Parents of young people with disabilities or a mental impairment within the meaning of the Mental Capacity Act 2005 (MCA 2005) are all too often faced with a stark change in regime once their child reaches majority. Having been the decision maker throughout their child's life, unless they are successfully granted the status of personal welfare deputies, parents then become consultees rather than decision makers after the age of 18 years. That change in status and in the approach of professionals around the family can lead to distress and confusion, and proper transition planning is vital. In the case of *Re Lawson, Mottram and Hopton (Appointment of Personal Welfare Deputies)*,[7] it was held that:

> 'Whilst there is no special alchemy that confers adulthood on a child on his or her 18th birthday, it nevertheless marks a transition to an altered legal status, which carries both rights and responsibilities. It is predicated on respect for autonomy. The young person who may lack capacity in key areas of decision making remains every bit as entitled to this respect as his capacitous coeval. These are fundamental rights which infuse the MCA 2005 and are intrinsic to its philosophy. The extension of parental responsibility beyond the age of eighteen, under the aegis of a PWD, may be driven by a natural and indeed healthy parental instinct but it requires vigilantly to be guarded against. The imposition of a legal framework which is overly protective risks inhibiting personal development and may fail properly to nurture individual potential. The data which I have analysed (paragraph 26 above) may, I suspect, reflect the stress and anxiety experienced in consequence of the transition from child to adult services. As a judge of the Family Division and as a judge of the Court of Protection I have seen from both

---

6 As per Lord Denning MR, *Re Agar-Ellis (No 2)* (1883) 24 Ch D 317, at 326.

7 [2019] EWCOP 22.

> perspectives the acute distress caused by inadequate transition planning. The remedy for this lies in promoting good professional practice. It is not achieved by avoidably eroding the autonomy of the young incapacitous adult'. (Hayden J, §53(b))

8.07 The *Lawson* case involved applications for personal welfare deputies by parents of young adults. Whilst the wording of the Mental Health Act 1983 Code of Practice suggests that such deputyships will only be required in the most difficult cases, Mr Justice Hayden held that that should not be regarded as a starting point, and that the code in that respect required to be revisited. In the interim, parents and families continue to experience the severe distress recognised by the court as consequent to poor planning for transition.

DUTIES OF LOCAL AUTHORITIES TOWARDS ADULTS OVER THE AGE OF 18 YEARS

8.08 Once over the age of 18 years, young people are faced with a myriad of overlapping and inconsistent legislation. This relates to the duties owed by local authorities towards vulnerable adults who live in their area. As a result of the fragmented and confusing system, this group of vulnerable adults are at risk of slipping through the net due to the number of different regimes.

CARE-EXPERIENCED ADULTS

8.09 A distinct category of individuals to whom duties are owed is care experienced adults, or as referred to in the legislation, care leavers. For the purposes of local authority duties and responsibilities, a child is a care leaver if, after the age of 14, they have spent 13 weeks or more (not necessarily in one block) as a looked after child, and have been in care on or after their 16th birthday.[8] Once their status as a care leaver is triggered, they are entitled to specific support.

8.10 Care leaver duties were first introduced into the Children Act 1989 (CA 1989) by the Children (Leaving Care) Act 2000 which made various amendments to the CA 1989. The CA 1989, s 23C now sets out the duties and obligations imposed on a local authority in relation to care leavers:

> '(2) It is the duty of the local authority to take reasonable steps—
>
> (a) to keep in touch with a former relevant child whether he is within their area or not; and
>
> (b) if they lose touch with him, to re-establish contact.
>
> (3) It is the duty of the local authority—
>
> (a) to continue the appointment of a personal adviser for a former relevant child; and
>
> (b) to continue to keep his pathway plan under regular review.

8 Children (Leaving Care) Act 2000, s.1.

(4) It is the duty of the local authority to give a former relevant child—

(a) assistance of the kind referred to in section 24B(1), to the extent that his welfare requires it;

(b) assistance of the kind referred to in section 24B(2), to the extent that his welfare and his educational or training needs require it;

(c) other assistance, to the extent that his welfare requires it.'

8.11 The duties owed to care leavers have developed further since the 2000 Act. The Children and Social Work Act 2017 was enacted with the publicly stated intention of 'improving the standards of social work and transforming the outcomes of children in care', as stated by the Prime Minister's office on the day that the Bill was first published. The Act deals expressly with transition cases at ss 2 and 3, extending the duties contained with the CA 1989, s 23C to former relevant children aged between 21 and 25 years old 'if the former relevant child informs the local authority that he or she wishes to receive advice and support under the section'.[9] These include access to a personal adviser, assessments and a pathway plan. The assessments carried out under the 2017 Act are with a view to determining whether any services offered by the authority may assist in meeting his or her needs, and if so what advice and support it would be appropriate to provide. That advice and support must be provided at least once in every 12 months.[10]

8.12 The Children and Social Work Act 2017, s 2 sets out the details of the local offer which must be published by a local authority. These include services relating to:

(a) health and well-being;

(b) relationships;

(c) education and training;

(d) employment;

(e) accommodation;

(f) participation in society.

8.13 Importantly, the Act extends the duties of local authorities in the CA 1989, s 23C, to care leavers up to the age of 25 years. This will apply to care leavers over the age of 21, who inform the authority that they wish to receive services until 25 years. At that stage, the authority will have a duty to carry out an assessment and prepare a pathway plan to determine what services would assist. Advice and support must also be provided (although this is limited to only at least once every 12 months), as well as a personal adviser.

8.14 However, these duties are expressed as existing only towards those young adults who inform the authority that they wish to receive services. The difficulties

9 Children and Social Work Act 2017, s 3(2).

10 Children and Social Work Act 2017, s 3(2), (7).

of engaging with care leavers is well known, although the research often involves self selecting participants and is therefore limited.[11] The most vulnerable are very unlikely to be those who will actively engage. A recent scoping review carried out by Bangor University found that barriers to engagement included: identity, independence, trust in services and inadequate support.[12] The authors recommended enabling factors such as persistent and consistent support, time and turning points, and the identification of an authentic trusted professional.

8.15 The care leaver provisions set out within the legislation provide a framework of duties, but they are only one part of the jigsaw of assessments and responsibilities owed by a local authority to young adults.

CARE ACT 2014

8.16 The most recent consideration of community care law, which has impacted on the area of transitions for care leavers can be found in the Care Act 2014 (CA 2014). The CA 2014 sought to bring coherence and consistency to an area of law previously governed by a myriad of competing legislation, with overlapping and often contradictory provisions for community care services previously being found in over 50 different Acts of Parliament.[13] The CA 2014 places the wellbeing of individuals at the heart of the scheme, described in the statutory guidance as relating to the following areas in particular:

(a) personal dignity (including treatment of the individual with respect);

(b) physical and mental health and emotional wellbeing;

(c) protection from abuse and neglect;

(d) control by the individual over day-to-day life (including over care and support provided and the way it is provided);

(e) participation in work, education, training or recreation;

(f) social and economic wellbeing;

(g) domestic, family and personal;

(h) suitability of living accommodation;

(i) the individual's contribution to society.

8.17 The CA 2014 is supported by the Care and Support (Eligibility Criteria) Regulations 2014**,** which set out the specified outcomes which are used as criteria for support needs. The CA 2014, s 9 says that:

---

11 What Works for Children's Social Care *'An Exploratory Study of the Emotional Well-being Needs and Experiences of Care Leavers in England'* (2023).

12 Prendergast, Louise; Davies, Ceryl Teleri; Seddon, Diane; Hartfiel, Ned; Edwards, Rhiannon Tudo *'Barriers and enablers to care-leavers engagement with multi-agency support: A scoping review' Children and Youth Services Review, 159, Article 107501* (2024).

13 Spencer-Lane, *Care Act Manual (3rd Edition, Sweet and Maxwell 2014).*

> 'Where it appears to a local authority that an adult may have needs for care and support, the authority must assess—
>
> (a) whether the adult does have needs for care and support, and
>
> (b) if the adult does, what those needs are.'

8.18 The assessment of children, in the planning of their support needs post-18, is set out at the CA 2014, s 58 as detailed below. The duty applies regardless of whether the child or their carer is in receipt of services prior to them turning 18 years old. The CA 2014 aims to assist the young person themselves, as well as their carer, or young carers and was the first time that such a duty was imposed by legislation.[14]

Care Act 2014, ss 58–66

8.19 The format and details to be included in a Care Act assessment of a child are set out at ss 58 to 66. The Care Act guidance (updated in March 2024) deals with the criteria and content of transitions assessments at Chapter 16. The CA 2014 is also supported by the Care and Support (Children's Carers) Regulations 2014. The Care Act guidance identifies effective person-centred transition planning as essential to help young people and their families to prepare for adulthood, with the wellbeing principle again underpinning decision making. There are specific assessments for each group: a child's needs assessment, a young carer's assessment, and a child's carer's assessment. Collectively, the assessments are referred to as 'transition assessments'.

8.20 The duty to conduct a transition assessment applies when someone is likely to have needs for care and support, or support as a carer, under the CA 2014 when they or the person they care for transition to adult social care. It should be carried out when it will be of significant benefit to the young person. This requires consideration of the following factors, which may contribute to establishing the right time to assess, set out as a non-exhaustive list in the guidance:

(a) the stage they have reached at school and any upcoming exams;

(b) whether the young person or carer wishes to enter further/higher education or training;

(c) whether the young person or carer wishes to get a job when they become a young adult;

(d) whether the young person is planning to move out of their parental home into their own accommodation;

(e) whether the young person will have care leaver status when they become 18;

(f) whether the carer of a young person wishes to remain in or return to employment when the young person leaves full time education;

(g) the time it may take to carry out an assessment;

---

14 Social Care Institute for Excellence (SCIE) 2016.

(h) the time it may take to plan and put in place the adult care and support;

(i) any relevant family circumstance;

(j) any planned medical treatment.

8.21 There is significant overlap with the Children and Families Act 2014 (CFA 2014) which addresses the needs of children and young people with special educational needs or disabilities at the CFA 2014, Pt 5. The CFA 2014 introduced Education and Health Care Plans in the place of the previous statements of Special Educational Needs.

8.22 For the purposes of the CFA 2014, preparation for adulthood must begin from year 9, aged 14 years. This is consistent with the NICE guidance for transition planning. There is recognition within the guidance of the importance of combining multiple assessments where possible, to avoid the young person and their repeating the process for a number of different assessments. The power set out in relation to adult assessments, that enables joined up assessments, applies equally to the assessment of young people. It is recognised that being asked to repeat a story more than once can risk traumatising young people and the duplication of assessments and recounting of life story narratives can only add to this risk.[15]

8.23 The content of a Care Act transitions assessment should include, in addition to the factors relevant to adult assessments:

(a) current needs for care and support and how these impact on wellbeing;

(b) whether the child or carer is likely to have needs for care and support after the child in question becomes 18;

(c) if so, what those needs are likely to be, and which are likely to be eligible needs;

(d) the outcomes the young person or carer wishes to achieve in day-to-day life and how care and support (and other matters) can contribute to achieving them.

8.24 A significant difficulty in working with this age group often relates to consent. In all cases, the young person in question must agree to the assessment, where they have mental capacity to agree, or are competent.[16] Where a local authority is satisfied that the young person lacks the requisite capacity, it can still go ahead with the assessment if it is satisfied that it is in the young person's best interests.

8.25 In relation to consent, it is vital to remember that safeguarding needs should override consent. In the serious case review relating to Steven Hoskin, it was highlighted that vulnerable adults who are known to social care, and who choose to discontinue their services, should continue to be supported if there are safeguarding

---

15 Design Patterns for Mental Health, '*Tell the story once*' https://designpatternsformentalhealth.org/patterns/tell-the-story-once/.

16 Care and support statutory guidance, 2024 para 16.37.

concerns.[17] In Steven's case, the review cited periods of time when he discontinued his communication with social care, and his choices were not discussed with him in any meaningful way:

> '5.13 It is essential that health and social care services review the implications of acceding to people's 'choice' if the latter is not to be construed as abandonment (e.g. Flynn, Keywood and Fovargue 2003). Steven's 'choice' to terminate contact with Adult Social Care was not investigated or explored with him, or other key agencies involved in his care, even though such choices may compound a person's vulnerability; may be made on the basis of inadequate or inappropriate information; or result from the exercise of inappropriate coercion from third parties. Steven's murder has confirmed that the choices of adults with learning disabilities in relation to their health care decision-making (Flynn, Keywood and Fovargue, 2003) can be transposed to social care as follows:
>
> - the process of determining that people are making 'choices' is frequently neither specific nor very explicitly discussed;
> - the discourse of 'rights' and the ideology of 'normalisation' are often implicated in the guise of people's 'choices';
> - the 'choices' are often not discussed with people's GPs, members of Primary Care Teams, support personnel in routine contact;
> - the fatal complications of 'choices' are not always considered.'
>
> (Flynn 2007).

8.26 The CA 2014 expressly requires services to remain in place pending assessment, under the principle of continuity of services.[18] This provision should ensure a smooth transition of care from children to adult services. However, as families often experience, it is not always as straightforward.

Funding

8.27 Once a young person turns 16, they are able to claim benefits in their own right. The nature of the benefits may change from those claimed as a child, for example from the Disability Living Allowance to the Personal Independence Payment. Universal credit also becomes available in some cases. Child benefit and child tax credit are only payable after the age of 16 years if a child remains in full time education, and is not in receipt of universal credit.

8.28 However, the receipt of some types of benefit, for example universal credit, can lead to the young person being means assessed for aspects of their care as they move into adult services. The CA 2014, section 14, gives local authorities the power to charge adults for care and support, including for their identified and eligible needs. Funding provisions are complex and can be found in:

---

17 Flynn, Cornwall Adult Protection Committee, *'The murder of Steven Hoskin: A serious case review'* (2007).

18 CA 2014, s 66.

The Care and Support (Charging and Assessment of Resources) Regulations 2014

The Care and Support (Deferred Payments) Regulations 2014

The Care and Support (Direct Payments) Regulations 2014

The Care and Support and Aftercare (Choice of Accommodation) Regulations 2014

The Care and Support (Preventing Needs for Care and Support) Regulations 2014

8.29 Recent guidance has introduced a care cap; the maximum contribution that anyone can be required to make towards their care costs for their lifetime, as provided for within the CA 2014, s 15.[19]

8.30 If the young person lacks capacity to manage their benefits, then a parent or carer, (in some cases the local authority), can apply to the Department of Work and Pensions to become their appointee, and deal with benefits on their behalf. For some young people, if they lack mental capacity to manage their property and affairs, and if the level of funds justifies the intervention, it will be preferable for a financial deputy to be appointed by an application to the Court of Protection. This can be a family member or a professional, for example a solicitor. Once appointed, the deputy can manage the estate in accordance with the young person's best interests, and with the oversight of the Office of the Public Guardian.

8.31 Whilst the cost of residential care becomes means tested and therefore liable to contributions, there are also other sources of funding available from the age of 18, in the form of NHS Continuing Healthcare (CHC) for relevant cases. This is fully funded care by the NHS and only available to those that meet the criteria of having a 'primary health need'. The National Framework on NHS Continuing Care defines CHC as care to meet needs arising as a result of disability, accident or illness. The package of care includes health and social care services, and sometimes accommodation if that is part of the patient's needs, as set out in the Framework. Therefore, access to CHC funding removes the young person from the means tested scheme of local authority care, and provides free care under NHS funding. It is only available however from the age of 18 years.

8.32 In addition, the local authority may look towards the use of direct payments for a young person to manage their personal budget directly, often with a family member nominated to manage the fund. These are governed by the CA 2014, s 31, and the Care and Support (Direct Payments) Regulations 2014, and are available to all over 16-year olds other than those dealing with drug or alcohol dependency as listed in Sch 1 to the regulations. If a direct payment is requested and the person concerned meets the criteria, then the local authority is obliged to deal with funding in that way. The regulations set out the conditions attached to direct payments and

19 Department of Health and Social Care '*Operational Guidance to implement a lifetime cap on care costs*' (2023).

the terms under which it can be paid. Direct payments can form part of the EHC plan, which should confirm the personal budget, pursuant to the CFA 2014, s 49.

8.33 One complex area in relation to the funding of care arises when a young person has been placed out of area, and then transitions to adult social care whilst in that out of area placement, or moves again. This can occur in social care or educational settings, and also as part of discharges from repeated detentions under the Mental Health Act 1983 (MHA 1983). In these cases, disputes often arise between the local authorities as to which authority should be responsible for the costs of care and the concept of ordinary residence falls to be considered.

ORDINARY RESIDENCE

8.34 Ordinary residence disputes arise between local authorities in the context of young people placed out of their original area due to the need for specialist care that may only be available at a distance from their home. It is a concept that applies to both children and adult social care disputes and is therefore of importance in transitions cases. Ordinary residence is a statutory concept, distinct (but similar) to habitual residence used to decide residence in international dispute cases. Taken at its most simplistic level, ordinary residence considers which local authority is responsible for a person's care needs, and therefore the costs of that care.

8.35 The classic test for 'ordinary residence' is set out in *Shah v London Borough of Barnet*:[20]

> 'unless … it can be shown that the statutory framework or the legal context in which the words are used requires a different meaning I unhesitatingly subscribe to the view that 'ordinarily resident' refers to a man's abode in a particular place or country which he has adopted voluntarily and for settled purposes as part of the regular order of his life for the time being, whether of short or long duration.'

8.36 In relation to children, their ordinary residence usually follows that of the parent. They are unable to make voluntary or settled decisions for themselves. Equally, adults who lack the capacity to make decisions about residence and accommodation will be unable to make voluntary or settled decisions for themselves, and therefore *Shah* becomes of limited relevance.

8.37 The CA 1989, s 105 sets out what is commonly referred to as the 'deeming' provisions for those age under 18 years:

> '(6) In determining the 'ordinary residence' of a child for any purpose of this Act, there shall be disregarded any period in which he lives in any place—
>
> (a) which is a school or other institution;
>
> (b) in accordance with the requirements of a supervision order under this Act

[20] [1983] 1 All ER 226.

(ba) in accordance with the requirements of a youth rehabilitation order under Part 1 of the Criminal Justice and Immigration Act 2008; or

(c) while he is being provided with accommodation by or on behalf of a local authority.'

8.38 Therefore, the ordinary residence of a child is usually that of a parent or carer with whom they were residing before they moved into care. This is often the area in which the trigger events arose for a removal to care under the CA 1989, s 31(8), explored at chapter 6. Once the young person reaches the age of 18 years, the CA 2014 contains similar 'deeming' provisions at s 39:

'(1) Where an adult has needs for care and support which can be met only if the adult is living in accommodation of a type specified in regulations, and the adult is living in accommodation in England of a type so specified, the adult is to be treated for the purposes of this Part as ordinarily resident—

(a) in the area in which the adult was ordinarily resident immediately before the adult began to live in accommodation of a type specified in the regulations, or

(b) if the adult was of no settled residence immediately before the adult began to live in accommodation of a type so specified, in the area in which the adult was present at that time.

(2) Where, before beginning to live in his or her current accommodation, the adult was living in accommodation of a type so specified (whether or not of the same type as the current accommodation), the reference in subsection (1)(a) to when the adult began to live in accommodation of a type so specified is a reference to the beginning of the period during which the adult has been living in accommodation of one or more of the specified types for consecutive periods.'

8.39 Therefore, under either the CA 1989 or the CA 2014, a person placed 'out of area' is deemed to remain ordinarily resident in the area of the placing authority. The Care and Support (Ordinary Residence) (Specified Accommodation) Regulations 2014 provide that the deeming provisions apply if the person is accommodated in a care home, shared lives accommodation or supported living. In *R (Greenwich) v Secretary of State and Bexley*[21] Charles J held that the deeming provisions should be treated as applying also where a person 'should have been' provided with the relevant accommodation. Accordingly, a local authority cannot avoid the effect of the deeming provisions through failure to comply with its statutory duties.

8.40 Disputes between local authorities in respect of ordinary residence are referred to the Secretary of State for resolution. There are a number of significant case law decisions, particularly when considering aftercare for a young person following discharge from a Mental Health Act detention, pursuant to the MHA 1983, s 117.

---

21 [2006] EWHC 2576 (Admin).

8.41 In *R (on the application of Cornwall Council) v Secretary of State for Health*[22] it was held that a man who lacked capacity to decide where he lived was ordinarily resident for the purposes of adult social care in Wiltshire despite having no current links current with the area. This was because it was Wiltshire Council who had arranged a foster placement for him while a child, in South Gloucestershire, meaning it retained ordinary residence for the purposes of the CA 1989, and that this responsibility continued when he became an adult and fell under the jurisdiction of the then National Assistance Act 1948. It was irrelevant for ordinary residence purposes that his family was then resident in Cornwall, whom the then health secretary had previously deemed to be responsible for his care, in a determination in 2012:

> '……..it follows that PH's placement in South Gloucestershire by Wiltshire is not to be regarded as bringing about a change in his ordinary residence. Throughout the period until he reached 18 he remained continuously where he was placed by Wiltshire, under an arrangement made and paid for by them. For fiscal and administrative purposes his ordinary residence continued to be in their area, regardless of where they determined that he should live.' (as per Lord Carnwarth, para 60)

8.42 Under the MHA 1983, s 117(3) the relevant local authority is determined by the place where the person was ordinarily resident immediately before their detention for treatment. As confirmed by the Care Act guidance this remains the case even if they are discharged for aftercare to a different area, and even if they moved to a third area.[23] However, the Care Act guidance goes on to say that if the person is detained again while receiving aftercare in a second or third area, it would be the local authority for *this* area that would take over responsibility for their aftercare.[24]

8.43 The Supreme Court has now held that 'ordinarily resident' should be given its ordinary meaning (determined by the facts of where a person lives), in the case of *R ((Worcestershire County Council) v Secretary of State for Health and Social Care*.[25] Applying the *Shah* test[26], residence must be voluntarily adopted and there must be a degree of settled purpose:

> 'unless … it can be shown that the statutory framework or the legal context in which the words are used requires a different meaning I unhesitatingly subscribe to the view that ordinarily resident refers to a man's abode in a particular place or country which he has adopted voluntarily and for settled purposes as part of the regular order of his life for the time being, whether of short or long duration'.

8.44 The case concerned a dispute about which local authority, Swindon or Worcestershire, was under a duty to arrange after care pursuant to the MHA 1983, s 117. JG was first detained under the MHA 1983, s 3 when she lived in Worcestershire. She was placed in Swindon on discharge, in a care home. At that

22 [2015] UKSC 46.
23 Care and Support Statutory Guidance, 2024, para 19.64.
24 Ibid.
25 [2023] UKSC 31.
26 *R v Barnet London Borough Council, Ex p Shah* [1983].

stage, Worcestershire continued to fund the placement. JG was then detained again, from Swindon, and a dispute arose as to the funding of the placement following her second discharge.

8.45 The Secretary of State originally determined that the responsibility should stay with the second placing Council, in this case Swindon. Swindon appealed and the Secretary of State reversed that decision and found that Worcestershire were then responsible. In doing so, he applied the Cornwall decision, and said that the area in which she was 'immediately before being *first* detained' was responsible. At first instance, Worcestershire sought judicial review of the substituted decision[27] and were successful:

> 'Although any change in the patient's ordinary residence after discharge will affect the local authority responsible for their social care services, it will not affect the local authority responsible for commissioning the patient's section 117 after-care. Under section 117 of the 1983 Act, as amended by the Care Act 2014, if a person is ordinarily resident in local authority area (A) immediately before detention under the 1983 Act, and moves on discharge to local authority area (B) and moves again to local authority area (C), local authority (A) will remain responsible for providing or commissioning their after-care. However, if the patient, having become ordinarily resident after discharge in local authority area (B) or (C), is subsequently detained in hospital for treatment again, the local authority in whose area the person was ordinarily resident immediately before their subsequent admission (local authority (B) or (C)) will be responsible for their after-care when they are discharged from hospital.'

8.46 The Secretary of State appealed to the Court of Appeal. The appeal was allowed and the Court of Appeal found that Worcestershire as the originating authority should meet the funding, as JG continued to be ordinarily resident in Worcestershire before her second period of detention.

8.47 In the Supreme Court, the issue turned on where JG had been ordinarily resident immediately before being detained for the purposes of the MHA 1983, s 117(3)(a). JG was ordinarily resident in Worcestershire before her first detention and that authority was therefore obliged to provide her with services after her first discharge. Worcestershire sought to argue that its duty to provide after care services ended upon the second discharge, or alternatively at the start of the second detention.

8.48 The court held, allowing Worcestershire's appeal, that under the MHA 1983, s 117(2) the duty exists until such time as the relevant authorities are satisfied that the person concerned is no longer in need of such services. At no time had Worcestershire made such a decision. However, JG had been living in Swindon immediately before her second detention. Giving the words 'ordinary resident' their usual meaning, the court found that she had been ordinarily resident in Swindon.

8.49 The case now provides some clarity in the area of ordinary residence and s 117 aftercare, although individual cases continue to pose complex problems.

27 *R (Worcestershire County Council) v Secretary of State for Health and Social Care* [2021] EWHC 682 (Admin).

Importantly for individuals, the guidance is clear that notwithstanding funding disputes, patients should receive ongoing care whilst those disputes are resolved.[28] Authorities must also meet any urgent needs for care and support regardless of the person's ordinary residence.[29]

PROTECTIVE MEASURES AVAILABLE TO OLDER TEENAGERS AND ADULTS

8.50 In the final section in this chapter, we will look at two further ways in which a local authority can act to protect vulnerable young people and adults. The first, wardship, only applies to those under the age of 18 years. It is echoed however in the use of the inherent jurisdiction as it relates to vulnerable adults.

Wardship

8.51 The use of the inherent jurisdiction, the procedure and framework are examined elsewhere in this book. The use of wardship as a protective measure is perhaps one of the oldest ways in which the inherent jurisdiction may be deployed, vesting responsibility for the child's welfare in the court. Wardship has its roots in the feudalism of the Middle Ages when the custody of a ward could be passed to a local Lord in the event of the death of a tenant. Wardship at that time could be bought and sold, with the selling of wards into marriage, or the receipt of the ward's profits of estates until their majority. Wardship has subsisted in one form or another since that time, but gathered a greater emphasis on child protection in the 19th century.

8.52 Since the passage of the CA 1989, wardship no longer exists as the mechanism by which a child can be placed into the care of a local authority. It now exists within the inherent jurisdiction; the great safety net, to only be commenced if it is clear that the issues concerning the child cannot be resolved under the CA 1989.[30] The grounds for a wardship application now often relate to emergency medical treatment, forced marriage or child abduction.

8.53 Importantly, due to the restrictions imposed by the CA 1989, the jurisdiction cannot be used to require an authority to accommodate a child.[31] These restrictions have been considered by the court in the decision of *Re M (Children)*.[32] That case involved a child who had previously been in the care of the local authority and subject to an interim care order. Upon the child reaching the age of 17, the court effectively 'swapped' the care order with one in wardship, approving the same care plan and leaving the arrangements on the ground unchanged. It was argued on appeal that as the local authority agreed to this course of action, and was agreeable to providing the

---

28 Care and Support Statutory Guidance, 2024, para 19.11.

29 CA 2014, s 19.

30 Family Procedure Rules 2010, Practice Direction 12D.

31 CA 1989, s 100(2).

32 [2016] EWCA Civ 937.

ward with accommodation, it had not been 'required' to do so, and that all the court had done was endorse the agreed way forward. In those circumstances it was said that it was appropriate for the wardship to continue.

8.54 The Court of Appeal response was clear; the inherent jurisdiction cannot be used to create a care order over a 17-year old. It is a distinct jurisdiction. It does not vest parental responsibility in the local authority, but does mean that no significant decision should be taken in respect of the ward's arrangements without oversight of the court. It can be invoked when a child is also voluntarily accommodated by the local authority under the CA 1989, s 20.[33]

8.55 Once the wardship is granted, which takes place immediately upon the issuing of the originating summons[34], the court retains oversight of the decisions made in relation to placement, contact and medical treatment. Although day to day care and control of the ward is given to (usually) a local authority, no important step can be taken in the child's life without the court's consent.

8.56 Commonly, the application is brought with a request for injunctive relief to protect the ward either from undesirable associations, relating to medical treatment or to protect abducted children. Orders commonly sought include:

(a) orders to restrain publicity;

(b) orders to prevent an undesirable association;

(c) orders relating to medical treatment;

(d) orders to protect abducted children, or children where the case has another substantial foreign element; and

(e) orders for the return of children to and from another state[35].

8.57 The jurisdiction expires at age 18, although in *Re M (Children)* above,[36] an unsuccessful attempt was made to extend the wardship beyond minority;

> '46. By a Respondent's Notice the local authority sought to establish that the protection of wardship and the inherent jurisdiction provided by the judge's order should continue beyond T's 18th birthday. Mr McCarthy submitted that an extension of the order could be achieved under the inherent jurisdiction, notwithstanding the fact that Senior Courts Act 1981, s 41 describes the use of wardship only with respect to 'minors'. As an illustration of a recent occasion where the court has extended wardship orders into adulthood reference was made to the decision of Baker J in *Re SO (Wardship: Extension of Protective Injunction Order)* [2015] EWHC 935 (Fam).
>
> 47. Re SO concerned a girl, who was by then aged 17 years and who had been the subject of wardship proceedings for many years aimed at protecting her from her father who had previously abducted her and who was serving a prison sentence for

33 *E (A Child)* [2012] EWCA Civ 1773.

34 Senior Courts Act 1981, s 41.

35 Family Procedure Rules 2010, Practice Direction 12D.

36 [2016] EWCA Civ 937.

inciting the murder of her mother. In view of the child's impending 18th birthday, the mother applied for an extension of the protective injunctions into adulthood. Baker J held that an order made during the currency of wardship proceedings may be extended into adulthood (applying the dicta of Thorpe LJ in *Re F (Adult: Court's Jurisdiction)* [2000] 2 FLR 512). Having considered the merits of the application Baker J made an order extending the injunction.

48. I regard Re SO as an uncontroversial example of the use of the inherent jurisdiction to protect a vulnerable individual, be they either a child or an adult, in the particular circumstances of that case by granting or extending an injunction. At no stage does Baker J contemplate the extension of the status of wardship beyond the age of 18 years and the extension of wardship was not a prerequisite for the court's jurisdiction to extend the injunctions. The authority of Re SO does not in any manner assist the local authority in the present appeal in establishing the adventurous submission that the court has jurisdiction to extend wardship into adulthood.' (as per McFarlane LJ)

PROTECTION OF VULNERABLE ADULTS

8.58 As set out above, whilst wardship may not extend into adulthood, other protective orders granted within the inherent jurisdiction are capable of protecting vulnerable adults. Prior to the implementation of the MCA 2005, the inherent jurisdiction was described as 'in substance and reality, a jurisdiction in relation to incompetent adults which [was] for all practical purposes indistinguishable from its well-established parens patriae or wardship in relation to children'.[37]

8.59 The use of the inherent jurisdiction to protect the vulnerable adult was described in the judgment of Mr Justice Munby, (as he then was), in the case of *Re SA (Vulnerable Adult with Capacity: Marriage).*[38] SA had been a ward of court as a child, and there was a significant risk that she would be taken abroad to be married. The case predated the availability of forced marriage orders. The High Court invoked the inherent jurisdiction to protect her and used its authority to prohibit SA from being taken to Pakistan, or entering into a marriage contract without her consent.

8.60 In the *Re SA* judgment, Munby J stated that:

> '[i]n the context of the inherent jurisdiction I would treat as a vulnerable adult someone who, whether or not mentally incapacitated, and whether or not suffering from any mental illness, or mental disorder, is or may be unable to take care of him or herself, or unable to protect him or herself against significant harm or exploitation, or who is deaf, blind, or dumb, or who is substantially handicapped by illness, injury or congenital deformity. This, I emphasise, is not and is not intended to be a definition. It is descriptive, not definitive; indicative rather than prescriptive'. (§82).

8.61 The list above is not prescriptive. The question of whether or not a young person has lost capacity as a result of third party influence, or are vulnerable for other

37 *E v Channel Four News & Ors* [2005] 2 FLR 913, para 55.

38 [2006] 1 FLR 867.

reasons but have mental capacity, may arise in a variety of contexts. An application to the court may require consideration of expert evidence, to establish the cause of the individuals' vulnerability, whether that is related to a third party or not.

8.62 Following the introduction of the MCA 2005 and the reformed Court of Protection in 2007, there had been some doubt as to the ongoing existence of the 'Munby vulnerable' jurisdiction. These were resolved by the decision of the Court of Appeal in *A Local Authority v DL & Ors*.[39] It is now settled law that the inherent jurisdiction remains an available forum for those that have capacity within the meaning of the MCA 2005, but still need protection, as a result of external influence, coercion or control.[40] In the case of *A Local Authority v BF*,[41] it was reiterated that the jurisdiction extends to those outwith the MCA 2005, to provide an additional protection. In any case in which there is evidence to suggest that the adult lacks the capacity to make the decision, then the correct recourse is to the Court of Protection. The use of the inherent jurisdiction is a last resort when a person is vulnerable but otherwise has capacity.

8.63 The test for engaging the inherent jurisdiction is whether the proposed intervention is necessary and proportionate, (*DL* at paragraphs 66 (per McFarlane LJ) and 76 (per Davis LJ)). The starting point is to facilitate unencumbered decision making by the adult, rather than taking the decision on their behalf. The court is naturally reluctant to make orders involving the compulsion of vulnerable adults and will ordinarily look to formulate the orders sought as against the third party instead.

8.64 In all cases, the inherent jurisdiction should only be used if no other legislative mechanism can adequately safeguard against the risk of harm. For example, if contact between adults is the issue, then it may be possible to regulate the relationships via the Family Law Act 1996, or the Serious Crime Act 2015 in relation to controlling or coercive behaviour. Domestic violence protection exists in a number of criminal statutory provisions, or within civil remedies such as the Protection from Harassment Act 1997. If the protection sought would be available under statute, then the inherent jurisdiction cannot be resorted to in the event that statute does not produce the desired outcome. As has been observed by the High Court:

> 'The inherent jurisdiction cannot be used to simply reverse the outcome under a statutory scheme, which deals with the very situation in issue, on the basis that the court disagrees with the statutory outcome'.[42]

8.65 One issue for young adults is the continuation of injunctive relief that was granted whilst they were under the age of 18 years. Whether or not injunctions granted within the inherent jurisdiction can be continued was resolved by the case of

39 [2012] EWCA Civ 253.

40 *LBL v RYJ and VJ* [2010] EWHC 2665 (CoP).

41 [2018] EWCA Civ 2962.

42 *JK v A Local Health Board* [2019] EWHC 67 (Fam), para 57.

Re SO[43] in which Baker J held that he was in 'no doubt' that the court had the power to make the order:

> '(1) Following *Re F* (2001) Fam 38 and *Re SA* (2006) EWHC 2942, that where a court has ruled a young person is at risk at harm and has granted protective injunctions, it has to power to extend the order beyond the child's 18th birthday. This originates in the protective nature of the jurisdiction and is supported by articles 2,6 and 8 of the ECHR.
>
> (2) Where the court had jurisdiction at the start of the proceedings on the grounds of habitual residence that jurisdiction continues until the conclusion of proceedings even if the child becomes habitually residence elsewhere.
>
> (3) On the facts of the case it was imperative that the court makes orders to protect the child.'

8.66 It is sometimes the case that individuals lack capacity in respect of certain decision making domains, such as residence or care, but have capacity to make decisions about contact with others. In those instances, where there are safeguarding concerns in respect of the contact, or the control that a third party is exercising over the young person, it is possible to make applications to both the Court of Protection and the inherent jurisdiction to run concurrently in court, before an appropriate judge. The use of the inherent jurisdiction can assist in the interim, whilst further assessments are carried out.[44]

8.67 The focus of any use of the inherent jurisdiction is to be facilitative, not dictatorial.[45] One of the purposes of the use of the jurisdiction is to provide a safe space for the vulnerable adult to make their own decisions, free from external influence, and to remove whatever barrier is existing to prevent their own autonomy being exercised.[46] Care should be taken to avoid the 'protection imperative':

> 'the risk that a capacity assessment will be unduly influenced by a perceived need to protect the individual rather than guided by a purely objective analysis'.[47]

8.68 The purpose of the inherent jurisdiction is to promote independent decision making, and to provide protection. Any order made must respect the individual's Article 8 rights under the ECHR, their dignity and autonomy. Orders sought should be necessary and proportionate, and least interventionist.

---

43 [2015] EWHC 935 (Fam).

44 *Wakefield MDC and Wakefield CCG v DN and MN* [2019] EWHC 2306 (Fam); *London Borough of Wandsworth v M & Ors* [2017] EWHC 2435.

45 *DL v A Local Authority* [2012] EWCA Civ 253.

46 Although this is not the limit of the jurisdiction, see *Westminster City Council v C* [2008] EWCA Civ 198.

47 *Oldham MBC v GW and PW* [2007] EWHC 136 (Fam).

Limits of the jurisdiction

8.69 However, there are some limits to the inherent jurisdiction. In the case of *A City Council v LS & Ors,*[48] set out above, it was held that it could not be used to authorise secure accommodation and therefore a deprivation of liberty of a young person who had not been looked after previously by the local authority, and was in effect, carrying out criminal activities. Both the 17-year old and his mother opposed the deprivation. McDonald J held that 'it is clearly established that the High Court cannot exercise its inherent jurisdiction to grant authority to the local authority to accommodate *a child where the local authority would not otherwise be able to do so under the statutory scheme'*, making reference to *Re E (A Child)* [49] and *Re M (Jurisdiction: Wardship).*[50]

8.70 Another limit to the jurisdiction is the use of injunctions against the vulnerable adult themselves, which are theoretically possible but would require specific evidence that the individual has capacity to understand and abide by such an order.[51] Injunctions can only be enforceable if the subject of the order understands the terms. It maybe that the court considers that the young person needs protection from their own behaviour, but the use of the court's powers to provide that protection does not promote autonomy, and care needs to be taken in that regard. In accordance with the well-established principles of the MCA 2005, individuals have the right to make unwise decisions.

INHERENT JURISDICTION AND DEPRIVATION OF LIBERTY OF ADULTS

8.71 It is also doubtful that the inherent jurisdiction can be used to deprive a capacitous adult of their liberty. There have been a number of recent decisions relating to this issue. If a vulnerable adult has capacity to make decisions about where to live, but is putting their life at risk by choosing to live with a violent or abusive family member, the natural response of safeguarding authorities is to seek to remove them from that situation. That may involve a removal to a care home, from which they are not permitted to leave. If the result of the orders sought meet the 'acid test' of *Cheshire West* (explained in chapter 3), then there will be a deprivation of liberty for the purposes of Article 5(1) of the ECHR.[52] However, the use of the inherent jurisdiction in that respect is fraught with difficulty. Not least, the terms of Article 5, which remind us that:

> 'Everyone has the right to liberty and security of person. No one shall be deprived of his liberty save in the following cases and in accordance with a procedure prescribed by law:

---

48 [2019] EWHC 1328 (Fam).

49 [2012] EWCA Civ 1773 at para 16.

50 [2016] EWCA Civ 937 at para 39.

51 *Redcar and Cleveland Borough Council v PR and others* [2019] EWHC 2305.

52 *Cheshire West and Chester Council v P* [2014] UKSC 19.

e) the lawful detention of persons …….., of persons of unsound mind…

…

Susceptibility to malign external influences, or vulnerability due to ill health does not render an otherwise capacitous adult 'of unsound mind'.'

8.72 In the early decision of *Re PS (Incapacitated or Vulnerable Adult)*,[53] it was held that:

'[§16] It is in my judgment quite clear that a judge exercising the inherent jurisdiction of the court (whether the inherent jurisdiction of the court with respect to children or the inherent jurisdiction with respect to incapacitated or vulnerable adults) has power to direct that the child or adult in question shall be placed at and remain in a specified institution such as, for example, a hospital, residential unit, care home or secure unit. It is equally clear that the court's powers extend to authorising that person's detention in such a place and the use of reasonable force (if necessary) to detain him and ensure that he remains there: see *Norfolk and Norwich Healthcare (NHS) Trust v W* [1996] 2 FLR 613 (adult), *A Metropolitan Borough Council v DB* [1997] 1 FLR 767 (child), *Re MB (Medical Treatment)* [1997] 2 FLR 426 at page 439 (adult) and *Re C (Detention: Medical Treatment)* [1997] 2 FLR 180 (child).'

…

'[§23] if the inherent jurisdiction is to be invoked to justify the detention of someone like PS in somewhere like the T unit, the following minimum requirements must be satisfied in order to comply with Article 5:

i) The detention must be authorised by the court on application made by the local authority and before the detention commences.

ii) Subject to the exigencies of urgency or emergency the evidence must establish unsoundness of mind of a kind or degree warranting compulsory confinement. In other words, there must be evidence establishing at least a prima facie case that the individual lacks capacity and that confinement of the nature proposed is appropriate.

iii) Any order authorising detention must contain provision for an adequate review at reasonable intervals, in particular with a view to ascertaining whether there still persists unsoundness of mind of a kind or degree warranting compulsory confinement.'

8.73 Therefore a need was identified for evidence of unsoundness of mind, to establish that the individual lacks capacity.

8.74 In a number of cases, the court has been asked to consider using the inherent jurisdiction to deprive capacitous adults of their liberty. In the follow up to the permission decision of *A Local Authority v BF*,[54] cited as *Southend-on-Sea Borough Council v Meyers*,[55] it was held that:

---

53 [2007] EWHC 623 (Fam).

54 [2018] EWCA Civ 2962.

55 [2019] EWHC 399 (Fam).

'However well motivated the State may be in seeking, paternalistically, to protect people from their own unwise decisions, it is a dangerous course which has the potential to threaten fundamental rights and freedoms.... the inherent jurisdiction is should be utilised sparingly.'(§42)

8.75 Mr Meyers had the capacity to decide where he wanted to reside and with whom. He did not therefore satisfy the Article 5(1)(e) criteria of being of 'unsound mind'. His son was considered by the court to be 'needy, irrational, frequently out of control…'. The court declined to authorise any deprivation of liberty to prevent Mr Meyers from living at his property with his son. It did however find that it was a permissible restriction to impose a condition on his return to his home, that being that his son should be excluded from the property. The court held that a restriction to that extent was a necessary and proportionate interference with Mr Meyers' Article 8 rights.

8.76 In *Mazhar v Birmingham Community Healthcare Foundation NHS Trust & Ors* ,[56] the Court of Appeal considered the question of deprivation of liberty under the inherent jurisdiction. The court at first instance had heard an ex parte and without notice application under the inherent jurisdiction enabling Mr Mazhar to be removed from his home and taken to hospital to receive urgent medical treatment. There was no suggestion that Mr Mazhar lacked mental capacity to make decisions about residence. On appeal, the court noted that this was the first time that the question of deprivation of liberty of a vulnerable adult with capacity had reached the Court of Appeal. However, due to procedural matters, the court held that it did not need to determine the question. It was observed that there was authority in each direction, and the qualification in the case of *Winterwerp*[57], for 'emergency cases' suggested that some departure from the criteria was possible.

8.77 In relation to out of hours inherent jurisdiction applications, the court emphasised that due to the emergency nature of those applications, it was vital that the applicant should spell out the evidence on which it relies, the appropriate test and the submissions to be made. It was said that there may be a greater risk of the protective imperative when the court was operating at speed, and particular care is needed. The court found that Mr Mazhar's Article 6 rights under the European Convention on Human Rights had been breached by the out of hours without notice application, and there had been a flagrant denial of justice. Guidance was given for this type of application at paragraph 74 of the judgment.

8.78 In *Wakefield Metropolitan District Council & Anor v DN & Anor*,[58] the court was concerned with a 25 year old man, who was not 'significantly intellectually impaired' and was 'capable of clear thinking'. As part of his community order arising from criminal convictions, he was required to live at a supported living placement. He was objectively deprived of his liberty. Mr Justice Cobb (as he then was) held that he was not a person of unsound mind, nor was he vulnerable. He had a diagnosis

---

56 [2020] EWCA Civ 1377.

57 *Winterwerp v The Netherlands* (1979) 2 EHRR 387.

58 [2019] EWHC 2306 (Fam).

of autism, general anxiety disorder and traits of emotionally unstable personality disorder. It was not argued that he lacked capacity to make decisions about residence. He consented to the confinement, and had he refused, he would have been likely to serve a sentence of imprisonment. The court held that the inherent jurisdiction should not be used to deprive a capacitous person of their liberty, and as a result the restrictions in place would have to be reduced.

8.79 The view taken in DN above differs from that in *Hertfordshire County Council v AB*[59] in which Mrs Justice Knowles authorised the deprivation of liberty of a patient subject to the MHA 1983, ss 37 and 41, a restricted patient, who had been conditionally discharged to a setting which amounted to a deprivation of liberty. The judgment considered the position in relation to mental health patients, and the findings of the Supreme Court in *Secretary of State for Justice (Respondent) v MM (Appellant)* ,[60] which held that the MHA 1983 does not permit either the First Tier Tribunal or the Secretary of State to impose conditions on discharge amounting to a deprivation of liberty. The court in AB was persuaded that the inherent jurisdiction could be used to authorise deprivation in those circumstances.

8.80 However, in the more recent decision of *Cumbria, Northumberland Tyne & Wear NHS Foundation Trust & Anor v EG*,[61] Mrs Justice Lieven refused to authorise a deprivation of liberty in the inherent jurisdiction. The court was faced with an issue arising under the MHA 1983, in the aftermath of the *Re MM* decision. Mrs Justice Lieven found that it was possible for the case to be dealt with through a construction of the MHA 1983, s 72. She went on however, in obiter, to express her very clear view that the inherent jurisdiction does not extend to the deprivation of liberty of adults with capacity, on the basis both of European jurisprudence and also the focus on the inherent jurisdiction as facilitative rather than dictatorial.

8.81 The issue of the use of the inherent jurisdiction to deprive someone with capacity of their liberty is yet to be decided by the Court of Appeal or Supreme Court. Whilst the preponderance of High Court decisions suggest that it is beyond the reach of the inherent jurisdiction, until we have a determination on appeal, it remains a difficult issue.

CONCLUSION

8.82 This chapter has looked at some of the concerns that arise when a young person with additional vulnerabilities reaches the age of 18 years. They continue to be faced with various different legal regimes and changes in the social care and health provision, which can seem impossible to navigate without expert advice and assistance.

---

59 [2018] EWHC 3103 (Fam).

60 [2018] UKSC 60.

61 [2021] EWHC 2990 (Fam).

Chapter 9

CASE LAW SUMMARIES

INTRODUCTION

9.01 This chapter contains summaries of the facts and decisions from the key cases which relate to children and young people who are or may be deprived of their liberty. This chapter is not an exhaustive overview of all reported decisions in this area, but includes the case law where key principles arose or were determined. This chapter is up to date from the date of publication, but there will no doubt be significant decisions which follow publication of this book which may impact the legal position going forward.

CASES

Hewer v Bryant [1970] 1 QB 357

9.02 This Court of Appeal decision concerned the interpretation of 'custody' in respect of a parent's custody of their child. In this case, the child, H, lived with his parents until the age of 15 when he left home to attend a farm training centre. Following his training, H remained living outside of the family home as he began work on a farm. For the application before it, the court was required to determine whether the child was in the custody of his parents at various points of his childhood. As part of its analysis, the court recognised that the legal powers of H's parents to physically control him and his movements diminished as H got older. Lord Denning MR described the extent of parental control as:

> '...the legal right of a parent to the custody of a child...is a dwindling right which the courts will hesitate to enforce against the wishes of the child, and the more so the older he is. It starts with a right of control and ends with little more than advice.'[1]

Guzzardi v Italy 7367/76 [1980] ECHR 5

9.03 The European Court of Human Rights heard this case, brought by Mr Guzzardi, concerning what he claimed to have been an unlawful deprivation of his liberty. Mr Guzzardi was imprisoned in Milan in 1973 for offences of conspiracy and abduction. Mr Guzzardi was transferred from prison to the island of Asinara under

---

1 *Hewer v Bryant* [1970] 1 QB 357 at 369.

a regime of special supervision provided for in domestic law and recommended because of the perceived dangerousness of Mr Guzzardi. Whilst living in Asinara, Mr Guzzardi described that he was confined to a radius of 800 metres in which those persons under special supervision were permitted to live. Permission had to be sought for inhabitants to travel outside of their designated area, usually on medical grounds. Mr Guzzardi was required to be in his place of residence between 10.00pm and 7.00am unless permission had been sought in advance. Permission was required for the inhabitants to be joined on the island by their family. Employment was difficult to source and telephone communications to the outside world were subject to monitoring. Mr Guzzardi summarised his circumstances within his application, describing 'the arbitrary action of the Italian authorities' which required him to reside on a scrap of land, unable to work or keep his family with him, unable to practise religion and as being 'barbarous imprisonment, the most degrading and pernicious incarceration.'[2] The government, responding to the application, argued that Mr Guzzardi was not deprived of his liberty by virtue of his residence on Asinara and if he were, this would be justified under Article 5(1)(e) of the European Convention of Human Right (ECHR), that Mr Guzzardi was lawfully detained for the prevention of spreading infectious diseases, persons of unsound mind, drug addicts or vagrants.[3]

9.04 In determining whether or not Mr Guzzardi was deprived of his liberty, the court reminded itself that it is to be concerned with the physical liberty of the relevant person and that no person should be 'dispossessed of this liberty in an arbitrary fashion'.[4] The court proceeded to evaluate Mr Guzzardi's circumstances, noting that 'the starting point must be his concrete situation and account must be taken of a whole range of criteria such as the type, duration, effects and manner of implementation of the measure in question'.[5] The court then described its approach to the analysis of the regime with a phrase that has persisted throughout subsequent jurisprudence: '[t]he difference between deprivation of and restriction upon liberty is nonetheless merely one of degree or intensity, and not one of nature or substance.'[6]

9.05 It was recognised that Mr Guzzardi was not confined in the traditional sense to a cell or tiny area secured by a physical boundary, but this feature or absence of feature was not determinative of whether Mr Guzzardi was deprived of his liberty. The court instead was concerned with the cumulative measures in place and what they amounted to holistically. Taking into account the limited area in which Mr Guzzardi was permitted to move, the oversight and supervision by authorities of Mr Guzzardi's daily life, his limited social contacts, and the duration of his stay, the court determined that Mr Guzzardi had been deprived of his liberty by virtue of his compulsory residence on Asinara.[7]

9.06 The court then turned to the government's argument that any deprivation of liberty was permissible under Article 5(1)(e) of the ECHR in that Mr Guzzardi, as

---

2 *Guzzardi v Italy* 7367/76 [1980] ECHR 5, para 53.
3 *Guzzardi v Italy* 7367/76 [1980] ECHR 5, para 57.
4 *Guzzardi v Italy* 7367/76 [1980] ECHR 5, para 92.
5 *Guzzardi v Italy* 7367/76 [1980] ECHR 5, para 92.
6 *Guzzardi v Italy* 7367/76 [1980] ECHR 5, para 93.
7 *Guzzardi v Italy* 7367/76 [1980] ECHR 5, para 95.

a mafiosi, could be considered a vagrant.[8] Taking the word 'vagrant' on its ordinary meaning, the court did not agree with the government's argument and did not find that Article 5(1)(e) was applicable to Mr Guzzardi. Having considered the other possible routes to a lawful deprivation of liberty set down by Article 5, the court did not find that any of the other exceptions applied and Mr Guzzardi's Article 5 rights had been breached.

Gillick v West Norfolk and Wisbech Area Health Authority [1986] AC 112

9.07 This case, decided by the House of Lords, was a fundamentally important judgment relating to the rights of a parent and the appropriate exercise of those rights. Although this case did not directly involve the issue of a deprivation of liberty, it is frequently referred to in cases which do because of the guiding principles which arose in respect of the appropriate exercise of parental consent and the consent of the child.

9.08 The case was initially brought by Mrs Gillick, a mother, with five daughters under the age of 16. Mrs Gillick was concerned about her daughters being provided with contraceptive advice and treatment without her knowledge or consent, whilst they remained under 16. She considered that to do so would be unlawful, and sought a declaration of the same from the court. In order to decide the issue, the court was tasked with determining three questions: whether a girl under 16 has the legal capacity to give valid consent to contraceptive advice and treatment including medical examination; whether giving such advice and treatment to a girl under 16 without her parents' consent infringes the parents' rights; and, whether a doctor who gives such advice or treatment to a girl under 16 without her parents' consent incurs criminal liability. The first two of those questions are relevant insofar as they relate to the scope of parental responsibility and the ability of a child to provide valid consent.

9.09 Beginning with the first question and the ability of children under 16 to consent to contraceptive advice, examination and treatment, the court examined the existing law relating to the ability of under 16s to make decisions for themselves. It was recognised that at that time, the law did not distinguish contraceptive advice and treatment from other forms of medical advice provided to children. The court logically considered that it would be 'verging on the absurd to suggest that a girl or a boy aged 15 could not effectively consent, for example, to have a medical examination of some trivial injury to his body or even to have a broken arm set.' Going further, the court held that when a child is capable of understanding what is proposed and expressing their wish about it, there is no good reason to say that the child lacks capacity to express a valid wish and authorise a medical professional to undertake an examination and provide treatment. This decision has since been formulated into a test which can be used to establish whether or not the child concerned is able to consent to medical advice and treatment. Following Lord Scarman's words, that test, labelled now as the test of *Gillick* competence, is whether the child demonstrates

8 *Guzzardi v Italy* 7367/76 [1980] ECHR 5, para 97.

sufficient understanding and intelligence to understand fully what is proposed. If the child is able to demonstrate the requisite understanding and intelligence, they are able to consent to medical advice, examination and treatment themselves.

9.10 Moving to the second question, the court was tasked with determining the scope of a parents' rights and duties in respect of the medical treatment of their child. Setting a background to the question, the House of Lords considered the general notion of parental rights and their boundaries. It confirmed that the rights of a parent exist for the benefit of the child, not their parent, and should only be exercised insofar as they enable a parent to perform their duties towards their children. The court recognised that most parents will relax the control they have over their children as they get older, and that the degree of control exercised by a parent will vary depending on the child's understanding and intelligence. Parental rights were described as 'dwindling' over time. Although the court was unable to set down a rigid limit on parental rights in reference to a child's age, it accepted that the rights of a parent do not wholly disappear until a child reaches 18. The principle of law distilled by Lord Scarman was 'that parental rights are derived from a parental duty and exist only so long as they are needed for the protection of the person and property of the child.'

9.11 Guarding against the difficulties which may ensue in the formulation of a rigid test, Lord Scarman explained:

> 'Certainty is always an advantage in the law, and in some branches of the law it is a necessity. But it brings with it an inflexibility and a rigidity which in some branches of the law can obstruct justice, impede the law's development and stamp on the law the mark of obsolescence where what is needed is the capacity for development. The law relating to parent and child is concerned with the problems of the growth and maturity of the human personality. If the law should impose on the process of 'growing up' fixed limits where nature knows only a continuous process, the price would be artificiality and a lack of realism in an area where the law must be sensitive to human development and social change.'

9.12 It was faced with this dilemma that the House of Lords declined to set any definite limits on the exercise of parental rights based upon the age of the child concerned. Instead, the court set down a generalised principle that the 'parental right yields to the child's right to make his own decisions when he reaches a sufficient understanding and intelligence to be capable of making up his own mind on the matter requiring decision.' Relating this principle to the decision at hand, the court held that parents will retain their right to determine whether or not their child under the age of 16 will have medical treatment until that child develops sufficient understanding and intelligence to make the decision themselves.

9.13 Lord Fraser went on to set out some guidelines which should be adopted when medical treatment is proposed for a child, proceeding on the basis of the child's consent. The guidelines apply to doctors who may be providing advice or treatment to children without the consent or knowledge of their parents. In order for such a course of action to be justified, the court suggested, in the context of this case, that: the doctor should be satisfied that the child understands the advice given;

that the child cannot be persuaded to inform their parents or allow the doctor to do so; that the child is likely to begin or continue to have sexual intercourse with or without contraceptive treatment; that unless the child receives contraceptive advice or treatment, their physical or mental health are likely to suffer; and that the child's best interests requires the doctor to provide contraceptive advice, treatment or both without parental consent.

Nielsen v Denmark (1988) 11 EHRR 175

9.14 This case was heard in the European Court of Human Rights and is widely known as one of the first fundamental cases assessing whether a child is deprived of their liberty. The case was determined by a narrow majority and continues to be the source of conflicting opinions from practitioners as case law has developed over time.

9.15 The case concerned a 12-year old boy and his detention in a child psychiatric ward at the request of his mother. The child was admitted onto a psychiatric ward following recommendations by medical professionals who considered such admission to be necessary owing to the child's presentation with neurosis.[9] This admission was supported by the child's mother who was the sole holder of parental responsibility for him. When on the ward, the child was provided environmental therapy and treatment but he was not medicated.[10] The ward operated a locked door policy and the child was only allowed to leave the ward with permission. However, when leaving the ward with staff supervision, the child was permitted to visit playgrounds and other recreational activities. He visited school friends and his parents. The ward conditions were described as being as close as possible to a normal home. He remained on the ward for five and a half months.[11]

9.16 In relation to the regime in place, the court found that the restrictions on the child's liberty were akin to those imposed in other hospital settings.[12] They therefore were not, in the court's view, of sufficient nature or degree to cause the child's objective confinement beyond what would be normal for a child of a similar age who may be admitted to hospital.[13] Considering the subjective element of the alleged deprivation of liberty, the court found that the child's admission to hospital and detention there was a 'responsible exercise by his mother of her custodial rights in the interests of the child.'[14] Although this case preceded the formulation of the *Storck* limbs and the focus on an absence of valid consent, it has been drawn from the judgment of the European Court of Human Rights that the involvement of the child's mother in the arrangements was appropriate and agreeing to the detention fell within her role as a person exercising parental responsibility.

---

9 *Nielsen v Denmark* (1988) 11 EHRR 175, paras 19-20 and 70.

10 *Nielsen v Denmark* (1988) 11 EHRR 175, paras 28-29.

11 *Nielsen v Denmark* (1988) 11 EHRR 175, para 70.

12 *Nielsen v Denmark* (1988) 11 EHRR 175, para 70.

13 *Nielsen v Denmark* (1988) 11 EHRR 175, para 72.

14 *Nielsen v Denmark* (1988) 11 EHRR 175, para 73.

Re K (A Child) (Secure Accommodation Order: Right to Liberty) [2001] Fam 377

9.17 The Court of Appeal considered this case brought on behalf of AK, a 15-year old, in relation to his detention in secure accommodation. AK was described as having displayed challenging, aggressive and sexualised behaviour from a young age. He was assessed a number of times during his childhood. At different junctures, he was considered to be suffering learning difficulties, Hyperkinetic Conduct Disorder, complex social and educational needs, mental health problems and a cognitive age below his years.[15] AK's parents struggled to manage his behaviours and an interim care order was granted to the local authority following elongated periods of time in local authority accommodation. At 11 years old, a recommendation was made for AK to reside within secure accommodation. Following a marked deterioration in his behaviour, AK was placed in a secure accommodation unit in December 1998 by court order.[16]

9.18 AK began to make progress within the secure facility but continued to be assessed by those working with him as presenting a risk of harm to himself and others.[17] The appeal before the court related to whether the provisions of the Children Act 1989 (CA 1989), s 25 were compatible with AK's right to liberty under Article 5 of the ECHR. The argument was divided into two components: whether a secure accommodation order involved a deprivation of liberty and, if so, whether that deprivation came within the permitted categories set out within Article 5(1).[18] The court quickly made clear that in AK's circumstances, the relevant provision of Article 5 would be Article 5(1)(d), the detention of a minor for the purpose of educational supervision.

9.19 In answering the first question, whether AK's residence in secure accommodation involved a deprivation of his liberty, the court looked at whether the regime was consented to by his parents and if so, whether this was a reasonable exercise of their parental responsibility. The court recognised without hesitation that the regime in secure accommodation was restrictive. The very purpose of secure accommodation is to restrict the liberty of the child.[19] The court went on to comment that '[i]f a parent exercised those powers by detaining a child in a similar restrictive fashion and was challenged to justify such detention, for my part, I doubt whether the general rights and responsibilities of a parent would cover such an exercise of parental authority.'[20] It follows from that analysis that the court found that AK was deprived of his liberty in secure accommodation and the apparent consent of his parents did not negate that.

---

15 *Re K (A Child) (Secure Accommodation Order: Right to Liberty)* [2001] Fam 377, paras 3-9.
16 *Re K (A Child) (Secure Accommodation Order: Right to Liberty)* [2001] Fam 377, para 7.
17 *Re K (A Child) (Secure Accommodation Order: Right to Liberty)* [2001] Fam 377, paras 11-12.
18 *Re K (A Child) (Secure Accommodation Order: Right to Liberty)* [2001] Fam 377, para 17.
19 *Re K (A Child) (Secure Accommodation Order: Right to Liberty)* [2001] Fam 377, para 29.
20 *Re K (A Child) (Secure Accommodation Order: Right to Liberty)* [2001] Fam 377, para 29.

9.20 Exploring this conclusion further, Judge LJ explained that the very definition of secure accommodation lends itself to the suggestion that it will implement measures which go beyond what a normal parent could provide or be reasonably expected to provide.[21] The regime within a secure accommodation unit could not be likened to the 'grounding' of a child by their parents. The very requirement of statute for any detention in a secure accommodation unit to be court authorised made the clear inference that such an arrangement involved more than 'ordinary parental control.'[22]

9.21 The court then turned to the question of whether AK's circumstances fell within a permissible exception to deem his deprivation of liberty lawful under Article 5 of the ECHR. The exception relevant to AK's circumstances was Article 5(1)(d), that the detention was for the purpose of educational supervision.[23] AK was receiving an education from which he was benefitting and making progress. However, it was argued on AK's behalf that due to his placement in secure accommodation being unrelated to the provision of education, and the CA 1989, s 25 making no reference itself to education, the regime was insufficient to satisfy Article 5(1)(d).[24] The court rejected this argument and found that the provisions of s 25 were sufficient to comply with Article 5(1)(d), therefore the domestic law was not incompatible with the ECHR.[25] The court drew a distinction between what may be said to be a local authority taking a step in line with statute which may breach Article 5, and a complaint that the statute itself is incompatible with Article 5. The court found that the CA 1989, s 25 can be interpreted in a manner which is compatible with Article 5 and therefore declined to make a declaration of incompatibility.

HL v The United Kingdom [2004] ECHR 471

9.22 In this important decision, the European Court of Human Rights set the foundations for how to decipher when a person is deprived of their liberty. The case concerned the applicant, HL, and his alleged detention in a psychiatric institution which he submitted amounted to a violation of his Article 5 right to liberty under the ECHR. HL was diagnosed with autism spectrum condition, he was unable to speak and had been assessed as lacking capacity to consent to or object to medical treatment. HL spent over three decades living in a hospital setting. He was discharged to a community setting with a package of care which was successful for over three years; however, in July 1997, HL experienced significant agitation and, displaying self-harming behaviours, he was taken to hospital for medical assistance. HL was assessed by a consultant psychiatrist and deemed to require inpatient treatment.[26] It was not considered necessary at the time to admit HL under the Mental Health Act 1983 (MHA 1983) as he was complying with medical advice and did not resist his admission. HL was therefore admitted to hospital as an informal inpatient.

---

21 *Re K (A Child) (Secure Accommodation Order: Right to Liberty)* [2001] Fam 377, para 101.
22 *Re K (A Child) (Secure Accommodation Order: Right to Liberty)* [2001] Fam 377, para 101.
23 *Re K (A Child) (Secure Accommodation Order: Right to Liberty)* [2001] Fam 377, para 35.
24 *Re K (A Child) (Secure Accommodation Order: Right to Liberty)* [2001] Fam 377, para 25.
25 *Re K (A Child) (Secure Accommodation Order: Right to Liberty)* [2001] Fam 377, para 41.
26 *HL v The United Kingdom* [2004] ECHR 471, para 12.

9.23 Upon re-assessment during his inpatient stay, HL was diagnosed with a severe learning disability, autistic traits and a possible cyclical mood disorder.[27] When in hospital, health care professionals exercised complete and effective control over HL's care and his movements.[28] HL's contact with his carers who had been looking after him in the community was controlled by hospital staff and his treating team had a 'clear intention… to exercise strict control over his assessment, treatment, contacts and, notably, movement and residence'.[29] Although labelled as an informal inpatient, HL would not be released from the hospital unless and until it was deemed appropriate by the medical team, and if HL had tried to leave the ward sooner, he would have been detained within the hospital pursuant to the MHA 1983.

9.24 Having reviewed the measures that HL was subjected to, the court summarised that 'the concrete situation was that the applicant was under continuous supervision and control and was not free to leave. Any suggestion to the contrary was, in the court's view… 'stretching credulity to breaking point' and a 'fairy tale'.'[30] Accordingly, the court found that HL had been deprived of his liberty on the psychiatric ward. Although the ward being locked or lockable was raised as an issue in assessing whether HL was deprived of his liberty, the court did not consider this to be determinative of whether a deprivation of liberty arose, recognising that a deprivation of liberty does not require a person to be in a locked space.[31]

9.25 The court distinguished the facts before it from the decision in *HM v Switzerland* in which it was held that the elderly applicant's residence in a foster home to ensure medical care and satisfactory living conditions was not a deprivation of the applicant's liberty.[32] The court drew attention to the fact that *HM* was not established as being 'legally incapable' of agreeing to the arrangements in place for her and had expressed a willingness to live in the foster home.[33] A further distinguishing feature was the stark contrast in the restrictive measures implemented, with *HM*'s placement being an open one which allowed freedom of movement and did not restrict contact with the outside world.

9.26 The court went on to consider whether HL's detention in hospital could be deemed as lawful in accordance with Article 5(1)(e) of the ECHR.[34] This would require HL to be established as being of unsound mind. The applicable test was regurgitated for the purposes of the judgment, being that: HL must be reliably shown to be of unsound mind; the mental disorder must be of a kind or degree warranting compulsory confinement; and the validity of continued confinement will depend upon the persistence of such a disorder. Having analysed the evidence pertaining to HL's mental disorder, the court was satisfied that this limb of Article 5 was available in HL's circumstances to form the basis of a lawful deprivation of liberty. Going on to

---

27 *HL v The United Kingdom* [2004] ECHR 471, para 16.

28 *HL v The United Kingdom* [2004] ECHR 471, para 91.

29 *HL v The United Kingdom* [2004] ECHR 471, para 91.

30 *HL v The United Kingdom* [2004] ECHR 471, para 91.

31 *HL v The United Kingdom* [2004] ECHR 471, para 92.

32 *HM v Switzerland* 39187/98 [2002] ECHR 157.

33 *HL v The United Kingdom* [2004] ECHR 471, para 93.

34 *HL v The United Kingdom* [2004] ECHR 471, para 95.

consider whether the detention was in fact lawful, the court looked to the doctrine of necessity relied upon by the government to satisfy the requirement of Article 5 that any detention was in accordance with a procedure prescribed by law.[35] HL argued against this proposition, considering the doctrine of necessity to be insufficiently precise and bring with it insufficient safeguards to comply with the requirements of Article 5 which protect against arbitrary detentions.[36] The court accepted that there was an absence of sufficient procedural safeguards when relying upon the doctrine of necessity to prevent arbitrary deprivations of liberty.[37] On this basis, the court did find that HL's Article 5 rights had been violated.

Storck v Germany 61603/00 [2005] ECHR 406

9.27 This landmark judgment was handed down by the European Court of Human Rights in relation to an 18-year old woman (the applicant) and her placement within a psychiatric institution at the demand of her father which spanned a period of 20 months.[38] At the time of her admission, the applicant was considered by her father to be suffering psychosis. She was therefore placed in a private psychiatric institution for the purposes of receiving medical treatment. When on the ward, the applicant was confined to the clinic, being a locked ward, and was unable to contact others outside of the clinic.[39]

9.28 In order to ascertain whether the applicant had been deprived of her liberty, the court considered her circumstances as a whole including the type, duration and manner of implementation of the restrictive measures. The court ascertained, and it was not disputed, that the applicant had been under continuous supervision and control within the clinic and was not free to leave for the entirety of her stay there.[40] The court referred to an occasion whereby the applicant had attempted to flee and it was 'necessary to fetter her in order to secure her stay in the clinic.'[41] It was held that objectively, the measures imposed upon the applicant had deprived her of her liberty for the purposes of Article 5 of the ECHR.

9.29 The court then moved to consider whether the arrangements for the applicant amounted to her deprivation of liberty based upon whether they had been validly consented to.[42] The court in its analysis confirmed that a person is only to be considered to be deprived of their liberty if they have not provided valid consent to the confinement in place. This element was disputed between the parties. In the circumstances of this case there was no question as to the applicant's ability to provide valid consent, should she wish to, as she was an adult and had not been assessed as

35 *HL v The United Kingdom* [2004] ECHR 471, para 102.
36 *HL v The United Kingdom* [2004] ECHR 471, paras 108 – 113.
37 *HL v The United Kingdom* [2004] ECHR 471, para 124.
38 *Storck v Germany* 61603/00 [2005] ECHR 406, paras 15-15 and 73.
39 *Storck v Germany* 61603/00 [2005] ECHR 406, paras 16, 69 and 73.
40 *Storck v Germany* 61603/00 [2005] ECHR 406, para 73.
41 *Storck v Germany* 61603/00 [2005] ECHR 406, para 73.
42 *Storck v Germany* 61603/00 [2005] ECHR 406, para 74.

lacking capacity to consent to her admission and treatment in hospital.[43] However, what was controversial was whether the applicant's presentation at the clinic at the commencement of her stay could be taken as implied consent to her detention there. Following admission, the applicant had on several occasions tried to flee and had to be returned to the clinic by police on one occasion when she had escaped. The court was clear in its view that these actions did not represent a person who was validly consenting to their continued detention at the clinic.[44] In the alternative, the court commented that in any event, the applicant's treatment during her inpatient stay with 'strong medicaments' may have rendered her unable to provide valid consent.[45]

9.30 The final factor considered by the court in determining the presence of a deprivation of liberty was the responsibility of the State for the arrangements for the applicant. This was a relevant factor as the wording of Article 5 of the ECHR places two positive obligations on signatory States. The first is to refrain from active infringement in a person's right to liberty, and the second is to take appropriate steps to provide protection against unlawful interferences with those rights. In the applicant's case, the State was both directly involved in her detention at the clinic and had upon it an obligation to protect her against interferences with her liberty as carried out by private persons. Based upon the facts before it, the court was satisfied that the applicant's detention brought about a responsibility of the State.[46]

9.31 This judgment has been subsequently distilled into a test of three salient elements which must all be satisfied for a deprivation of liberty to arise. They are:

(a) the objective component of confinement in a particular restricted place for a not negligible length of time;

(b) the subjective component of a lack of valid consent; and,

(c) the attribution of responsibility to the state.

Stanev v Bulgaria 36760/06 [2012] ECHR 46

9.32 This decision of the European Court of Human Rights concerned an application alleging a breach of a number of the applicant's rights under the ECHR. Principally, the applicant submitted that he had been unlawfully deprived of his liberty pursuant to Article 5 of the ECHR.

9.33 The applicant, a man in his 60s, was diagnosed with schizophrenia and had lived in the community until his placement in a care home.[47] He had no relatives willing to act as his guardian and therefore the domestic state authorities determined that he should be moved into a care home and placed under a partial guardianship. The applicant was duly moved into a care home in an isolated area which housed

43 *Storck v Germany* 61603/00 [2005] ECHR 406, para 75.
44 *Storck v Germany* 61603/00 [2005] ECHR 406, paras 76-77.
45 *Storck v Germany* 61603/00 [2005] ECHR 406, para 76.
46 *Storck v Germany* 61603/00 [2005] ECHR 406, para 89.
47 *Stanev v Bulgaria* 36760/06 [2012] ECHR 46, para 9.

residents suffering mental illness. The applicant shared a bedroom with four other residents, and the conditions in the care home were poor.[48] The applicant's access to stimulating activities and the community was limited, his ability to send letters outside of the home was made difficult by staff and his access to the bathroom was limited.[49]

9.34 It was the applicant's case that the totality of the regime in which he was living amounted to his deprivation of liberty. The factors which he drew to the court's attention were: the remote location of the placement, isolating him from society; the applicant's inability to leave if he chose to as he had no money or identity papers; his inability to leave the care home without permission; the fact that if he left with permission and did not return when required, the police would be instructed to search for him; his occupational activities, treatment and movements were subject to supervision by staff at the care home; his daily routine was strict and imposed; and that he had no free choice which restricted his formation of relationships with others.[50]

9.35 The argument to the contrary advanced by the government was that the applicant had not been deprived of his liberty because the arrangements for him were protective and taken in his interests.[51] In coming to a conclusion, the court considered the totality of the measures in place.[52] The court reiterated the established principle that the question of whether the applicant is locked into a building or not is not decisive of whether there is a deprivation of liberty.[53] The court was not in doubt that the applicant's daily life was subject to controls and restrictions, even during periods where he was permitted to leave the physical placement itself. The court considered that the regime in its entirety amounted to constant supervision and that the applicant was 'not free to leave the home without permission whenever he wished'.[54]

9.36 Moving to consider the subjective element of the deprivation of the applicant's liberty, the court held that the applicant had not consented to the placement such as to negate a deprivation of liberty.[55] The applicant's views about moving to the placement were not sought in advance of or during his stay and the applicant had explicitly expressed a wish to leave.[56] Whilst the court recognised that there may be situations in which a person 'with impaired mental faculties' may validly have their wishes replaced by another acting in a protective way, the fact that a person lacks legal capacity does not mean they are unable to comprehend a situation and express a

48 *Stanev v Bulgaria* 36760/06 [2012] ECHR 46, para 21.
49 *Stanev v Bulgaria* 36760/06 [2012] ECHR 46, paras 22-23 and 29-30.
50 *Stanev v Bulgaria* 36760/06 [2012] ECHR 46, paras 102-105.
51 *Stanev v Bulgaria* 36760/06 [2012] ECHR 46, para 108.
52 *Stanev v Bulgaria* 36760/06 [2012] ECHR 46, paras 124-129.
53 *Stanev v Bulgaria* 36760/06 [2012] ECHR 46, para 124.
54 *Stanev v Bulgaria* 36760/06 [2012] ECHR 46, para 128.
55 *Stanev v Bulgaria* 36760/06 [2012] ECHR 46, para 130.
56 *Stanev v Bulgaria* 36760/06 [2012] ECHR 46, para 130.

view about it.[57] The domestic law at the time gave particular weight to the applicant's wishes which, when expressed, were to leave the care home.

9.37 In finding that the requisite elements of a deprivation of liberty were satisfied, the court then considered whether the deprivation was lawful pursuant to Article 5 of the ECHR. The court concluded that the deprivation of liberty was unlawful as insufficient evidence had been provided to satisfy the criteria establishing that the applicant was of unsound mind, under Article 5(1)(e).[58]

Surrey County Council v P; Cheshire West and Chester Council v P [2014] UKSC 19

9.38 The case of *Cheshire West* brought about a landscape-changing decision in respect of the deprivation of liberty of children, young people and adults. The judgment delivered by the Supreme Court concerned three adults, MIG, MEG and P. The case arrived at the Supreme Court following an appeal against conclusions of the Court of Appeal that the three relevant people were not deprived of their liberty. The ultimate question before the court was whether or not the circumstances for these three people amounted to their deprivation of liberty when taking into account their disabilities and individual circumstances.

9.39 MIG and MEG were sisters in their 20s at the time of the judgment being handed down. Both were diagnosed with a learning disability and experienced different challenges in their communication. They had a turbulent childhood and experienced neglect when living within their family.[59] As children, they were both removed into placements arranged for them by the local authority and within which they were provided support to meet their care needs. MIG resided in foster care and was provided intensive support in most aspects of her daily living. She was not permitted to leave the home alone.[60] MEG lived in a residential home for adolescents with learning disabilities and complex needs. She too was supervised continuously and had to be accompanied in the community.[61] P was aged 38 and was diagnosed with cerebral palsy and Down's syndrome. He required 24-hour care to meet his needs.[62] He lived with his mother for the majority of his life until her health began to deteriorate and an alternative provision was required. P moved to a bungalow which he shared with two other residents and was arranged for him by the local authority. The bungalow had two staff present during the day and one member of staff overnight. P also had 98 hours of one to one (1:1) support each week to support him to leave the bungalow. P had other activities arranged for him during the week and within which he was supported by care staff.[63]

57 *Stanev v Bulgaria* 36760/06 [2012] ECHR 46, para 130.
58 *Stanev v Bulgaria* 36760/06 [2012] ECHR 46, paras 151-159.
59 *Surrey County Council v P; Cheshire West and Chester Council v P* [2014] UKSC 19, paras 11-12.
60 *Surrey County Council v P; Cheshire West and Chester Council v P* [2014] UKSC 19, para 13.
61 *Surrey County Council v P; Cheshire West and Chester Council v P* [2014] UKSC 19, para 14.
62 *Surrey County Council v P; Cheshire West and Chester Council v P* [2014] UKSC 19, para 16.
63 *Surrey County Council v P; Cheshire West and Chester Council v P* [2014] UKSC 19, para 17.

9.40 The Court of Appeal concluded for MIG, MEG and P that they were not being deprived of their liberty. This court had looked to the 'relative normality' of each person's circumstances in reaching its conclusion.[64] These decisions were brought together as a challenge before the Supreme Court, asking it to determine when a person with disabilities is to be considered to be deprived of their liberty. The Supreme Court clarified early on in its judgment that there were features arising in the present case which had not, as a combination of facts, been previously subject to consideration by the European Court of Human Rights. These issues were: the relevant person lacks capacity to decide where to live but has not indicated a dissatisfaction with their residence arrangements; the placement is not a hospital or care home and is as close as possible to 'normal' home life; and, the placement had been initially authorised by the court as being in that person's best interests.[65] The combination of these novel factors provided a different lens through which to consider the appropriate test for determining if a person is deprived of their liberty.

9.41 The Supreme Court was focused on the first element of the *Storck* criteria: the objective deprivation of MIG, MEG and P's liberty and whether they were being confined to a particular restricted place for a not negligible length of time. The court was tasked with determining whether the relative normality of the arrangements for MIG, MEG and P when compared with others living with similar disabilities impacted upon the analysis of whether they were being deprived of their liberty. As part of this discussion, Lady Hale stated at paragraph 46:

> 'Those rights include the right to physical liberty, which is guaranteed by article 5 of the European Convention. This is not a right to do or to go where one pleases. It is a more focussed right, not to be deprived of that physical liberty. But, as it seems to me, what it means to be deprived of liberty must be the same for everyone, whether or not they have physical or mental disabilities. If it would be a deprivation of my liberty to be obliged to live in a particular place, subject to constant monitoring and control, only allowed out with close supervision, and unable to move away without permission even if such an opportunity became available, then it must also be a deprivation of the liberty of a disabled person. The fact that my living arrangements are comfortable, and indeed make my life as enjoyable as it could possibly be, should make no difference. A gilded cage is still a cage.'

9.42 Following this rationale, Lady Hale rejected the appropriateness of comparing the relative normality of a person's living situation to others with similar diagnoses or disabilities in order to establish if they were being objectively deprived of their liberty.[66] Lady Hale recognised that for MIG and MEG, the Court of Appeal had compared their living situations not with other disabled young women but women of a similar age who may be living at home. However, the Supreme Court still reached the conclusion that even on that comparison, their lives were not the same as those being led by teenagers of the same age and the assessment of their

64 *Surrey County Council v P; Cheshire West and Chester Council v P* [2014] UKSC 19, paras 15 and 18.

65 *Surrey County Council v P; Cheshire West and Chester Council v P* [2014] UKSC 19, para 32.

66 *Surrey County Council v P; Cheshire West and Chester Council v P* [2014] UKSC 19, para 47.

placement as being 'home-like' did not provide an answer to whether they were being deprived of their liberty.

9.43 Lady Hale went on to consider the formulation of an 'acid test' which may be applied to a set of circumstances to determine whether or not they meet the objective criteria of a deprivation of liberty.[67] Drawing upon the case law which came before, the court considered the key elements of which the objective element is comprised is that a person is under constant or continuous supervision and control, and that they are not free to leave.[68] Lady Hale made clear that what will not be relevant in deciphering if a person is deprived of their liberty is their compliance or lack of objection; the relative normality of the placement on any comparator; and the reason or purpose behind the placement.[69] In reviewing the judicial treatment of P's circumstances, Lady Hale provided a helpful steer on the correct approach to determining if a person is deprived of their liberty. This includes consideration of the degree and intensity of the measures implemented, whether or not the person is free to leave and 'whether those treating and managing the person exercise complete and effective control of the person's care and movements.'[70]

9.44 The court also considered the approach to restrictive measures when they are essential components of a person's care and support, and they are essential for a person's survival. Lady Hale dismissed this potential argument against the finding of a deprivation of liberty on the basis that it would 'resurrect the comparison with other people sharing their disabilities' and 'deny them the same concept of liberty as everyone else.'[71]

9.45 Lord Kerr's judgment, agreeing with Lady Hale, then brought a focus on the deprivation of liberty of young people. He summarised that:

> '[t]he question whether one is restricted (as a matter of actuality) is determined by comparing the extent of your actual freedom with someone of your age and station whose freedom is not limited. Thus a teenager of the same age and familial background as MIG and MEG is the relevant comparator for them. If one compares their state with a person of similar age and full capacity it is clear that their liberty is in fact circumscribed. They may not be conscious, much less resentful, of the constraint but, objectively, limitations on their freedom are in place.'[72]

9.46 Considering how this applies practically to children, Lord Kerr recognised that it is an essential component of raising a child that they will be subjected to some level of restraint which will wane as they age.[73] It is therefore imperative that any exercise of comparison is tailored to the age and relative maturity of the child or young person concerned.

---

67 *Surrey County Council v P; Cheshire West and Chester Council v P* [2014] UKSC 19, para 48.

68 *Surrey County Council v P; Cheshire West and Chester Council v P* [2014] UKSC 19, paras 49 and 63.

69 *Surrey County Council v P; Cheshire West and Chester Council v P* [2014] UKSC 19, para 50.

70 *Surrey County Council v P; Cheshire West and Chester Council v P* [2014] UKSC 19, para 51.

71 *Surrey County Council v P; Cheshire West and Chester Council v P* [2014] UKSC 19, para 55.

72 *Surrey County Council v P; Cheshire West and Chester Council v P* [2014] UKSC 19, para 77.

73 *Surrey County Council v P; Cheshire West and Chester Council v P* [2014] UKSC 19, para 78.

9.47 Touching upon the subjective element of a deprivation of liberty, Lord Kerr confirmed that this must involve the absence of valid consent to the deprivation which is not the same as 'passive acquiescence to the deprivation'.[74] He went on to confirm that '[b]enevolence underpinning a regime which restricts liberty is irrelevant to an assessment of whether it in fact amounts to a deprivation'.[75] The court reaffirmed the principles of past European judgments that each case will turn on its own facts.

Re D (A Child) (Deprivation of Liberty: Parental Responsibility) [2015] EWHC 922 (Fam)

9.48 This matter, also referred to as *Trust A v X (A Child)*, was heard in the Family Division of the High Court by Keehan J. It concerned D, a 15-year old boy, diagnosed with attention deficit hyperactivity disorder, asperger's syndrome (now autism spectrum condition or disorder), Tourette's syndrome and a mild learning disability.[76] This was the first reported decision concerning D, prior to the matter reaching the Supreme Court in 2019 in *Re D*, discussed at paragraph 9.66 onwards.[77]

9.49 The issues before the court were: whether D's circumstances living in hospital satisfied the acid test as set down in *Cheshire West*; if they did, were the parents able to consent to the arrangements within the scope of their parental responsibility; and if the arrangements fell outside the scope of parental consent, should the court exercise its inherent jurisdiction to declare lawful D's deprivation of liberty in hospital.

9.50 D's circumstances were that he was living in a hospital as an informal inpatient following a recommendation by his treating psychiatrist that D required hospital admission for assessment and treatment.[78] D's parents had struggled to care for him in the family home due to D's challenging behaviour which included verbal and physical aggression. The hospital in which D was placed provided mental health services to children and young people. It also had an education provision on site. D was visited regularly by his parents and brother: he also visited the family home for periods on the weekends with staff supervision.[79] The unit on which D was living had 24-hour staffing, the front door was locked and D was prevented from leaving the ward without a staff member or family member supervising him. D was checked on by a staff member every 30 minutes, although he would seek out more frequent contact with staff. Any access to the community was undertaken with one-to-one support. This was something D felt more comfortable with as opposed to going out alone. D was assessed as not being *Gillick* competent and therefore was unable to consent to his residence and care arrangements which may have amounted to

---

74 *Surrey County Council v P; Cheshire West and Chester Council v P* [2014] UKSC 19, para 81.

75 *Surrey County Council v P; Cheshire West and Chester Council v P* [2014] UKSC 19, para 82.

76 *Re D (A Child) (Deprivation of Liberty: Parental Responsibility)* [2015] EWHC 922 (Fam), paras 1 and 12.

77 [2019] UKSC 42.

78 *Re D (A Child) (Deprivation of Liberty: Parental Responsibility)* [2015] EWHC 922 (Fam), para 14.

79 *Re D (A Child) (Deprivation of Liberty: Parental Responsibility)* [2015] EWHC 922 (Fam), para 16.

the deprivation of his liberty.[80] D was not considered suitable for detention under the MHA 1983, and by August 2014, he was assessed as fit for discharge from the hospital, although remained there awaiting the identification of a suitable community placement.

9.51 With the ultimate agreement of the state bodies involved in the case, the court first determined that D's circumstances did satisfy the acid test set down in *Cheshire West* and as such, the objective element of the criteria for a deprivation of liberty was satisfied.[81] In reaching that decision, the court was tasked with considering whether or not the test arising from *Cheshire West* applied to D at all because he was under 16. The court found that the core definition of the objective component of a deprivation of liberty did apply to D, reiterating the comments of Lady Hale that what it means to be deprived of liberty is 'the same for everyone, whether or not they have a physical or mental disability'.[82]

9.52 The court then turned to the issue of consent: the subjective component of a deprivation of liberty. D was unable to consent to the arrangements, and so the relevant consent to be considered was that of his parents. The Trust, who had brought the application, was uncomfortable with the proposition that D's deprivation of liberty may be negated by the consent of his parents in circumstances where he had been detained in hospital for 15 months and the use of parental consent did not provide sufficient safeguards to protect D's rights under Article 5 of the ECHR.[83]

9.53 In reaching a decision, the court considered it relevant to take into account D's diagnoses, stating: 'they are important and fundamental factors to take into account when considering his maturity and ability to make decisions about his day to day life'.[84] The court's summary of its approach to parental responsibility in D's circumstances is helpful to set out in full:

> '56. An appropriate exercise of parental responsibility in respect of a 5 year old child will differ very considerably from what is or is not an appropriate exercise of parental responsibility in respect of a 15 year old young person.
>
> 57. The decisions which might be said to come within the zone of parental responsibility for a 15 year old who did not suffer from the conditions with which D has been diagnosed will be of a wholly different order from those decisions which have to be taken by parents whose 15 year old son suffers with D's disabilities. Thus a decision to keep such a 15 year old boy under constant supervision and control would undoubtedly be considered an inappropriate exercise of parental responsibility and would probably amount to ill treatment. The decision to keep an autistic 15 year old boy who has erratic, challenging and potentially harmful behaviours under constant supervision and control is a quite different matter; to do otherwise would be neglectful. In such a case I consider the

---

80 *Re D (A Child) (Deprivation of Liberty: Parental Responsibility)* [2015] EWHC 922 (Fam), para 19.

81 *Re D (A Child) (Deprivation of Liberty: Parental Responsibility)* [2015] EWHC 922 (Fam), paras 40 and 52.

82 *Re D (A Child) (Deprivation of Liberty: Parental Responsibility)* [2015] EWHC 922 (Fam), para 43.

83 *Re D (A Child) (Deprivation of Liberty: Parental Responsibility)* [2015] EWHC 922 (Fam), para 49.

84 *Re D (A Child) (Deprivation of Liberty: Parental Responsibility)* [2015] EWHC 922 (Fam), para 55.

decision to keep this young person under constant supervision and control is the proper exercise of parental responsibility.'

9.54 The court therefore reached the conclusion that whilst D's circumstances did meet the criteria to satisfy the objective element of a deprivation of his liberty, D was not deprived of his liberty because his parents had appropriately consented to the arrangements for him in the hospital ward.[85] The court placed emphasis on the fact that the arrangements for D were made in his best interests and the general exercise by the parents of their parental responsibility had been wholly appropriate in light of D's diagnoses and presentation. The court commented that it may have reached a different conclusion in respect of the appropriateness of relying on parental consent if D's parents had acted contrary to medical advice or had allowed D's placement in hospital and subsequently abandoned him.[86] However, for D, his parents remained very involved in his day to day life and continued to act in accordance with the advice provided to them by professionals. This allowed the court to conclude that consenting to D's deprivation of liberty fell within the appropriate scope of his parents' parental responsibility.

Re AB (A Child)(Deprivation of Liberty: Consent) [2015] EWHC 3125 (Fam)

9.55 This matter came before Keehan J, concerned with the arrangements for a 14-year old boy, AB, who was diagnosed with a moderate severe learning disability and attention deficit hyperactivity disorder.[87] AB lived in a children's home and was subject to an interim care order. AB had been subjected to physical abuse and neglect in his father's care and was ultimately removed into the children's home.[88] Whilst in local authority care, AB began displaying sexualised and challenging behaviour.[89] As a result, measures of supervision, monitoring and restriction were implemented. These included: staff being always aware of where AB was; observations of AB every 15 minutes by staff; AB not being left alone with another resident at the placement; AB being supervised when taking his medication; and AB not being allowed to leave the placement unaccompanied.[90] AB had been assessed as not having the requisite level of understanding and intelligence to make decisions about his residence and care arrangements.[91]

9.56 The first question before the court was which route should be taken to authorise AB's deprivation of liberty. The court promptly made clear that neither AB nor the placement met the criteria which would allow the court to consider a secure accommodation order under the CA 1989, s 25.[92] However, the criteria for leave

85 *Re D (A Child) (Deprivation of Liberty: Parental Responsibility)* [2015] EWHC 922 (Fam), para 65.
86 *Re D (A Child) (Deprivation of Liberty: Parental Responsibility)* [2015] EWHC 922 (Fam), para 62.
87 *Re AB (A Child)(Deprivation of Liberty: Consent)* [2015] EWHC 3125 (Fam), para 12.
88 *Re AB (A Child)(Deprivation of Liberty: Consent)* [2015] EWHC 3125 (Fam), para 6.
89 *Re AB (A Child)(Deprivation of Liberty: Consent)* [2015] EWHC 3125 (Fam), paras 8 and 13.
90 *Re AB (A Child)(Deprivation of Liberty: Consent)* [2015] EWHC 3125 (Fam), paras 13-15.
91 *Re AB (A Child)(Deprivation of Liberty: Consent)* [2015] EWHC 3125 (Fam), para 17.
92 *Re AB (A Child)(Deprivation of Liberty: Consent)* [2015] EWHC 3125 (Fam), paras 31-32.

to invoke the inherent jurisdiction was satisfied in AB's circumstances. The court concluded that if its jurisdiction was not exercised for AB, he was likely to suffer significant harm.[93] A third potential route to authorisation was canvassed by the local authority, being for the court to grant an interim care order and approve a care plan which included AB's deprivation of liberty, and by virtue of endorsing the plan, the deprivation would be authorised by the court. The court rejected this argument, concluding that such a proposal would not provide AB the necessary safeguards in order to comply with the requirements of Article 5 of the ECHR.[94]

9.57 Having determined it necessary and proportionate to invoke the inherent jurisdiction to authorise the arrangements in place for AB, the court continued to provide some observations in relation to the deprivation of liberty of children who are 'in need' or looked after by the local authority.[95] It is helpful to set out these observations in full:

> '(1) Local authorities are under a duty to consider whether any children in need, or looked-after children, are, especially those in foster care or in a residential placement, subject to restrictions amounting to a deprivation of liberty.
>
> (2) The Cheshire West criteria must be rigorously applied to the individual circumstances of each case.
>
> (3) The comparison to be made is not with another child of the same age placed in foster care or in a residential home but simply with another child of the same age.
>
> (4) A deprivation of liberty will be lawful if warranted under statute; for example, under s.25 of the Children Act 1989 or the Mental Health Act 1983 or under the remand provisions of LASPO 2012 or if a child has received a custodial sentence under the PCCSA 2000.
>
> (5) Where a child is not looked after, then an apparent deprivation of liberty may not in fact be a deprivation at all if it falls within the zone of parental responsibility exercised by his parents… The exercise of parental responsibility may amount to valid consent, with the consequence that the second limb of Cheshire West is not met. In those circumstances, the court will not need to make any declaration as to the lawfulness of the child's deprivation of liberty.
>
> (6) Where a child is a looked-after child, different considerations may apply, regardless of whether the parents consent to the deprivation of liberty.
>
> (7) Where a child is the subject of an interim care order or a care order, it is extremely unlikely that a parent could consent to what would otherwise amount to a deprivation of liberty. In those circumstances, a local authority cannot consent to a deprivation of liberty.
>
> (8) The local authority must first consider whether s.25 of the Children Act is applicable or appropriate in the circumstances of the individual case. This will require an analysis of (1) whether any of the regulations disapply s.25, (2) whether the intended placement is accommodation provided for the purposes of restricting liberty and, thus, secure accommodation within s.25 and (3) whether the test set out in s.25.1(a) or (b) is met.

---

93 *Re AB (A Child)(Deprivation of Liberty: Consent)* [2015] EWHC 3125 (Fam), para 34.

94 *Re AB (A Child)(Deprivation of Liberty: Consent)* [2015] EWHC 3125 (Fam), para 36.

95 *Re AB (A Child)(Deprivation of Liberty: Consent)* [2015] EWHC 3125 (Fam), para 38.

(9) If it is not, then the s.100(4) leave hurdle is likely to be crossed on the basis that any unlawful deprivation of liberty is likely to constitute significant harm.

(10) Irrespective of the means by which the court authorises the deprivation of a child's liberty, whether under s.25 or the inherent jurisdiction, the local authority should cease to impose such deprivation as soon as (1) the s.25 criteria are not met, or (2) the reasons justifying the deprivation of liberty no longer subsist. Authorisation is permissive not prescriptive.'[96]

Re A-F [2018] EWHC 138 (Fam)

9.58 In this case before the Family Division of the High Court, the then President of the Family Division, Sir James Munby, handed down a significant decision regarding the deprivation of liberty of children and young people. The case involved seven children whose proceedings were brought together as 'test cases', raising similar issues which were dealt with by the court together. The children were aged between 11 and 16. They will be referred to collectively as 'children' for the purposes of this summary even though the eldest had reached 16. Each child was the subject of a care order made in favour of the same local authority. The children each had some level of difficulties in respect of their behaviour, presentation or relating to diagnoses they had. They resided in different types of placements, some in foster care and others in specialist placements, and all were subject to some level of restriction on their movement or liberty.[97]

9.59 For clarity, and in a practice which has now been adopted by other judges, the court referred to the objective element of the deprivation of liberty as 'confinement' throughout. This distinguished it from the circumstances which should be properly referred to as a deprivation of liberty wherein all three elements of the *Storck* criteria are made out. The court undertook an analysis of each element of the *Storck* criteria within its judgment, determining whether the circumstances of the children fit within that criteria and whether they were deprived of their liberty.

9.60 The court considered first limb (c) of the *Storck* criteria, being the attribution of responsibility to the State for the arrangements for the children. The court comfortably concluded that when a care order is in force in respect of a child, there is clear involvement and responsibility by the State which satisfies this element of the *Storck* criteria.[98]

9.61 Turning then to component (b) of the *Storck* criteria and the absence of valid consent, the court again reached a swift conclusion on the facts before it. The court reiterated the existing case law which confirmed that when a child is subject to a care order, a local authority is unable to exercise its parental responsibility as corporate parent, to provide valid consent for the purposes of a child's confinement.[99] The

96 *Re AB (A Child)(Deprivation of Liberty: Consent)* [2015] EWHC 3125 (Fam), para 38.

97 *Re A-F* [2018] EWHC 138 (Fam), para 3.

98 *Re A-F* [2018] EWHC 138 (Fam), para 10.

99 *Re A-F* [2018] EWHC 138 (Fam), para 12.

court further confirmed that in those circumstances, where parental responsibility is shared between a local authority and parents, the parents were also unable to exercise their parental responsibility to provide valid consent under limb (b) of the *Storck* criteria.

9.62 The court then moved on to the trickier element of its analysis which concerned limb (a) of the *Storck* criteria and the objective confinement of the children. The court referred itself to the acid test set down in *Cheshire West* and its essential components of the child being under complete supervision and control and not being free to leave. Sir James Munby P was careful to recognise that for children, the application of this test would be more convoluted as children were, by virtue of their age and level of maturity, subject to restrictions imposed by their parents during the course of ordinary parenting. A parent implementing boundaries and restrictions on their child as part of parenting them would not usually be confining them for the purposes of Article 5. The court considered whether it was possible to identify a minimum age, under which a child could not meet the *Cheshire West* criteria based upon an expectation that other children of the same age would be subject to similar controls enacted by their parents. As a rule of thumb, the court suggested that:

> '1. A child aged 10, even if under pretty constant supervision, is unlikely to be "confined" for the purposes of Storck component (a).
>
> 2. A child aged 11, if under constant supervision, may in contrast be so "confined", though the court should be astute to avoid coming too readily to such a conclusion.
>
> 3. Once a child who is under constant supervision has reached the age of 12, the court will more readily come to that conclusion.'[100]

9.63 In setting down this framework, Sir James Munby P was cautious to warn that each case will turn on its facts and the attributes of the regime imposed on each individual child should be carefully considered. The court was not persuaded that the analysis of a child's circumstances should differ if that child is the subject of a care order.[101]

9.64 Within its analysis, the court provided some helpful comments in relation to the workings of the inherent jurisdiction. It was first clarified that the exercise of the inherent jurisdiction is open to the High Court (including its Family Division) but not the Family Court.[102] Sir James Munby P confirmed that the exercise of the inherent jurisdiction extended to authorising the detention of a person, including a child, within a setting and using reasonable force to affect that detention. Any exercise of the inherent jurisdiction must, the court recognised, comply with the substantive and procedural requirements of Article 5 of the ECHR. To that end, Sir James Munby P explained that the confinement of a child will be lawful in substance if it is both necessary and proportionate, being the least restrictive regime which aligns with

---

[100] *Re A-F* [2018] EWHC 138 (Fam), para 43.

[101] *Re A-F* [2018] EWHC 138 (Fam), para 44.

[102] *Re A-F* [2018] EWHC 138 (Fam), para 27.

meeting the child's welfare needs. Procedurally, to be lawful, that confinement must then also be authorised by a judge sitting in the Family Division of the High Court.[103]

9.65 Moving to consider the process of authorisation, the court urged practitioners to make an application to the court for authorisation when the circumstances in which the child is living or will be living '*arguably*' amount to a deprivation of liberty when adopting a realistic view.[104] For the process of authorisation to comply with Article 5 of the ECHR, the court held that there must be an oral hearing to consider authorisation; the child must be a party to proceedings and be represented by a guardian; and evidence in support of an application will be required. That evidence should address the nature of the regime for the child, the child's circumstances which give rise to the need for a deprivation of liberty, detail on why the proposed regime is necessary and proportionate and that no less restrictive regime will do, and the views of the child.[105] Continuing review of any deprivation of liberty was determined by the court to be a central element of the process allowing the authorisation to be lawful for the purposes of Article 5. The court held that a review by a judge must take place at least once every 12 months, although this may be undertaken on the papers if there has been no significant change in circumstances since the previous review hearing.[106]

Re D [2019] UKSC 42

9.66 This decision followed an initial reported judgment within the case, coming from the High Court in 2015 and summarised at **9.48** onwards. The Supreme Court was concerned with whether or not a parent or parents can consent to the living arrangements for their 16 or 17-year old when those living arrangements would, without consent, amount to a deprivation of the young person's liberty. As part of tackling this question, the court also looked at what difference it would make if the child had capacity to make their own decisions about their residence and care regime, and what the difference would be if it were the local authority holding parental responsibility rather than (or alongside) the parents.[107] During the course of proceedings, the court also raised the question of whether the restrictions on accommodation under the CA 1989, s 25 apply to other restrictive placements not governed by s 25.

9.67 The young person subject to proceedings was D, aged 20 at the time of judgment being delivered. D was diagnosed with attention deficit hyperactivity disorder, asperger's syndrome (now autism spectrum condition/disorder), Tourette's syndrome and a mild learning disability. During his childhood, D's parents struggled to manage his challenging behaviour at home and D was admitted informally to a hospital in 2013, when he was 14 years old.[108] In 2014, the Hospital Trust sought an order authorising the deprivation of D's liberty in hospital. The application first came

---

103 *Re A-F* [2018] EWHC 138 (Fam), para 47.
104 *Re A-F* [2018] EWHC 138 (Fam), para 48.
105 *Re A-F* [2018] EWHC 138 (Fam), para 51.
106 *Re A-F* [2018] EWHC 138 (Fam), para 55.
107 *Re D* [2019] UKSC 42, para 3.
108 *Re D* [2019] UKSC 42, para 6.

before Keehan J who considered D's circumstances at 15 years' old and determined that his parents could consent to his arrangements, resulting in there being no deprivation of liberty.[109]

9.68 Following his 16th birthday, D subsequently moved from hospital to a residential placement. He was living there pursuant to consent provided by his parents under the CA 1989, s 20 for him to be accommodated in local authority care. D was therefore a looked after child but the local authority did not have parental responsibility for him. At the residential placement, the external doors were locked, D could not go out of the building without asking a staff member to unlock the door, D was not allowed to leave the premises apart from attending school or planned activities, and D had 1:1 support during waking hours with constant staff attendance overnight.[110] The parties agreed that these arrangements satisfied the objective element of the criteria for D's deprivation of liberty. The question arising was whether D's parents could consent to those arrangements now that he had turned 16. This issue was heard by Keehan J sitting in the Court of Protection in January 2016. Keehan J determined that D's parents could not consent to his confinement because he had reached the age of 16 and parliament had been clear that this brought with it a different legal status to that of children.[111]

9.69 The decision of Keehan J was appealed by the local authority. Before the appeal was heard, D moved to a new residential placement but his living arrangements were very similar and his parents continued to agree to his accommodation in local authority care. The Court of Appeal agreed that the accommodation of D was attributable to the state (a matter resolved before the case reached the Supreme Court), but allowed the appeal on the ground that Keehan J was wrong to hold that a parent could not consent to arrangements for their 16 or 17-year old child which amounted to their confinement when they lacked capacity to consent themselves.[112]

9.70 That decision was subsequently appealed to the Supreme Court by the Official Solicitor acting on D's behalf. The Official Solicitor's primary position was that that no person could consent to the confinement of a young person who lacks capacity to consent themselves.[113] The Official Solicitor was concerned with the compliance with Article 5 of the ECHR and the need to have appropriate safeguards in place when a person's physical liberty is being restricted. It was argued that this would not be achieved if parental consent was used to prevent a deprivation of liberty arising. The Supreme Court undertook a thorough analysis of the relevant law and determined that D was deprived of his liberty when living in the restrictive arrangements put in place by the local authority following his 16th birthday. The court came to this conclusion on the basis that his parents could not, pursuant to their parental responsibility, consent to these arrangements and therefore the essential second element of the deprivation of liberty criteria (an absence of valid consent)

---

109 *Re D (A Child) (Deprivation of Liberty)* [2015] EWHC 922 (Fam).
110 *Re D* [2019] UKSC 42, para 9.
111 *Birmingham City Council v D (by his litigation friend, the Official Solicitor)* [2016] EWCOP 8.
112 *Re D* [2019] UKSC 42, para 13.
113 *Re D* [2019] UKSC 42, para 14.

was present.[114] D was unable to consent to the arrangements himself as he lacked capacity in this domain.

9.71 The Supreme Court explained that the conclusion that D had been deprived of his liberty was drawn irrespective of the fact that the arrangements for D were agreed to be in his best interests.[115] The court was instead concerned with the scope of parental responsibility and whether, for 16 and 17-year olds, this extended to consenting to measures which infringed on a young person's human rights. The court also commented that, whilst it had not been tasked with considering whether this principle would apply to younger children, that would be logical.[116] The court was clear not to set down any binding judgment applicable to children under 16.

9.72 Lady Black went on to consider the question arising in relation to the CA 1989, s 25. This was whether the restrictions of that statutory provision apply to children such as D who are living in accommodation which restricts their liberty but which is not secure accommodation for the purposes of s 25. The court found that the CA 1989, s 25 could not be interpreted so widely as to catch children such as D in its provisions.[117] The focus in ascertaining whether a child's circumstances fall within section 25 should be on the accommodation itself, not upon the care regime. The court did not alter the existing definition set down by Wall J in *Re C (Detention: Medical Treatment)* [1997] 2 FLR 180, that secure accommodation will include accommodation that is 'designed for' or has 'as its primary purpose' the restriction of liberty[118].

A City Council v LS [2019] EWHC 1384 (Fam)

9.73 In this matter before MacDonald J, the High Court was concerned with whether its powers under the inherent jurisdiction extended to authorise the placement of a 17-year old in secure accommodation when the young person is not looked after by the local authority and the young person's parents object.[119]

9.74 The young person whose circumstances were being considered by the court was KS, a 17-year old boy. KS lived with his mother and was deemed by professionals to be at risk of criminal exploitation.[120] The police believed KS to be an active member of an organised crime group that was involved in drug trafficking. In 2018, KS had been found in possession of heroin, cocaine and weapons. Later that year, he was convicted of possessing an offensive weapon and assault occasioning actual bodily harm.[121] Following his conviction, KS was attacked in the street by men carrying a machete and a knife. Moving into 2019, KS continued to be involved

114 *Re D* [2019] UKSC 42, para 49.
115 *Re D* [2019] UKSC 42, para 49.
116 *Re D* [2019] UKSC 42, para 50.
117 *Re D* [2019] UKSC 42, para 113.
118 *Re D* [2019] UKSC 42, para 115.
119 *A City Council v LS* [2019] EWHC 1384 (Fam), para 1.
120 *A City Council v LS* [2019] EWHC 1384 (Fam), para 6.
121 *A City Council v LS* [2019] EWHC 1384 (Fam), para 8.

in criminal activity and was arrested on suspicion of attempted murder.[122] The police considered that KS was at risk of reprisal from an opposing gang who may attempt to kill him.

9.75 The local authority involved with KS had therefore issued an application for authorisation of his deprivation of liberty. An order authorising an extensive list of restrictions was initially granted by a different judge.[123] That order included powers to detain KS, remove him from where he was living and transport him to a place identified in which he could be kept safe. KS was accordingly moved into a non-secure placement and deprived of his liberty there.[124] Shortly after the move, KS absconded and had not been located by the time of the hearing before MacDonald J. He had however provided instructions to inform the court that he wished to return to his mother's care.[125] KS's mother also sought his return to her care.

9.76 The question therefore arose of whether the court could, under its inherent jurisdiction, authorise for KS to be returned to a placement arranged by the local authority and deprived of his liberty there. The issue was complicated owing to KS' age and status. KS was 17 and was not a 'looked after child'. The local authority was unable to take steps to make KS a 'looked after child' as he was 17, and his mother was unwilling to provide her consent for KS to be looked after.[126] He therefore fell outside of the scope of the CA 1989, s 25, meaning the inherent jurisdiction was the only possible route by which a deprivation of liberty may be authorised. However, the inherent jurisdiction could only be exercised in accordance with the CA 1989, s 100.[127] This section prohibits the exercise of the inherent jurisdiction in order to require a child to be placed in the care of or accommodated by a local authority.

9.77 Having analysed the statute and case law, MacDonald J concluded that it was not a permissible use of the inherent jurisdiction to authorise KS's deprivation of liberty in secure accommodation which would in effect require his accommodation in local authority care.[128] The court held that the CA 1989, s 100(2) prevented such a course of action in circumstances where the order sought would 'have the effect of authorising his removal from his mother's care without her consent for this purpose in circumstances where his mother, who retains exclusive parental responsibility for him, objects to this course of action.'[129] The court summarised that any order in the terms sought would bring about KS' removal from his mother which would be granting the local authority with powers to accommodate KS which would not otherwise be available under the CA 1989. For this reason, the inherent jurisdiction could not be exercised.[130]

---

122 *A City Council v LS* [2019] EWHC 1384 (Fam), para 11.
123 *A City Council v LS* [2019] EWHC 1384 (Fam), para 15.
124 *A City Council v LS* [2019] EWHC 1384 (Fam), para 17.
125 *A City Council v LS* [2019] EWHC 1384 (Fam), para 18.
126 *A City Council v LS* [2019] EWHC 1384 (Fam), para 33-34.
127 *A City Council v LS* [2019] EWHC 1384 (Fam), para 37.
128 *A City Council v LS* [2019] EWHC 1384 (Fam), para 45.
129 *A City Council v LS* [2019] EWHC 1384 (Fam), para 48.
130 *A City Council v LS* [2019] EWHC 1384 (Fam), para 49.

Lancashire County Council v G and N [2020] EWHC 2828 (Fam)

9.78 This case came before MacDonald J sitting in the Family Division of the High Court concerning a 16-year old girl, G. The application before the court was made by the local authority seeking an order under the inherent jurisdiction to authorise the deprivation of G's liberty. The local authority had also, during their involvement with G, applied for an order pursuant to the CA 1989, s 25. G was the subject of a care order, granted when she was four years old, and she had lived in foster care for the majority of her childhood.[131] G's mental health seemingly deteriorated in January 2020 and she had a number of hospital admissions following self-harm and suicidal ideation. By the time of the hearing, G was continuing to demonstrate high risk behaviours including cutting, ligaturing and refusing water. G had been diagnosed with post-traumatic stress disorder.[132]

9.79 At the time of the hearing, G was detained under the MHA 1983, s 2 and was living in an adult mental health ward due to a lack of CAMHS psychiatric intensive care beds. The court had been provided with evidence confirming that G did not meet the criteria for her continued detention under the MHA 1983. Despite G's continuing extreme and dangerous behaviours which persisted whilst she was on the hospital ward, she was considered to not be displaying an underlying diagnosable mental disorder which required her clinical treatment in hospital.[133]

9.80 Alongside there being no available adolescent mental health bed, there was no secure accommodation placement for G in the country.[134] The local authority's plan was therefore for G to be discharged to a non-secure placement but with an order in place permitting her deprivation of liberty there. The only placement that could be found by the local authority was an unregulated provision which was not willing to apply for Ofsted registration.[135]

9.81 The options before the court were bleak. If no order was made and G was discharged from her detention in hospital, G would have to return to community living wherein there was a significant risk of her causing harm to herself which may have been fatal.[136] The only alternative presented to the court was for it to authorise G's deprivation of liberty in the community, which would result in her placement in an unregulated and unregistered facility. This alternative caused concern for the court as the proposed community placement was not subject to scrutiny by the regulatory body, Ofsted, which was designed to secure the welfare of the children in its care.

9.82 As part of its evaluation of the circumstances, the court considered whether its use of the inherent jurisdiction would cut across the statutory scheme of the CA 1989, s 25, therefore making the exercise of the inherent jurisdiction

---

131 *Lancashire County Council v G and N* [2020] EWHC 2828 (Fam), para 10.

132 *Lancashire County Council v G and N* [2020] EWHC 2828 (Fam), para 11.

133 *Lancashire County Council v G and N* [2020] EWHC 2828 (Fam), para 20.

134 *Lancashire County Council v G and N* [2020] EWHC 2828 (Fam), para 5.

135 *Lancashire County Council v G and N* [2020] EWHC 2828 (Fam), para 6.

136 *ancashire County Council v G and N* [2020] EWHC 2828 (Fam), para 8.

impermissible. The issue arose as the local authority had accepted that G met the criteria to be placed in secure accommodation and if a placement were available, an application for a secure accommodation order would be pursued. The court was satisfied that to use the inherent jurisdiction in the circumstances would not cut across the statutory scheme because not all of the criteria for making a secure accommodation order were met. A key part of the criteria for a secure accommodation order was that the proposed placement was secure accommodation. In G's case, the proposed placement was not secure accommodation.[137]

9.83 The court then turned its focus to Article 5 of the ECHR and what may amount to a lawful deprivation of liberty. In G's case, the proposed limb of Article 5(1) under which her arrangements would fall was Article 5(1)(d), being G's detention for the purposes of educational supervision.[138] MacDonald J clarified that this 'is not meant to denote that educational supervision is the only purpose for which a child may be detained'.[139] Turning to whether G was objectively deprived of her liberty, whether she was under continuous supervision and control and not free to leave, the court summarised the principles arising from the case law which came before it:

> 'i) 'Free to leave' does not mean leaving for the purpose of some trip or outing approved by those managing the institution; it means leaving in the sense of removing himself permanently in order to live where and with whom she chooses…;
>
> ii) It is accepted wisdom that a typical fourteen or fifteen-year old is not free to leave her home…;
>
> iii) The terms 'complete' or 'constant' define 'supervision' and 'control' as indicating something like 'total', 'unremitting', 'thorough', and/or 'unqualified'…;
>
> iv) It does not matter whether the object is to protect, treat or care in some way for the person taken into confinement…;
>
> v) The comparative benevolence of living arrangements should not blind the court to their essential character if indeed those arrangements constitute a deprivation of liberty…;
>
> vi) What it means to be deprived of liberty must be the same for everyone, whether or not they have physical or mental disabilities…;
>
> vii) The person's compliance or lack of objection, the relative normality of the placement (whatever the comparison made) and the reason or purpose behind a particular placement are not relevant factors…;
>
> viii) The distinction between deprivation and restriction is a matter of "degree or intensity" and "in the end, it is the constraints that matter"…;
>
> ix) The question whether a child is restricted as a matter of fact is to be determined by comparing the extent of the child's actual freedom with someone of the child's age and station whose freedom is not limited…;

137 *Lancashire County Council v G and N* [2020] EWHC 2828 (Fam), para 34.
138 *Lancashire County Council v G and N* [2020] EWHC 2828 (Fam), para 37.
139 *Lancashire County Council v G and N* [2020] EWHC 2828 (Fam), para 37.

x) The sensible and humane comparison to be drawn is that between the situation of the child with the ordinary lives which young people of their ages might live at home with their families…;

xi) The 'acid test' has to be directly applied on each case to the individual circumstances of the individual under review. Where that individual is a child or young person, particular considerations apply…'.[140]

9.84 The court then reiterated what it saw as a number of relevant factors when assessing a child's concrete situation, including: the 'extent to which the child is actively prevented from leaving the placement' and the extent of efforts made to return the child if they were to leave; the extent of restraint used within the placement including the 'nature, intensity, frequency and duration'; the supervision and monitoring that is in place, including its level and nature; how far the rules and sanctions in place differ from other settings for children of the same age; the level of community access; and, the regulations upon time spent outside of the placement including for the purpose of transport.[141] Applying these considerations to G's circumstances, the court was in no doubt that if G was discharged to the proposed placement under the regime put forward by the local authority, she would be objectively deprived of her liberty.[142] The regime included locked car and placement doors; three-to-one supervision at all times in the placement; for G to be escorted at all times outside of the placement; physical restraint to be used when reasonable and proportionate; and 'waking watch' throughout the night.

9.85 With limited options before it, the court authorised G's deprivation of liberty in the community, despite the proposed setting being unregistered with Ofsted and unwilling to register.[143] The court expressed 'deep reservations' in coming to its conclusion, describing the placement proposal as 'sub-optimal from the perspective of meeting G's identified welfare needs'.[144] MacDonald J reiterated the extensive list of published judgments which had come before expressing the current crisis in provision of suitable and regulated placements for children in similar circumstances to G. He expressed that:

> 'It is plain that despite the issue being highlighted in multiple court decisions since 2017, and by the Children's Commissioner, the shortage of clinical provision for placement of children and adolescents requiring assessment and treatment for mental health issues within a restrictive clinical environment, the shortage of secure placements and the shortage of regulated placements remains. In this context, children like G with highly complex needs and behaviour continue to fall through the gaps that exist between secure accommodation, regulated accommodation and detention under the mental health legislation.'[145]

140 *Lancashire County Council v G and N* [2020] EWHC 2828 (Fam), para 42.
141 *Lancashire County Council v G and N* [2020] EWHC 2828 (Fam), para 43.
142 *Lancashire County Council v G and N* [2020] EWHC 2828 (Fam), para 63.
143 *Lancashire County Council v G and N* [2020] EWHC 2828 (Fam), para 65.
144 *Lancashire County Council v G and N* [2020] EWHC 2828 (Fam), para 65.
145 *Lancashire County Council v G and N* [2020] EWHC 2828 (Fam), para 59.

Re Z (A Child)(Deprivation of Liberty: Transition Plan) [2020] EWHC 3038 (Fam)

9.86 Knowles J, sitting in the Family Division of the High Court, was concerned with an application by a local authority for the inherent jurisdiction to be invoked to authorise a transition plan for the child, Z, which amounted to his deprivation of liberty. Z was 14 years old at the time of the hearing and lived with his parents and sibling. Z had presented with challenging behaviours for a significant proportion of his childhood and aged six was diagnosed with attachment difficulties.[146] At the age of ten, Z was further diagnosed with autism spectrum condition, traits of pathological demand avoidance and attachment disorder. He struggled to regulate his emotions and was frequently violent, experiencing anxiety and intrusive thoughts.

9.87 Z's violent behaviour progressed as he got older and by February 2020, the plan for him was to transition into a residential school for 38 weeks per year which would be able to meet his needs and reduce the impact of his behaviours on his sibling at home.[147] However, that plan and the to-and-fro between home and school prompted an escalation in violent and dysregulated behaviour by Z. A different residential placement was required for Z where he could live all year round.[148] When informed of the proposed placement, Z became violent. The proposed placement was a school which specialised in caring for children with autism spectrum condition and pathological demand avoidance.[149] Z's parents considered this specialist school to be suitable for Z and they agreed with the local authority's proposal for him to move there.

9.88 Although the detail of the care plan for Z at the specialist school are not set out within the judgment, Knowles J records that it was agreed between the parents and the local authority that the arrangements for Z when at the specialist school did not require authorisation of the court.[150] The parents provided their consent to Z being accommodated there, and any use of reasonable force required was to be carried out in accordance with the Education and Inspections Act 1996, s 93 and linked statutory provisions.[151] However, what did require authorisation was the transition plan for Z's move to the specialist school. The proposed transition was to be a staged approach with the least invasive measures being adopted first and, if unsuccessful, the level of intervention progressing.[152] The height of the restrictions proposed in the transition plan, if required, included the use of secure transport, medication, the assistance of police and physical restraint.[153]

9.89 In assessing the proposed transition, Knowles J undertook an assessment of the law in relation to what a parent may consent to on behalf of their child. This

---

146 *Re Z (A Child)(Deprivation of Liberty: Transition Plan)* [2020] EWHC 3038 (Fam), para 5.
147 *Re Z (A Child)(Deprivation of Liberty: Transition Plan)* [2020] EWHC 3038 (Fam), para 11.
148 *Re Z (A Child)(Deprivation of Liberty: Transition Plan)* [2020] EWHC 3038 (Fam), paras 11-12.
149 *Re Z (A Child)(Deprivation of Liberty: Transition Plan)* [2020] EWHC 3038 (Fam), para 15.
150 *Re Z (A Child)(Deprivation of Liberty: Transition Plan)* [2020] EWHC 3038 (Fam), para 18.
151 *Re Z (A Child)(Deprivation of Liberty: Transition Plan)* [2020] EWHC 3038 (Fam), para 38.
152 *Re Z (A Child)(Deprivation of Liberty: Transition Plan)* [2020] EWHC 3038 (Fam), para 20.
153 *Re Z (A Child)(Deprivation of Liberty: Transition Plan)* [2020] EWHC 3038 (Fam), para 22.

included consideration of an excerpt from *A Metropolitan Borough Council v DB*[154] which confirmed that a parent can permit the use of reasonable force on their child pursuant to their parental responsibility where the child is in a life-threatening situation or immediate and significant harm to the child will occur if force is not used.[155] However, in Z's circumstances and in the context of the proposed transition plan, Knowles J found that 'what was contemplated here strained the boundaries of what was permitted by a parent with respect to the exercise of their parental responsibility. There was no immediacy of significant harm in this case as would be recognised by necessity.'[156] She went on to confirm that '[t]he measures contemplated appeared to be at, if not beyond, the limits of what a parent could consent to within the proper exercise of their parental responsibility.'[157] The court was also concerned that enacting the transition plan based upon the consent of Z's parents would remove the safeguards of the court process for Z along with the objective scrutiny it provided.[158]

9.90 Accordingly, the court confirmed that in circumstances where Z could not himself consent to the arrangements, it was also not possible for his parents to provide valid consent which would negate a deprivation of liberty. In the circumstances, the court found the proposed transition plan to be necessary, proportionate and in Z's best interests and it was duly authorised pursuant to the inherent jurisdiction.

Tameside MBC v L (Unavailability of Regulated Therapeutic Placement) [2021] EWHC 1814 (Fam)

9.91 Before MacDonald J sitting in the Family Division of the High Court, this matter concerned the deprivation of liberty of a 17 year old young man, L. This decision concerned issues which were, at the time, awaiting determination by the Supreme Court in *Re T* (below). However, in L's circumstances, the court could not await the Supreme Court's decision before providing its judgment. The court had before it an application made by a local authority seeking to extend the authorisation of L's deprivation of liberty within his placement. L's parents opposed the application on the basis that they sought a plan to be implemented for L to return home. L's guardian could not support the application as being in L's best interests.[159]

9.92 L was adopted by his parents when he was four. He began to present with difficulties in 2012, relating to his social communication, emotional vulnerability and educational progress.[160] By 2015, L's challenging behaviour had escalated and included making threats with a knife, smearing faeces, food hoarding, arson, aggression to the family pet and sexualised behaviour. L was described as presenting with an increasing preoccupation with violence. L remained in the care of his parents until 2016. During this time, a number of recommendations were made for

154 [1997] 1 FLR 767.

155 *Re Z (A Child)(Deprivation of Liberty: Transition Plan)* [2020] EWHC 3038 (Fam), para 27.

156 *Re Z (A Child)(Deprivation of Liberty: Transition Plan)* [2020] EWHC 3038 (Fam), para 41.

157 *Re Z (A Child)(Deprivation of Liberty: Transition Plan)* [2020] EWHC 3038 (Fam), para 44.

158 *Re Z (A Child)(Deprivation of Liberty: Transition Plan)* [2020] EWHC 3038 (Fam), para 42.

159 *Tameside MBC v L* [2021] EWHC 1814 (Fam), para 3.

160 *Tameside MBC v L* [2021] EWHC 1814 (Fam), para 7.

therapeutic support although it was not clear on the evidence before the court what input had actually been provided to L.[161] L was accommodated by the local authority in December 2016, pursuant to consent provided by his parents. It was subsequently recommended that L receive a therapeutic programme within a specialist rehabilitation unit. L returned to his parents' care shortly after this recommendation and some therapeutic support was implemented.[162]

9.93 L's behaviours continued to deteriorate, including him taking an overdose in March 2017.[163] L was then placed in a residential placement and a care order was made. Since the granting of a care order in 2017, L was moved 13 times due to the placements he was in being unable to meet his level of need and unable to manage the violent and sexually inappropriate behaviour which L was displaying.[164] This behaviour was extreme and included L expressing a wish to murder children. By the time of the hearing before MacDonald J, L resided in a temporary placement which had been refused Ofsted registration due to concerns about the conditions of the home and poor compliance with policy and regulations.[165] The restrictive regime in place for L included permission for: three-to-one staff supervision in the placement; welfare checks every 30 minutes; L being unable to lock his bedroom or bathroom door; supervision of L in the community by two staff members as a minimum; the use of physical restraint; minimal furniture in L's bedroom; and L being unable to access the kitchen or any sharp objects.[166]

9.94 L had begun sleeping on the bathroom floor at the placement and was not accessing education. He continued to display worrying behaviour and thoughts, including expressing an intention to rape female staff, dreaming of killing people, assaulting staff, stabbing his bedroom walls with a screwdriver, attempting to grab a staff member's genitalia, and attempting to drag a staff member into his bedroom.[167] L's guardian described his situation bleakly, including that he has minimal stimulation, sleeps for long periods of time on the floor and was not washing.[168]

9.95 The court had no hesitation in concluding that the circumstances for L amounted to his deprivation of liberty for the purposes of Article 5 of the ECHR.[169] L lacked capacity to consent to the restrictive arrangements in place and no other person could provide valid consent.[170] What was troubling for the court was the proposition of authorising that deprivation of liberty as being in L's best interests given his circumstances. MacDonald J noted that the court must undertake an evaluation of L's best interests including considering his welfare in the widest sense,

---

161 *Tameside MBC v L* [2021] EWHC 1814 (Fam), paras 8-9.
162 *Tameside MBC v L* [2021] EWHC 1814 (Fam), para 10.
163 *Tameside MBC v L* [2021] EWHC 1814 (Fam), para 11.
164 *Tameside MBC v L* [2021] EWHC 1814 (Fam), para 12-16.
165 *Tameside MBC v L* [2021] EWHC 1814 (Fam), para 21.
166 *Tameside MBC v L* [2021] EWHC 1814 (Fam), para 21.
167 *Tameside MBC v L* [2021] EWHC 1814 (Fam), para 24.
168 *Tameside MBC v L* [2021] EWHC 1814 (Fam), para 28.
169 *Tameside MBC v L* [2021] EWHC 1814 (Fam), para 69.
170 *Tameside MBC v L* [2021] EWHC 1814 (Fam), para 51.

which will include his health, wellbeing and safety.[171] This necessarily included considering what alternatives may be available for the child or young person. MacDonald J commented:

> 'In circumstances where it is rarely, if ever, the case that a particular welfare option will meet perfectly all of a given child's welfare needs, safeguarding and promoting a child's best interests will almost invariably involve a degree of compromise. The extent to which a given welfare compromise is or is not acceptable will in turn depend, in part, on whether or not another welfare option that does not require such a compromise is or is not available. A course of action that can meet some of the child's needs may well not be acceptable where a course of action that meets all of the child's needs is available. But where a course of action that meets all of the child's needs is not available, a course that meets only some of the child's needs may become acceptable, particularly where the alternative is that none of the child's welfare needs will be met.'[172]

9.96 The only alternative to the local authority's application would have been to refuse to extend the deprivation of liberty authorisation, causing L to be free to leave his placement and likely cause significant harm to himself and others. The court balanced the limitations of L's placement in meeting his welfare needs against the risks to L were he not to be in that placement in light of his presenting behaviours and urges. The court ultimately authorised for a short period the deprivation of L's liberty within the placement on the basis that it was in his best interests owing to the high risk of harm if his liberty was not deprived.[173] MacDonald J summarised in saying 'I am further satisfied that that risk of harm to L is, at present, greater than the risks presented to him by the identified deficiencies in his current placement. Keeping L safe from harm is, at least in the short term… a legitimate function of current restrictions amounting to a deprivation of his liberty.'[174]

9.97 In concluding, MacDonald J took the opportunity to again highlight the crisis which is arising from a shortage in accommodation provision for children and young people with similar challenges to L.[175] The court stressed that children continue to fall through the gaps in appropriate provision which is exacerbating the difficulties for children like L. The final paragraphs urge practitioners to consider early intervention for children like L when they begin to present with difficulties, recognising that the early input of therapeutic support may prevent an escalation to such extreme behaviours like those with which the court was grappling.

Wigan MBC v Y [2021] EWHC 1982 (Fam)

9.98 In a second decision by MacDonald J following shortly after the decision in *Tameside MBC v L*, the court was concerned with issues surrounding the deprivation of liberty of Y. Y was 12 years' old and had suspected diagnoses of attention deficit

171 *Tameside MBC v L* [2021] EWHC 1814 (Fam), para 70.
172 *Tameside MBC v L* [2021] EWHC 1814 (Fam), para 71.
173 *Tameside MBC v L* [2021] EWHC 1814 (Fam), para 79.
174 *Tameside MBC v L* [2021] EWHC 1814 (Fam), para 79.
175 *Tameside MBC v L* [2021] EWHC 1814 (Fam), para 88.

hyperactivity disorder, autism spectrum condition and a diagnosis of epilepsy. Y had experienced a turbulent childhood and concerns had been raised by the local authority as to abuse and neglect of Y by his father.[176] The child protection concerns escalated and in July 2021, care proceedings were issued and Y was removed from the care of his family and placed in a residential placement. When at the residential placement, Y struggled and began attempting suicide.[177] He had been demonstrating extreme challenging, violent and self-harming behaviours including attempting to assault staff and expressing intentions to kill.[178]

9.99 Following an attempt to end his life, Y was taken to hospital. He was assessed as not meeting the criteria for detention under the MHA 1983 and there was no available placement in a therapeutic facility for him. At the time of the hearing, Y was placed on a clinical ward within a hospital where he was subjected to chemical and physical restraint and five-to-one staffing.[179]

9.100 The circumstances for Y on the ward were extreme. The ward had been shut to new admissions and parts of it closed entirely owing to the risks posed by Y. Other gravely ill children who were on the ward had to be moved to other hospitals and surgeries for those children had to be cancelled.[180] The hospital did not have staff trained to provide physical restraint to Y.[181] During episodes of heightened behaviour, the police were called upon to assist staff in managing Y and Y had been handcuffed to prevent him assaulting professionals.[182] On one occasion, 13 police officers were present on the ward over a three hour period to assist in restraining Y.[183] He was administered sedative medication on occasions up to a level exceeding the hospital's protocol. The hospital had also at times administered rapid effect tranquilisers by intramuscular injection to calm Y.[184]

9.101 The NHS Trust managing the hospital were parties to proceedings and had expressed their serious concerns as to Y's continued placement on the ward.[185] Y was presenting a risk to all other patients on the ward and to the staff. The Trust summarised their concern as follows:

> 'The situation on [the ward] is described by staff as harrowing, Y feels like he is being 'caged' and is frightened when Police are called by the ward who require assistance when his behaviour becomes a safety risk to himself and others. At all times Y still requires an incredibly high level of supervision, he is restrained often and is controlled by chemical sedation.'[186]

---

176 *Wigan MBC v Y* [2021] EWHC 1982 (Fam), para 10.
177 *Wigan MBC v Y* [2021] EWHC 1982 (Fam), para 12.
178 *Wigan MBC v Y* [2021] EWHC 1982 (Fam), paras 1 and 18-21.
179 *Wigan MBC v Y* [2021] EWHC 1982 (Fam), para 3.
180 *Wigan MBC v Y* [2021] EWHC 1982 (Fam), para 3.
181 *Wigan MBC v Y* [2021] EWHC 1982 (Fam), para 14.
182 *Wigan MBC v Y* [2021] EWHC 1982 (Fam), para 15.
183 *Wigan MBC v Y* [2021] EWHC 1982 (Fam), para 18.
184 *Wigan MBC v Y* [2021] EWHC 1982 (Fam), para 18.
185 *Wigan MBC v Y* [2021] EWHC 1982 (Fam), para 24.
186 *Wigan MBC v Y* [2021] EWHC 1982 (Fam), para 28.

9.102 In the context of Y's presenting behaviours and needs, the local authority had been unable to find an alternative placement for him. It had conducted a search of regulated residential placements, unregulated residential placements and secure accommodation.[187] The local authority had only two options in sourcing a placement for Y outside of the hospital. They were: obtaining a property in which to implement a bespoke package of care for Y, although no staff team could be found; or, returning Y to the care of his father in the context of Y expressing a wish to kill his father and the preceding child protection concerns.[188] Neither of these alternatives were set up and ready for Y to move to, and they both would come with significant welfare concerns for Y.

9.103 The court undertook an extensive analysis of the relevant law when considering whether or not to authorise Y's continued deprivation of liberty in hospital. This included the stipulation that in order to be lawful, any deprivation of Y's liberty must be considered to be in his best interests in light of his needs and whilst recognising the limited options available to him and the need for some compromise to be struck to achieve his safety. Having considered the evidence about Y's current situation, MacDonald J recognised that the approach to be taken must involve a 'consideration of whether the placement is so unsuitable as to breach Y's rights under Article 5 of the ECHR'.[189] The court did consider in the circumstances that the arrangements for Y were so unsuitable, to the extent that the court was unable to authorise his deprivation of liberty in the circumstances. MacDonald J summarised that 'Y's current situation on the hospital ward is that it is an inappropriate, demeaning and, quite frankly, brutal one for a 12-year old child.'[190] The evidence had not uncovered any positives in respect of Y's situation; he was making no discernible progress and his troubling behaviour was continuing.[191] Although recognising that there were no safe alternatives for Y, the court was so concerned with his current situation, and considered that situation fell so far outside of what was in Y's best interests, that the court held it was not within the jurisdiction of the High Court to authorise Y's deprivation of liberty on the ward.[192]

Re T (A Child) (Appellant) [2021] UKSC 35

9.104 The Supreme Court was concerned with the circumstances of T, a young woman who was 19 at the time the judgment was handed down. The court was faced with two questions relating to T's living and care arrangements during her childhood.[193] The first was whether or not the inherent jurisdiction could be invoked at all to authorise the deprivation of T's liberty. The second issue, which arose if the inherent jurisdiction was available to authorise a deprivation of liberty, was the role of the child's consent within the criteria for finding that they are deprived of

187 *Wigan MBC v Y* [2021] EWHC 1982 (Fam), para 31.
188 *Wigan MBC v Y* [2021] EWHC 1982 (Fam), para 32.
189 *Wigan MBC v Y* [2021] EWHC 1982 (Fam), para 52.
190 *Wigan MBC v Y* [2021] EWHC 1982 (Fam), para 53.
191 *Wigan MBC v Y* [2021] EWHC 1982 (Fam), para 58.
192 *Wigan MBC v Y* [2021] EWHC 1982 (Fam), para 59.
193 *Re T (A Child) (Appellant)* [2021] UKSC 35, paras 15-16.

their liberty. The questions which the court grappled with arose in the context of T's circumstances and, the court made clear, may arise for only a narrow group of children.[194] These are children who meet the criteria to be placed in secure accommodation for the purposes of the CA 1989, s 25 but who, the local authority proposes, are to be deprived of their liberty in another setting which is not within the definition of secure accommodation.

9.105 T first became the subject of proceedings relating to her care in 2017 when she was 15, and she lived in local authority care pursuant to a care order.[195] At the time the first application was made for the inherent jurisdiction to be invoked, T had already been living within secure accommodation which was approved by an order under the Social Services and Well-being (Wales) Act 2014 (SSWWA 2014), s 119. The local authority sought for T to move to a different setting which was not approved as secure accommodation but which could better meet her needs. This placement was not a registered children's home. The move was authorised by Mostyn J in July 2017 and T continued to live in this placement, deprived of her liberty, until March 2018 when the placement broke down. A different placement was sourced which was a registered children's home and in which it was proposed that T would live and continue to be deprived of her liberty.[196]

9.106 T appealed the authorisation of both placements in which she had been deprived of her liberty, initially basing her appeal upon the issue of consent which rendered court authorisation unnecessary.[197] T's representatives had argued in the Court of Appeal that her consent negated a deprivation of liberty arising and therefore it was not open to the court to authorise the arrangements. This argument fell away during the course of the Court of Appeal hearing, but T's representatives did argue that owing to T's consent, it had been inappropriate for the court to make the orders it had. The Court of Appeal did not agree and found that Mostyn J was right at first instance, to make the orders authorising the deprivation of liberty. Mostyn J had considered the orders necessary as he did not perceive T's consent to be authentic and enduring, which would be required to satisfy Article 5 of the ECHR.

9.107 The issues evolved as they came before the Supreme Court and somewhat unusually, the court was tasked with determining an issue which had not been the subject of consideration in the lower courts.[198] This was the availability of the inherent jurisdiction at all for children in T's circumstances who are deprived of their liberty. The reasons why it was contended that the inherent jurisdiction was unavailable was broken down into three strands.[199] The first argument was that the CA 1989, s 100(2)(d) prohibits the court using its inherent jurisdiction to authorise a deprivation of liberty for a young person in T's circumstances. This section of the CA 1989 specifically prohibits the use of the inherent jurisdiction to determine

---

194 *Re T (A Child) (Appellant)* [2021] UKSC 35, para 17.
195 *Re T (A Child) (Appellant)* [2021] UKSC 35, para 13.
196 *Re T (A Child) (Appellant)* [2021] UKSC 35, para 18.
197 *Re T (A Child) (Appellant)* [2021] UKSC 35, para 20.
198 *Re T (A Child) (Appellant)* [2021] UKSC 35, para 22.
199 *Re T (A Child) (Appellant)* [2021] UKSC 35, para 15.

questions which arise in connection with aspects of parental responsibility.[200] It was argued that the deprivation of a child's liberty was such a question and so s 100(2)(d) prohibited the inherent jurisdiction intervening.[201] The Supreme Court rejected that argument and found that section the CA 1989, s 100(2)(d) did not act to prevent the inherent jurisdiction being used to authorise the deprivation of a child's liberty in local authority accommodation.[202] This argument, explored in detail by Lady Black, did not hold up in the context of the provisions of s 100 as a whole and its clear intention to prevent the inherent jurisdiction being used to circumvent the provisions of the CA 1989, which the authorisation of a deprivation of liberty was not doing.[203] The court was satisfied that the inherent jurisdiction could and should be available to local authorities in circumstances where no statutory scheme can be used to authorise a child or young person's deprivation of liberty, and that deprivation of liberty is necessary for their safety.

9.108 The second argument in relation to the unavailability of the inherent jurisdiction was that using it in T's circumstances would cut across the statutory scheme of the CA 1989 and/or its use was not in accordance with a procedure prescribed by law as required by Article 5.[204] If either of those sentiments were found to be correct by the Supreme Court, the inherent jurisdiction's scope would have to be curtailed so as to not include the ability to authorise the deprivation of a child or young person's liberty. The statutory schemes referred to are the CA 1989, s 25 and the SSWWA 2014, s 119. In unpicking the argument, the court considered the definition of secure accommodation, continuing the discussion emerging from *Re D* [2019] (above).[205] Lady Black was cautious to comment that secure accommodation needs to be interpreted to include the protections intended by the statute, but to not be so widely defined as to prevent local authorities from meeting the needs of children in a variety of settings when they may not meet the criteria set down in s 25. The Supreme Court found ultimately that to authorise the deprivation of a child's liberty under the inherent jurisdiction when the circumstances were such that secure accommodation could be used but was unavailable was a proper exercise of the inherent jurisdiction. The court did not find that such authorisation would cut across or clash with the statutory scheme. Lady Black noted that it was to be used when the statutory scheme could not be, and to prevent its use in those circumstances would contradict the very aims which the use of the inherent jurisdiction sets to achieve in safeguarding children who may fall through the gaps of the statutory provisions.[206]

9.109 The second limb of this argument related to whether the inherent jurisdiction is a procedure prescribed by law for the purposes of Article 5 of the ECHR, and therefore whether the process of authorising a deprivation of liberty in this way is

---

200 *Re T (A Child) (Appellant)* [2021] UKSC 35, para 107.
201 *Re T (A Child) (Appellant)* [2021] UKSC 35, para 111.
202 *Re T (A Child) (Appellant)* [2021] UKSC 35, paras 116-121.
203 *Re T (A Child) (Appellant)* [2021] UKSC 35, para 116.
204 *Re T (A Child) (Appellant)* [2021] UKSC 35, paras 127 and 150.
205 *Re T (A Child) (Appellant)* [2021] UKSC 35, paras 130-131.
206 *Re T (A Child) (Appellant)* [2021] UKSC 35, paras 141-143.

compliant with the ECHR's requirements.[207] The Supreme Court evaluated fully the safeguards in place by virtue of the exercise of the inherent jurisdiction and court process. This included the representation of the child within proceedings, and the judicial oversight which is encompassed in the application process.[208] Having done so, it rejected the argument that the exercise of the inherent jurisdiction was not a compliant procedure prescribed by law. The court clearly determined that to comply with this element of Article 5, a procedure need not be set out in statute but can be developed through case law which governs the court and domestic decisions.[209]

9.110 The final issue before the court related to consent, the subjective element of the *Storck* criteria. On T's behalf, questions were raised as to whether the court at first instance was right to make the orders it did and choose not to rely on T's consent, which would have led to there being no deprivation of liberty.[210] Lady Black summarised the point made on T's behalf as being that 'it would have been conducive to her welfare if the court had been prepared to put weight on her consenting to the restrictive placements, rather than making its own order.'[211] The Supreme Court did not interfere with the decision of the Court of Appeal in which it was confirmed that the court has jurisdiction to make a permissive deprivation of liberty order whether or not the child consents to the arrangements.[212] It is not a prerequisite of that authorisation that consent must be absent, as the court granting the authorisation need not have an active deprivation of liberty before it in order to make an order. The court instead needs detail of a proposed arrangement which, absent of consent, would amount to a deprivation of liberty in order to grant authorisation (if satisfied of the necessity and proportionality of the same).

9.111 In summarising the approach of the court to the use of its inherent jurisdiction, Lord Stephens made clear that it should be available to the court to make orders when '"there is absolutely no alternative, and where the child (or someone else) is likely to come to grave harm if the court does not act"'... and 'that it is a "permissible exercise of the inherent jurisdiction to authorise a local authority to place a child in an unregistered children's home in relation to which a criminal offence would be being committed"'... '[a]ccordingly, the courts, in the exercise of the inherent jurisdiction, must only authorise such a placement where there are "imperative considerations of necessity".[213]

Lincolnshire County Council v TGA & Ors [2022] EWHC 2323 (Fam)

9.112 This case came before Lieven J sitting in the High Court and concerned the purported deprivation of liberty of K. K was 14 years old and he was diagnosed

207 *Re T (A Child) (Appellant)* [2021] UKSC 35, para 150.
208 *Re T (A Child) (Appellant)* [2021] UKSC 35, paras 153-154.
209 *Re T (A Child) (Appellant)* [2021] UKSC 35, para 152.
210 *Re T (A Child) (Appellant)* [2021] UKSC 35, paras 156-158.
211 *Re T (A Child) (Appellant)* [2021] UKSC 35, para 158.
212 *Re T (A Child) (Appellant)* [2021] UKSC 35, paras 160-162.
213 *Re T (A Child) (Appellant)* [2021] UKSC 35, para 170.

with epilepsy, autism spectrum condition, attention deficit disorder and global developmental delay.[214] K was accommodated in a children's centre by a local authority with the consent of his guardians, provided under the CA 1989, s 20. K's parents were deceased and so parental responsibility for him was exercised by his guardians who were respondents to the application.[215]

9.113 The issue before the court was whether the subjective element of the criteria for a deprivation of liberty was met, namely whether or not K was deprived of his liberty in circumstances where his guardians had provided their consent to the arrangements in place.[216] This issue had arisen following the decision above in *Re D* [2019] and comments made within that judgment by Lady Hale and Lady Black as to the possible applicability of the principles therein to children under 16. Although the judgment in *Re D* did not hand down any binding decision in relation to under 16s, the inference drawn from the judgment was that it may be appropriate to apply its principles to younger children, going against the earlier decision of Keehan J in *Trust A v X and A Local Authority*.[217]

9.114 In considering the issue of parental consent, which was applied in the same way for K's guardians as it would be to his natural parents, Lieven J explored the relevant case law. She considered the key guiding principles which had been set down in relation to the appropriate exercise of parental responsibility and its scope. In particular, the court referred to the decision in *Nielsen v Denmark* and the determination that to consent to a child's confinement could fall within an appropriate exercise of parental rights and responsibilities.[218] The court emphasised that whatever decision is to be made by a holder of parental responsibility, in order to be appropriate, it must be within the child's best interests.[219]

9.115 Having undertaken an analysis of the law, Lieven J concluded that it was within the scope of parental responsibility for a parent to consent to the confinement of a child who is under 16 and lacks *Gillick* competence.[220] It was determined that this will only be appropriate when there is no dispute that implementing restrictions on the child's liberty is in that child's best interests.

9.116 Lieven J then turned to the principles of *Gillick* and how they may be applied to circumstances concerning a deprivation of liberty. Lieven J commented that both decisions around medical treatment and the liberty of a child are serious and have potentially significant consequences for the child. For that reason, she found the analysis of *Gillick* to be relevant to the question before her even though the court in *Gillick* was considering medical treatment and not liberty. Lieven J determined that her focus should be on establishing the maturity and intelligence of the particular child when considering what is an appropriate exercise of parental responsibility,

---

214 *Lincolnshire County Council v TGA & Ors* [2022] EWHC 2323 (Fam), para 1.
215 *Lincolnshire County Council v TGA & Ors* [2022] EWHC 2323 (Fam), para 1-3.
216 *Lincolnshire County Council v TGA & Ors* [2022] EWHC 2323 (Fam), para 5.
217 [2015] EWHC 922 (Fam).
218 *Lincolnshire County Council v TGA & Ors* [2022] EWHC 2323 (Fam), para 29.
219 *Lincolnshire County Council v TGA & Ors* [2022] EWHC 2323 (Fam), para 51.
220 *Lincolnshire County Council v TGA & Ors* [2022] EWHC 2323 (Fam), para 47.

rather than undertaking a comparative exercise about a hypothetical child of the same age.[221] In summarising the analysis, the court stated:

> 'More fundamentally, when dealing with children, whose ability to understand the issues will vary greatly depending not simply on their age, but on their psychological and emotional maturity, their family support and their life experiences, in my view it is more appropriate to consider the characteristics of the individual child than try to compare them with a hypothetical child of the same age. Whereas it is appropriate to assume that someone over the age of 16 will have capacity, and therefore there is a benchmark to compare the non-capacitous adult with, that is a much more difficult and arguably less possible exercise for children under 16.'[222]

Manchester City Council v CP (Refusal of Restrictions on Mobile Phone) [2023] EWHC 133 (Fam)

9.117 The Family Division of the High Court was concerned with the circumstances of P, a 16 year old girl, for whom a local authority sought an order authorising her deprivation of liberty. P was the subject of a care order granted shortly before this judgment was handed down.[223] P was diagnosed with attention deficit hyperactivity disorder and was assessed at working at the level of a 7-year old.[224] P had lived in local authority care since June 2021 and during that time had made a number of attempts to end her life. P had spent periods of time in hospital but was assessed three times in 2022 as not meeting the criteria for admission to a Tier 4 CAMHS bed.[225] A Tier 4 CAMHS bed is the label used for specialist inpatient services for children and young people who require input related to their mental health and includes secure and psychiatric intensive care placements. At the time of the hearing, P was the subject of an order authorising her deprivation of liberty which included an extensive list of restrictions on her mobile phone use. It was those restrictions which were the court's primary concern.

9.118 The existing order authorised that P must not have her mobile phone, tablet or laptop overnight; that she was unable to use the house phone; that she was to be supervised when calling friends and those calls would be recorded; that Wi-Fi at the placement may be turned off; that staff may access P's phone to delete recordings of themselves; that P was not to have her sim card topped up so she could only access social media by Wi-Fi; that P could not take her mobile phone into the bathroom; and that staff may check P's mobile phone or any other devices she was using.[226] These restrictions were submitted to be necessary and proportionate for P as she

---

[221] *Lincolnshire County Council v TGA & Ors* [2022] EWHC 2323 (Fam), paras 53-56.

[222] *Lincolnshire County Council v TGA & Ors* [2022] EWHC 2323 (Fam), para 57.

[223] *Manchester City Council v CP (Refusal of Restrictions on Mobile Phone)* [2023] EWHC 133 (Fam), para 1.

[224] *Manchester City Council v CP (Refusal of Restrictions on Mobile Phone)* [2023] EWHC 133 (Fam), para 4.

[225] *Manchester City Council v CP (Refusal of Restrictions on Mobile Phone)* [2023] EWHC 133 (Fam), para 6.

[226] *Manchester City Council v CP (Refusal of Restrictions on Mobile Phone)* [2023] EWHC 133 (Fam), para 8.

could be agitated following contact with friends online or by phone, and friends had encouraged P's aggressive behaviour. P had also shared her address with others online which the local authority considered may pose a risk to her safety. There were concerns that P was befriending people online who may pose a risk to her.[227]

9.119 On the basis of these risks, the local authority sought an order authorising the continuation of restrictions on P's access to her phone, social media and the internet.[228] The question before the court was whether these interventions amounted to a restriction on P which could properly fall within the Article 5 ECHR considerations of her deprivation of liberty. The contrary proposition was that restrictions on P's phone use, social media and internet access may fall within the exercise of parental responsibility for her by the local authority pursuant to the care order and the CA 1989, s 33.[229]

9.120 Having analysed the legal principles in respect of both a deprivation of liberty and the scope of parental responsibility, the court determined that restrictions on P's use of her mobile phone, tablet, laptop and access to social media were not restrictions amounting to a deprivation of liberty for the purposes of Article 5 of the ECHR.[230] The court instead held that the appropriate framework for 'mediating the removal of, or the restriction of the use of, P's mobile phone, tablet and laptop and use of social media is that provided to the local authority by the Children Act 1989, s 33(3)(b).'[231] The court's focus in reaching this conclusion was the clear definition of liberty for the purposes of Article 5 being physical liberty. Although the court accepted that P and other young people may perceive their phone and social media access to be a part of their liberty, when broadly defined, that went beyond the scope of the liberty with which Article 5 was concerned.[232] MacDonald J summarised that:

> 'in my judgment, the removal of, or the placing of restrictions on the use of, P's mobile phone, tablet and laptop and her use of social media do not by themselves amount to a restriction of her liberty for the purposes of Art 5(1). On the evidence currently before the court those restrictions do not act to deprive P of her physical liberty, but rather act to restrict her communication, so as to ensure her physical and emotional safety.'[233]

9.121 In accepting that the restrictions on mobile phone, tablet and laptop use may at times form part of the regime of continuous supervision and control, the court

---

227 *Manchester City Council v CP (Refusal of Restrictions on Mobile Phone)* [2023] EWHC 133 (Fam), para 9.

228 *Manchester City Council v CP (Refusal of Restrictions on Mobile Phone)* [2023] EWHC 133 (Fam), para 15.

229 *Manchester City Council v CP (Refusal of Restrictions on Mobile Phone)* [2023] EWHC 133 (Fam), para 21.

230 *Manchester City Council v CP (Refusal of Restrictions on Mobile Phone)* [2023] EWHC 133 (Fam), para 44.

231 *Manchester City Council v CP (Refusal of Restrictions on Mobile Phone)* [2023] EWHC 133 (Fam), para 44.

232 *Manchester City Council v CP (Refusal of Restrictions on Mobile Phone)* [2023] EWHC 133 (Fam), para 45.

233 *Manchester City Council v CP (Refusal of Restrictions on Mobile Phone)* [2023] EWHC 133 (Fam), para 46.

reaffirmed that those measures did not serve to restrict P's physical liberty. They were not implemented in order to bring effect to the measures preventing P leaving the placement. They were instead in place to prevent P broadcasting online and to prevent her contact with others that was encouraging harmful behaviour.[234] In that context, the measures were not related to P's physical liberty and so did not fall to form part of the regime in place which did deprive her of her physical liberty. Instead, regulating P's access to her mobile phone or social media was deemed to fall within the local authority's exercise of parental responsibility for her.[235] The court commented that 'it would not be unreasonable in my view for a parent who has become aware that the use by their 16-year old child of his or her mobile phone is placing them at risk of significant harm.... to seek to address that situation by removing or restricting the use of their teenager's mobile phone and other devices in the exercise of their parental responsibility.'[236]

9.122 In assessing further the restrictions on P's access to her mobile phone and social media, the court commented that if those steps did amount to an interference with P's rights under Article 8(1) of the ECHR relating to her right to respect for private and family life, they would likely be necessary and proportionate on the basis of the evidence and the harm that was presented to P by using her mobile phone and social media.[237]

Peterborough City Council v Mother & Ors [2024] EWHC 493 (Fam)

9.123 Lieven J, sitting in the High Court, provided this judgment relating to SM, a 12-year old girl and dealing with issues surrounding the application of the *Cheshire West* principles to children. SM had profound disabilities which impacted every aspect of her living and functioning. She had been diagnosed with Lissencephaly, epilepsy, global developmental delay and scoliosis.[238] She could not move independently and could not speak. SM's only body control was to push her hands away and to wriggle and roll.[239] A local authority applied for the authorisation of the measures in place for SM which, it said, amounted to her deprivation of liberty. Lieven J considered there to be two central issues with the argument advanced by the local authority.

9.124 Firstly, Lieven J looked at the measures which were submitted by the local authority to be restrictions and in their totality amount to SM's confinement. Lieven J distinguished a number of these measures as being part of SM's care provision and

---

234 *Manchester City Council v CP (Refusal of Restrictions on Mobile Phone)* [2023] EWHC 133 (Fam), para 48.

235 *Manchester City Council v CP (Refusal of Restrictions on Mobile Phone)* [2023] EWHC 133 (Fam), para 52.

236 *Manchester City Council v CP (Refusal of Restrictions on Mobile Phone)* [2023] EWHC 133 (Fam), para 55.

237 *Manchester City Council v CP (Refusal of Restrictions on Mobile Phone)* [2023] EWHC 133 (Fam), para 57.

238 *Peterborough City Council v Mother & Ors* [2024] EWHC 493 (Fam), para 3.

239 *Peterborough City Council v Mother & Ors* [2024] EWHC 493 (Fam), para 4.

not restrictions which fed into a holistic analysis of SM's deprivation of liberty.[240] Specifically, those restrictions which were better termed as care provision were: SM's supervision at home; SM being moved by her carers; SM's feeding and medication administration being managed by carers; SM being dressed, washed and her continence needs being met by carers; and bars being in place on SM's bed to prevent her falling and injuring herself. Lieven J summarised at paragraph 8 that '[t]here are many aspects of care which may intrude on an individual's privacy and autonomy, and which may interfere, albeit with justification, into the scope of Article 8. But they are not interferences with the right to liberty'.

9.125 The court then turned to the trickier issue of how to approach the objective test for a deprivation of liberty for children such as SM who have significant disabilities which impact their physical liberty and ability to exercise that right, separate to any restrictions imposed upon them.[241] Lieven J considered there to be a tension between the comparative approach to establishing an objective deprivation of liberty, being to compare the relevant child with another child of the same age and station, and achieving a logical outcome which properly reflects the regime in place for a severely disabled child. The court considered it unrealistic to compare SM with another 12-year old child in order to determine whether she was confined, principally due to SM's limited functioning which caused her to present as a very young child and not a child of the same chronological age.[242] Lieven J instead preferred a fact-specific approach. She noted of particular importance that when assessing if SM is free to leave and under constant supervision and control, her actual ability to leave has to be considered. SM did not have restrictions imposed upon her that prevented her leaving the placement, rather her disabilities rendered her unable to move independently which meant she was not free to leave.[243] When considering the level of supervision and control, Lieven J surmised that the close supervision of SM was not designed to impede her physical liberty but to meet her care needs.[244] For those reasons, the court found that SM was not deprived of her liberty within the meaning of Article 5 of the ECHR and consequently, no order for authorisation was required.[245]

240 *Peterborough City Council v Mother & Ors* [2024] EWHC 493 (Fam), para 8.
241 *Peterborough City Council v Mother & Ors* [2024] EWHC 493 (Fam), para 33.
242 *Peterborough City Council v Mother & Ors* [2024] EWHC 493 (Fam), paras 25 and 43.
243 *Peterborough City Council v Mother & Ors* [2024] EWHC 493 (Fam), paras 37-40.
244 *Peterborough City Council v Mother & Ors* [2024] EWHC 493 (Fam), para 37.
245 *Peterborough City Council v Mother & Ors* [2024] EWHC 493 (Fam), para 45.

INDEX

[all references are to paragraph number]